SORRY!

Contents

A note on the text

In quotations, spellings have been adjusted to conform to modern readers' expectations. I have also standardized the spellings of names.

1

The stars' tennis balls

or, a short introduction from
an unusual angle

In 1977 an eighteen-year-old American skipped his high school graduation to play tennis in Europe. Although an amateur, he competed against professionals – thrilling fans and maddening traditionalists with his prickly, passionate attitude. Even to people for whom tennis was of little interest, his behaviour seemed at once scandalous and magnetic. Two decades later a sociologist, E. Digby Baltzell, would assess the player's impact in his book *Sporting Gentlemen*. This had had a rather more catchy working title: *John McEnroe and the Decline of Civilization*.

Tennis mattered a lot to me when I was a child. Each summer I would go square-eyed watching Wimbledon. In the first couple of years that I was able to follow it, I registered McEnroe's sulky petulance, and registered also how violently it was at odds with the coolness of his great rival, Björn Borg. I liked Borg, the doleful-looking Swede who reputedly slept surrounded by his racquets, and was encouraged in this preference by my parents.

McEnroe was considered a disgrace because he flouted the norms of a sport steeped in tradition, showed no regard for authority, and always insisted that he was right, even when (and partly because) such insistence was guaranteed to be futile. His technique disclosed his angsty nonconformity. In a review of one of the player's televised matches, Clive James observed that McEnroe gave the impression of 'serving around the corner of an imaginary building'; his service motion, apparently developed to prevent back pain, seemed consonant with paranoia. Meanwhile his demeanour was 'as charming as a dead mouse in a loaf of bread'.[1] A further source of outrage was McEnroe's appearance: his air of dishevelment (wild hair, sloppy socks, a mystifying lack of muscle tone) meant that he looked like a dabbler, at a time when tennis was embracing the bland ruthlessness of professional sports management. McEnroe's manners grated. His defiance stemmed from a hatred of anything that seemed phoney; he suffered not from a lack of sensitivity, but from a tendency to be hypersensitive in situations where he was meant to be stoical.

Borg and McEnroe suggested two distinct ways of experiencing the world, two distinct ways of greeting fortune and misfortune. Borg was the embodiment of restraint and politesse, averting his gaze from his own excellence, whereas McEnroe was the embodiment of . . . well, of what E. Digby Baltzell considered calling the decline of civilization.

The choice between these two figures and their attitudes was presented to me explicitly. Neither was English, but I saw the drama of their rivalry in an English setting, and it spoke to an English audience. Here were two approaches to life: the mannerly and the unmannerly. One player kept his feelings locked up; the other expressed them continually. One had eliminated all trace of intimacy from his behaviour; the other was forever admitting us to an intimate place we didn't want to go.

Yet now the choice between Borg and McEnroe feels different: we find McEnroe's conduct authentic, even courageous, while Borg's seems that of an android. In his autobiography, *Serious*, McEnroe writes that 'Where money and publicity meet, there's always excitement, but good behaviour is rarely part of the mix. Manners are the operating rules of more stable systems . . . I thought tennis had had enough of manners. To me, "manners" meant sleeping linesmen at Wimbledon, and bowing and curtsying to rich people with hereditary titles who didn't pay any taxes.'[2]

To McEnroe, as to many people, the notion of manners seems old-fashioned and starchy, and it also means something divisive, corrupt, shamefully unquestionable – and quintessentially English. The manners of every society encode a particular view of the world. They can be understood as a system for producing a sense of togetherness or minimizing a sense of not-togetherness. But in the pantheon of national stereotypes, *English* and *manners* go together like *French* and *romance* or *German* and *efficiency*.

In the pages that follow, I examine English manners. I also examine Englishness. It therefore seems appropriate to say something about the words *English* and *British*. The distinction between them is one that English people often fail to observe; in the eyes of the Scottish and Welsh, it is much clearer. Britain is a political construct; the Act of Union in 1707 joined England, Wales and Scotland as 'one united kingdom by the name of Great Britain'. This construct, which blurred traditional divisions, was strengthened by a reaction against all that was encountered overseas. As a political concept, 'Britain' has worked, but at root the people of England, like the people of Scotland and Wales, feel that while 'British' may be the name for *what* they are, it is not *who* they are.

Because I have Welsh and Scottish antecedents as well as English ones, I call myself British. Yet to foreigners I undoubtedly seem deeply English. Some years ago, on a trip to Japan with students from a dozen other countries, I referred to myself as a European and was mocked for doing so by my generally charming companions. As one Belgian member of the group put it, 'The English really are not Europeans.' 'I'm not English,' I countered. The response was a chorus: 'Oh yes, you are.' What did Englishness mean to these citizens of Sweden, Portugal, Austria and Greece? Mainly it consisted of belligerence, xenophobia and crudeness, leavened by a chummy warmth. 'We like the English,' said one young woman from Barcelona, 'and we know you like us. But you're still, you know, different – the English, he's partly a friendly person who's polite and easy, and partly a guy who likes football and beer and is really loud.' It meant something to my companions to think of me as English, and when I said I was British I was regarded as invoking a technicality.

To speak of English manners, rather than of British ones, is to recognize something visceral. As I investigate this, in the chapters that follow, I also discuss manners in general. I could hardly not, for, as I shall show, the sources of many of our ideas to do with manners are not English at all. Manners are neither an English invention nor a modern one. A global history of the subject would reach back at least as far as the twenty-fifth century BC, when the Egyptian vizier Ptahhotep issued a set of maxims about appropriate behaviour. It would take in the Chinese thinker Confucius, the Roman statesman Cicero, the great compendium of Jewish lore known as the Talmud, and Abu Hamed Mohammad ibn Mohammad al-Ghazali, a scholar who almost 1,000 years ago wrote about *adab*, the code that provides Muslims with a model of respectfulness. The coverage of medieval Europe might start with Thomasin of Zerklaere, an Italian who produced a didactic poem about manners around 1215. Writing in German, Thomasin offered guidance on matters such as where to look when riding a horse (upwards, rather than at one's legs), and advised young men not to step on benches and women not to look over their shoulders.[3]

Guides to manners have not always begun as reactions to bad behaviour − attempts to halt social decline − yet implicit in every such work, and explicit in most of them, is an anxiety about slipping standards or a belief that tighter codes of conduct need defining. Today it is common to remark that the little civilities that make life bearable are vanishing, that people from whom you expect flawless behaviour instead act rudely, that conflict is more common than rapport. We seem to be inundated with stories of degeneracy: politeness is expiring. Thus, for instance, the *Daily Mail* in April 2008 reported a new study claiming that bad manners were the biggest problem facing society. Behaviours cited as giving especially grave offence included spitting and swearing.[4]

Complaints of this kind will strike a chord with readers who feel that the present moment is one of unique discourtesy. But here is a snippet from a report published by penal reformers in 1898: 'The tendencies of modern life incline more and more to ignore, or disparage, social distinctions, which formerly did much to encourage respect . . . [and it] is frequently asserted, that the manners of children are deteriorating, that the child of today is coarser, more vulgar, less refined, than his parents were.' Here is the churchman Robert Wallace in 1758, summing up an attitude prevalent among his contemporaries: 'There being now nothing in our constitution to give due check to our bad manners, their natural consequences must have their full effect, and we run the greatest risk of going to destruction.'⁵ And here is Baldassare Castiglione in 1528, in a book that would enjoy great popularity among English readers, condemning as an 'error' the tendency whereby 'nearly all praise the past and blame the present, revile our actions and behaviour and everything which they themselves did not do when they were young, and affirm, too, that every good custom and way of life, every virtue and, in short, all things imaginable are always going from bad to worse.'

I hope to avoid the error described by Castiglione, developing a true sense of the past, the present and their relationship. My book's structure is chronological, but sometimes I cut away from the main narrative to explore a subject such as table manners that belongs to no one historical moment. I have also canvassed the opinions of a few experts in the field – by which I mean complete strangers, people with whom I fell into conversation on the bus or while waiting in a queue. Here, for instance, are the views of Tia and Misha, teenage girls I met at the Elephant and Castle Shopping Centre. Tia: 'Manners is just another word for respect. And respect has to be *earned*.' Misha: 'How do you *earn* manners?' Tia: 'You *learn* them.' Misha:

'You *said* you earn them.' Tia: 'Like fuck I did.' And then to me, Tia: 'Sorry about this, man.'

Sorry. Lynne Truss says in her 2005 book *Talk to the Hand* that the word is 'near extinction'. Although that is not my experience, its force has diminished, and often today it does not express sorrow, penitence or even regret. It can be powerful when incorporated into a sincere apology, but when it stands alone may seem hollow – a punctuation mark, with a weight no greater than a comma, in the everyday discourse of selfishness. According to a report in the *Daily Telegraph* in September 2011, the average Briton says 'Sorry' eight times a day. The very existence of that report is worthy of remark: a lot of the time manners are treated as a minority concern, but they are guaranteed to interest the many readers of conservative newspapers such as the *Telegraph* and the *Mail*. It is apt that the *Telegraph* uses Old Testament terms when noting: 'That's 204,536 times in threescore years and ten.'[6]

The readiness of the English to apologize for something they haven't done is remarkable, and it is matched by an unwillingness to apologize for what they have done. This puts me in mind of an essential paradox that I have observed: the English are polite, and they are also rude. Extreme rudeness and elaborate politeness both stem from feelings of unease; they are different techniques for twisting one's way out of discomfiture.

Paradox will come up again and again in this book. A few examples: The English are proud of their stoicism and resilience, though often in practice they are hypochondriacs. 'Mustn't grumble,' the English say straight after grumbling, and in circumstances where complaint is not only justified but necessary. (The stiff upper lip, that fabled image of re-strained English fortitude in the face of adversity, seems to be American in origin.) The English advertise their simplicity, yet many of those who do so take pleasure in English culture's tangled mysteries. Although they like forming committees, even like the idea of sitting on them, they hate committee meetings. The English catchphrase 'I know my rights' belies a state of affairs in which legal rights are convoluted, and in which litigation is slow and costly. The very people who display greatest pride in the English past know nothing of their own families before their grandparents.

A final example, before we are borne back into that past: the people who speak most emotionally about the decline of manners, and who rejoice most in the sanctity of their under-standing of what English manners are, rarely express any curiosity about the origins of those manners or the authority and rationale on which they rest. But perhaps that isn't a paradox at all.

2

'I'ma get medieval on yo ass'

manners in the age of chivalry

When Marcellus Wallace in *Pulp Fiction* threatens another character with the words 'I'ma get medieval on yo ass', we have a pretty good idea what he means. He is likely, we sense, to wield some daunting instruments of torture; he specifically mentions pliers. The line works because it is unexpected yet not incongruous; the popular image of the medieval world involves a passion for violence – jousts, swordplay, beheadings, witch-burnings. This is an incomplete view, but it is fair to say that in medieval England violence was considered an unavoidable part of life. In the case of the trial by ordeal, which used a painful test to determine the guilt of an accused individual, violence was even carried out in the name of justice.

It was because of all this violence, rather than in spite of it, that manners mattered. A man surrendered his weapons when he visited equals or superiors. The way he greeted them was important in establishing his trustworthiness and creating rapport. He exercised care when eating in their presence. He would do what he could to maintain a clean, respectable appearance; that might not be much, but he would be aware that his face, hair, teeth and hands ought to be clean. This was not because of a concern with germs (it was only in the nineteenth century that the relationship between microbes and disease was established). Rather, it was because physical cleanliness was understood as a sign of spiritual cleanliness.

Let's for a moment project ourselves into this world. If you live in thirteenth-century England, your home is draughty and smoky. Unless you are rich and can sleep in a bed on linen sheets, you will be obliged to slumber on a clay floor strewn with rushes that have become ingrained with filth. Sleeping has in any case not yet been privatized; you are likely to share your space at night with other people, some of whom you would prefer not to be near. You may well receive visitors in your bedroom; in many houses, the bedroom is a busy place throughout the day. You may also share your bed with a stranger. Inhibitions are low, which is in some ways a good thing, but you see an awful lot of other people's dirty, blemished bodies. You blow your nose directly into your hand; the handkerchief will not be introduced into polite use, by Richard II, until around 1384, and will still be rare 200 years later.

Imagine a world in which you have no light in the evening save that of firesides, torches and candles, expensive to maintain in great number and perpetually hazardous. It's not just that you don't have electricity; you don't have matches, and make fire using a flint and steel. Your windows, instead of being glazed, may be covered with parchment or a cow's stretched-out placenta. And you have no pillows, cutlery, nightclothes, curtains or mattresses – never mind the internet, aeroplanes, telephones, refrigeration, combustion engines and, for that matter, form-fitting bras. Today some people relish camping, which they see as a return to natural and simple ways, but they for the most part have sleeping bags lined with down or thermal microfibres and are in vented tents that resist even the heaviest rain.

Imagine not having access to a bath or shower – or a flush lavatory, toilet roll and toothbrush – and needing constantly to disguise foul odours (including that of your own body) with perfume. It's easy to say 'Yes, yes, of course', and you may have experienced such privations on your travels (a chic slumminess or an all too real ruggedness), but imagine it fully: a life, a whole life, of grime. In a world without detergents, people did what they could to make themselves and their surroundings clean. Monks and monarchs had decent facilities; Edward I had running water in his bathroom, and Edward III had a number of bathrooms built and even had hot running water in some of them.[1] Others were less fortunate. Some medieval citizens could go to public baths, which were associated with bad behaviour and disease, and some could make use of ponds and rivers. But, while it was normal to wash one's hands several times a day, total immersion was rare. Water was something to use cautiously. People were less disturbed than you would be by the presence of lice and the pervasive aroma of shit. Until the late fourteenth century, urine was used to thicken cloth during its manufacture. Into the seventeenth century bad smells, though regarded as capable of harming the brain, were associated not with poverty, but with the bustle of urban progress; in the towns, unlike in the country, it was hard to get rid of bodily waste.

In this dangerous and largely rural world of feudalism and superstitions, the Church was vitally important. Ideas about manners grew out of religious teachings, in which manners were an expression of moral absolutes. As the subject began to be examined in greater detail, accounts of mannerly behaviour incorporated traditions that had developed in the monasteries. Treatises on self-discipline were no longer just for monks. Gradually manners took on a distinct identity, independent from religion. They were a terrestrial matter, not an ethereal one, and were touched by the particular demands of three different (but not easily separable) value systems: courtliness, courtesy and chivalry.[2] Their powerful convergence was manifest in a practical concern with acceptable and unacceptable behaviours at court, a distaste for excess and a desire to maintain systems of social status.

In medieval England, works expounding this concern explicitly assumed a noble and male coterie of consumers. One example was the twelfth-century Latin poem *Facetus* (essentially meaning 'polite man'), which presented a selection of maxims from which a youthful audience could learn basic courtesies. Also known as *Urbanus*, this didactic work is something of a hotchpotch, on the one hand rehashing the Ten Commandments and on the other warning about the dangers of accepting hospitality from someone who has red hair. A man should be careful about what he tells his wife, and yet should speak well of women, for speaking ill of them is a rustic habit. Mothers-in-law should be treated generously. If handling an object you are thinking about buying, you should do so gently. You should always choose a travelling companion with care and not cast him aside without a very good reason.

There was an English audience for the Latin text of *Facetus*, but there were also English translations of it, and soon there were derivative works setting out dicta about table manners, conversation, personal appearance and social life. In one form or another, *Facetus* was consumed in schools for more than 200 years, fading from use only in the early sixteenth century. Narrower in focus but similar in temper was the thirteenth-century Latin poem usually known by its opening words, '*Stans puer ad mensam*' (loosely, 'The child at the table'). This short work, sometimes attributed to the scholarly bishop Robert Grosseteste, was several times translated into English, most notably by John Lydgate, whose version became popular after being printed by William Caxton around 1476.

A businessman rather than a scholar, Caxton was keen on publishing what he knew would appeal to readers. '*Stans puer ad mensam*' was hardly the latest thing, but it was enduringly useful, providing young boys with rigorous guidance about conduct at table: slouching and scratching were condemned, as were shuffling, finger-wagging and the slurping of soup. Caxton also translated a book by the Augustinian friar Jacques Le Grand; *The Book of Good Manners* was intended to help 'the amendment of manners and the increase of virtuous living'. Lydgate for his part produced a widely disseminated poem, *The Dietary*, which presented moderation in the intake of food as desirable and as part of a more general personal moderation that was beneficial not just to the individual, but also to society at large.

The titles of these books are either prosaic or impenetrable, so it is interesting to come across *The Babees Book*, which sounds half twee, half provocative. Dating from about 1475, this was 'a little report of how young people should behave' addressed to young men of royal blood. It advises that they should stand 'as still as a stone' in the presence of their master, make eye contact with anyone who speaks to them, and avoid drinking while they have food in their mouths. Hand-washing matters. When eating, one's face should register appreciation of the food.

Works of this kind were precursors of modern manuals of etiquette. The word *etiquette* was not introduced into English until the eighteenth century, but the essential idea of etiquette was present: a code of conduct existed, and with it came the idea of self-control as a virtue. In the mid-fifteenth century John Russell, an usher in the service of Humphrey, Duke of Gloucester, produced the *Boke of Nurture*, a guide to standard practices in Humphrey's household. This gives general directions: a man shouldn't claw at his back as if looking for a flea, pick his nose or allow droplets to fall from it, belch, exhale over his superiors, or fiddle with his codpiece (the flap that covers and accentuates his genitals). By implication, becoming cleaner and shielding from view the less attractive parts of yourself enhances your sense of the integrity of your body.

These guides established a sense of what constituted correct behaviour in the presence of the king or another potentate. They were concerned with what we would now think of as public conduct. Today we identify more clearly a difference between the public and the private, and between the manners of these two domains. What we do in public is more formal than what we do at home. Partly this is because we in public present an ideal version of ourselves that we've assembled at home. Partly it is because in our private lives *we* define the boundaries of what's acceptable. In public, we often assume roles in which we are expected to show particular skills and behaviours; a certain poise is required. In intimate situations we feel able to give vent to a greater variety of behaviour – more emotion and more truth. Privacy allows us to test our ideas, share confidences, and lay aside the masks we wear the rest of the time (at our places of work, for instance). The contrast here is between the segmented and the diffuse, between expectation and exemption. We might assume that this is universal, but it isn't: at the risk of oversimplification, one can say that in India, Russia and Japan, public behaviour is in many respects less formal than behaviour at home.

In the Middle Ages the distinction between public and private was less clear. Although it had been drawn in Roman law, in Britain it was largely meaningless. Philippe Ariès has claimed that 'until the end of the seventeenth century, nobody was ever left alone': isolation was nigh on impossible.[3] Social life was certainly dense for medieval citizens; while they were capable of thinking in terms of trespass and nuisance, and sometimes spoke of them with a strong sense of grievance, what we would now think of as privacy – choosing to keep only the company we have selected – had negative connotations, if any. Solitude, which is in any case different from privacy, was associated with monks and hermits. Where we would speak of the private, it was usual to speak of the hidden or the secret. The word *privacy* itself would not gain currency until the seventeenth century, and even then was still sometimes muddled with the noun *privity*, a term for the genitals that had been used by Geoffrey Chaucer in the 1370s.

In medieval societies, the smooth running of what we would call public life was achieved to a large degree (perhaps surprising to us now) through the symbolic effects of gesture.

Facial expressions were remarked upon less than they are today; instead it was mainly the body that was examined – for signs that supported words, undercut them, or took their place. Ritual gesture was crucial to expressions of homage, deference, loyalty, piety, petition, penance and kindness. We may think of gesture as inherently demonstrative, but in a more concertedly gestural society the work of gesture could be circumspect. For every vigorous breast-beating there were dozens of less showy acts. A hand held up while an oath was sworn was a means of symbolizing one's submission. Going down on one knee, rather than both, was a way of holding back a certain amount of one's honour. In general, kneeling was associated with receiving and acknowledging benefits. Placing one's hands between the hands of one's overlord – not an unnatural thing to do – could be a sign that one recognized one was completely at his command. Other gestures had deprecatory effects: crossing one's legs was a mark of insouciance, while briefly closing the eyes could indicate contempt.[4] Overdoing any of these gestures could be a form of usefully ambiguous insult. By convention, when walking with a person one recognized as one's social superior one was expected to keep him on one's right and stay a pace behind him. The powerful fourteenth-century landowner Roger Mortimer attracted comment when he breached convention by walking ahead of the king (Edward II).

We still understand that placing someone on our right – which mainly happens at table – is an honour. This is merely one among the many polite behaviours that have antique explanations. Allowing one's superior to ride on one's right, for instance, made it easier for him to draw his sword, should the need arise; now one does it without any thought of swords and sheaths. Tipping one's hat is either a reduced form of uncovering one's head − an ancient mark of respect − or a relic of the practice of opening the visor of one's helmet so that the face could be seen. Firing an artillery salute is an announcement of trust: you respect your visitor's intentions and believe you can afford to discharge your weapons, showing both your own lack of hostility and your feeling that the visit is one for which you do not need to be armed.

Early guides to conduct specified ways in which one could, metaphorically speaking, disarm oneself. In due course, these principles of courtesy percolated down through society. But while writers on manners have tended to assume that good practices trickle down, often people seeking to climb the social ladder have reached up for them. The moment codes of behaviour are written down, they become accessible to people who have previously had only a limited, second-hand knowledge of them.

The process by which this has happened across Europe was the subject of groundbreaking research by Norbert Elias. A German sociologist of Jewish descent, Elias moved to Britain in 1935 to escape Nazi persecution. In 1939 he published his book *Über den Prozeß der Zivilisation*. It was not a good time to be making claims for the progress of civilized behaviour, and Elias's reputation bloomed only after the publication of an English translation of its first volume, under the title *The Civilizing Process*, in 1969.

Elias identifies the spread of civilization as a growth of inhibition. Being civilized is a matter of constraining natural impulses. To use the language of Sigmund Freud, we reconcile the pleasure principle with the reality principle: our desires are tempered by the demands of the world at large. Manners can be interpreted as symptoms of repression; when one views society from above, as if watching time-lapse footage shot from a hot-air balloon, collective repression looks useful, but to the individual it may seem a frustrating denial of life's zing and zest. It requires us to make sacrifices, conceal passions and hold back urges. In addition, it involves empathy. Self-control and empathy were not invented by Europeans of the early modern period (roughly 1500 to 1800); they existed already, but were now amplified. Self-discipline, exercised and toned a bit like a muscle, was a characteristic of the rising European bourgeoisie. Feelings of shame and repugnance became more common. As this happened, behaviour that had once seemed acceptable became problematic: for instance, you had to be much more scrupulous about disposing of your bodily waste, whether it was a question of blowing your nose discreetly or retreating to a special room to urinate.

The process Elias describes was not slick. But, with hindsight, its direction is clear. Aggression was dampened. The power of the monarch and his court increased. As London became more established as England's social and political centre, and as it became more clear that the court was the centre of power, so there developed a society in which different groups' functions and obligations were at once more sharply defined and more densely interwoven. Elias argues that the royal court stood at the heart of the social networks that initiated and maintained the civilizing process. The control of weapons was centralized, and so was the control of the people chosen to wield those weapons. Laws were stiffened: as a result, when people travelled, they no longer expected to have to fend off physical attack. Right across western Europe an upper class of knights was superseded by a more peaceable, literate upper class of courtiers.[5]

This transition – warriors to courtiers – was not absolutely decisive, as the categories were not mutually exclusive. Yet as the formal apparatus of government developed, the authoritarian state monopolized large-scale violence. Away from state-sanctioned wars, fatal acts of violence became much less common; crimes against the person diminished (outside the home, though perhaps not within it), and property became the main target for criminals. Increasingly, the authorities stigmatized violence and punished those who engaged in it.

As society became better regulated and safer, it seemed reasonable to think beyond the short term, to avoid doing now what would be likely to cause pain or displeasure in the future. More complex social relationships in any case made it more important to exercise foresight. Adolescents were recognized as a distinct group, in need of tutelage and supervision, and various means were found to control adolescent masculinity. Among these was popular entertainment, such as theatre, which allowed violent fantasies to be indulged – harmlessly, it was for the most part believed. As casual day-to-day violence receded, so sensitivity to threats and evidence of violence increased. By the middle of the seventeenth century there was a strong aversion to the sight of blood.[6] In defence of even the most passionate convictions, courtiers were likely to spill not blood, but ink.

Many of the basic principles of mannerly behaviour have existed, in a pretty stable form, since before this transition from warriors to courtiers. What's changed more has been the things we have to be mannerly *about*. Medieval courtesy books were preoccupied with table manners, almost to the exclusion of any other subject. In medieval England, the feast expressed an ideal image of society. The rituals that organized a feast were essential to the occasion's rewards. The Bible established the value of feasting (the Last Supper being just one of many biblical feasts), and medieval ideas of social behaviour, no matter how secular in appearance, were coloured by religion. Feasts were occasions to display social cohesion; leftovers could be given to the poor, who could be expected to pray for the souls of their benefactors.

Petrus Alfonsi, a Jew from Andalusia who converted to Christianity and served at the court of Henry I, wrote in a little book of wisdom he called *Disciplina Clericalis* that one should not speak with one's mouth full, allow crumbs to fall from one's lips, or lunge for the bread before any other food has reached the table. Henry's household propagated many ideas about good behaviour, and one young man who spent time there went on to be King David I of Scotland, whose innovations included a scheme to give tax rebates to those of his subjects who learned to consume their food more elegantly.

Daniel of Beccles, probably a member of the court of Henry II, was another who provided a wealth of advice for those attending feasts. In his Latin poem known as *Urbanus Magnus* or *Liber Urbani*, he wrote that while eating one should not put one's elbows on the table or play with one's cutlery, and one should never lick one's greasy fingers or speak with one's mouth full. He also emphasized the need for watchfulness and restraint as one sought to maintain peaceful relations with one's fellow citizens. One shouldn't attack an enemy while he is defecating, should avoid sharing secrets with one's wife, and ought to look towards the ceiling when belching.

Table manners, central to these medieval guides, remain important, and are interpreted as representing in miniature a person's whole repertoire of manners. They enable us to take a thin yet flavoursome slice of someone's character. In the nineteenth century it was alleged that the surest test of English people's table manners was to observe them in the act of eating asparagus, artichokes, oranges and grapes, while those of Americans could be assessed on the evidence of how a pie was consumed. The manner in which one eats peas has traditionally been subjected to similar scrutiny. It is sometimes alleged that candidates for fellowship at the exclusive Oxford college All Souls are served a fruit tart at dinner; those examining them watch to see what they do with the fruit's inedible pits. To quote a Victorian proverb: 'Every meal is a lesson learned.'

In the title of the *Liber Urbani* there is a clear sign of where Daniel of Beccles expected to find good manners. *Urbs* was the Latin for 'city', and in Latin culture it was usually understood to mean before all else Rome. *Liber Urbani* was literally a 'book of the city' – of city life and city ways. We now inevitably see a link here to the word *urbane*. This entered English in the sixteenth century; around 1600 *urbane* began to connote not just city manners but specifically an elegant form of manners. In 1623 Henry Cockeram published a dictionary in which he defines the adjective *urbane* as 'civil' or 'courteous'. By contrast, rusticity has conventionally been identified with a lack of manners, and the use of *rustic* in that sense began at around the time that *urbane* was beginning to denote courtesy. To this day, accounts of manners and guides to the subject tend to concentrate on what happens in urban life. Rural manners get less coverage, either because they are assumed not to exist (once the standard view) or because it is harder to find them documented (now the more credible explanation).

Urbanity in medieval England did not reach far. Even in the places it did reach, it could not blot out the norms of a world full of physical dangers.[7] War was an almost constant feature of life. England in the twentieth century was much less violent than England in the fourteenth century – about 95 per cent less so, according to the Harvard psychologist Steven Pinker. The medieval English were familiar with torture, cruel spectacles and capital punishment. Religious faith, often presented today as a great bulwark against chaos, did not make them safe.[8] But deep religious feeling was the norm. Although not everyone was pious and the clergy were often an object of animosity, medieval Christians, living at a time when terrestrial life was hard and there were few diversions to entice their attention, were intent on doing whatever they could to achieve salvation.

One apparent path to salvation was the Crusades, a series of experiments in colonialism that were informed by penitence yet ended in butchery. When Pope Urban II delivered the sermon at Clermont that led to the First Crusade, he turned a request for mercenaries from the embattled Byzantine emperor into a vision of armed pilgrimage. The ensuing conflicts with pagans and heretics were understood not only as a religious mission, but also as an opportunity for what we might today call personal development.

When we think of manners in this context, we think of chivalry. The word *chivalry* has been cheapened; today it calls to mind either knights protecting damsels in distress – which is the stuff of fairy tales – or a man helping a woman off the train with her heavy bag – something quaint, banal, perhaps problematic, and the cue for a joke about how this kind of thing is dying out or a retort about its being patronizing. But we know that chivalry once meant something more than this. Originally it was a collective term for knights who were ready for battle, typically mounted on horseback.

If it is a twentieth-century cliché that 'The age of chivalry is dead,' it is to the nineteenth century that we can trace the notion that chivalry is all about little courtesies. Sir Walter Scott's ballads and his novels with medieval settings fuelled an enthusiasm for reviving feasts and tournaments, as well as the (supposed) spirit of the Middle Ages. More remarkable was Kenelm Henry Digby's *The Broad Stone of Honour* (published in 1822 and later expanded), which originally set out to provide 'rules for the gentlemen of England'. Digby claimed that chivalry 'disposes men to heroic and generous actions, and keeps them conversant with all that is beautiful and sublime in the intellectual and moral world'.[9] Those inspired by Scott and Digby expended their efforts on acquiring the physical trappings of medieval Englishness, yet the business of reclaiming chivalry, even in this limited fashion, was seen as a means of recovering from the frivolity and moral laxity of the Regency period (1811–20). It was amid this rather fanciful rearmament that the adjective *chivalrous* became a term to denote what the *Oxford English Dictionary* (*OED*) calls being 'disinterestedly devoted in the service of the female sex'. It was at this time, too, that *chivalric* caught on as an alternative to *chivalrous*: *chivalric* was more strongly associated with real knightly qualities, *chivalrous* with an ideal and polished image of the halcyon days of gallantry.

The image of chivalry as a veneer of ceremony trivializes what was in the Middle Ages a serious code and a vocation with its own visual language (the heraldic insignia that would later be displayed by families as blazons of their noble histories). The concept of chivalry was probably born at the court of Charlemagne in the eighth and ninth centuries, if not before, though the word itself is not attested in English until around 1300. It flourished from 1100 to 1500, peaking in the thirteenth century, and at its heart was what the historian Maurice Keen calls 'the code and culture of a martial estate which regarded war as its hereditary profession'.[10] Keen's phrase does a good job of dispelling the romance summoned up by stories of heroic expeditions and derring-do.

In medieval society, chivalry was a means for a man to emphasize not just his bravery and valour, but his knightly bearing as well. It had a softening effect. While this is not to say that it made men actually seem soft, it moderated or channelled violent urges. Skill was prized above flamboyant attempts at heroism. Hunting, a favoured recreation and a good preparation for war, allowed a knight to perfect his handling of horses, the techniques for killing animals, and the dissection and distribution of each carcass. Tournaments, though another valuable means of preparing for warfare, were chiefly occasions for defining one's reputation, not least for being well equipped; from the thirteenth century, most of the weapons used in tournaments were blunted, and the festivities were controlled and carefully documented. Even battle, for all its material rewards and bloody thrills, was aestheticized, and although violence and vigour were commended, portraits of the best knights made much of their watchfulness and mastery of reconnaissance.

The literature of chivalry promoted an ideal of princely behaviour and the obligations of government. This informed the ideal of a Christian prince that was later expounded by the Dutch scholar Desiderius Erasmus among others. But the main legacy of chivalry was an idea of honour – something that it had itself inherited from earlier warrior codes. Honour was achieved through a life of action rather than through genteel inertia: prowess in the handling of arms, loyalty, generosity, courtesy and a frankly confident manner. Writers on the subject presented military service as not only a discipline and a profession, but also the expression of a sophisticated ethos in which horsemanship, Christian purpose and aristocratic virtue were bound together. Rather than promoting sterile conformism, chivalry emphasized that within the collective ethos of military virtue there was a special place for the individual and his journey.

We get a sense here of a world in which ideas about manners were mainly to do with male experience. So what about women? The heroic acts of the *chevalier* had an erotic stimulus. The imagination of the medieval upper classes was gripped by fantasies of love, which were inspired by works of literature. The *Roman de la Rose*, a long poem written in the thirteenth century by Guillaume de Lorris and Jean de Meun, exerted an especially strong influence, conceiving of love as a quest that develops in graduated steps. In England, Eleanor of Aquitaine in the twelfth century and Eleanor of Provence in the thirteenth played leading parts in propagating new ideas of love. These powerful women were, respectively, the wives of Henry II and Henry III. Their gift was the idea of 'courtly' love, an aristocratic sport in which the idealized mistress is an object of unstinting devotion for her adoring suitor, who hopes that his persistence will eventually be rewarded, though such an end seems almost unbearably remote. The modern Hollywood rom-com does not sound so very far away. While there was much more to courtly love than a mere code of procedures, the intricate behaviour it entailed often makes it look like an alternative to religion, and the idea of love as a surrogate for faith is a resonant one for us now, as is the idea that love, for all its supposedly organic qualities, is a ritual, a code of communication, a mechanism for establishing security and dependency.

In practice, courtly love made the woman an object. It exalted her, yet in a way that denied her individuality. Medieval women were classified according to their marital status; they were expected to be virgins, wives or widows. There was no link between employment and power, for only peasant women worked, perhaps brewing ale, mowing fields or laundering other people's clothes. The doctrine of courtly love, rather than providing women with a useful vision of their potential or of how to behave, simply enlarged the vocabulary used (by men) to talk about women.

There is no more arresting (male) literary portrait of a woman at this time than Chaucer's of the Prioress in *The Canterbury Tales*. When Chaucer introduces the Canterbury pilgrims, he gives a taste of their distinguishing characteristics. Instead of offering a lot of moralizing comment, he leaves it to his audience to form a view of precisely what is wrong with each pilgrim. Thus the open sore on the Cook's shin, readily visible, seems to suggest a sloppy approach to kitchen hygiene, and the detail is all the more pungent for being followed by the information that he makes a good sweet poultry pudding. The Pardoner's cache of spurious holy relics, besides allowing him to extract money from gullible folk, appears similarly insanitary. The Miller's liking for crude jokes, while hardly at odds with his line of work, seems as tediously inconsiderate as his passion for playing the bagpipes while the pilgrims pass through the London streets. Chaucer constructs these characters and their stories in what are often bawdy terms; in his world, unlike for much of the period since, people's particular forms of profanity were treated as evidence of their personalities and desires, rather than just as something to be blotted out and denounced.

By comparison with these figures the Prioress seems, on first view, delicate and highly civilized. She is described as demure and charitable, and we learn that she would weep if she saw a mouse in a trap. Her table manners are fastidious; she repeatedly wipes her upper lip, and in the following centuries this was frequently reproduced in courtesy books as an example of polite behaviour. But instead of being a paragon, the Prioress is guilty of a crime we know well: she is a good deal more fashionable than she should be. It is 'grease' that she wipes from her lip, and there may be a medieval pun here (lost to us because of words' changed sounds), for in so fussily removing every last trace of it, she is also eliminating all suggestion of 'grace'. The manners of Chaucer's Prioress suggest vanity, not morality. They are a shallow, worldly imitation of

French aristocratic habits, as well as echoing – unbefittingly – some tips on seduction given in the *Roman de la Rose*.

The Prioress looked to French examples because at this time there was in English no sustained guide to conduct specifically aimed at women. There would be none until the seventeenth century: Richard Brathwait's *The English Gentlewoman* (1631) has a claim to be the first work to fill the void. 'Honour' was a keyword for Brathwait. His idea of feminine 'decency' was narrow. A decent woman's 'propriety' could be perceived in the way she walks ('demurely'), her gaze (there should be no 'lightness' or 'wantonness'), her speech ('light' subjects were to be avoided) and her attire (which should show no sign of 'variety and inconstancy'). Brathwait stressed the need for women to concentrate on domestic matters, and claimed that a woman in mixed company should 'tip her tongue with silence'. Among young women especially, 'bashful silence is an ornament'. In short, a gentlewoman should be 'fashionably neat', 'formally discreet', 'civilly complete', 'amiably decent', 'precious in repute', 'affectionately constant', 'generously accommodated' (which is somewhat vaguely explained) and 'honourably accomplished'.[11]

These terms suggest a difficult balancing act. *The English Gentlewoman* was the forerunner of all those guides to female excellence that expect women to achieve an impossible array of skills and qualities – as wives and mothers, rounded but retiring, and gemlike but unobtrusive. It also inherited a medieval tradition of picturing the ideal woman as self-effacing, chiefly concerned with others' welfare rather than her own.

Before Brathwait, there were imported treatises providing similar instruction, but their focus was narrow: at their core was a concern with the preservation of honour through chastity. The fourteenth-century *The Book of the Knight of the Tower*, compiled by the Angevin nobleman Geoffroy de la Tour Landry for the instruction of his daughters, was twice translated into English in the century that followed, the second time by Caxton. It is mainly concerned with clarifying the difference between good and evil, to keep young women from surrendering their chastity to manipulative males. It is a paean to moderation, fixated on the need for women to dress in an unostentatious style. No woman should wear the sort of steepling headdress that obliges her to stoop like a stag entering a wood; hanging sleeves are out, and so are fancy caps. In literature of this kind, aimed at girls rather than grown women, examples were essential. Biblical stories were used to illustrate virtues. The story of the Virgin Mary – typically presented as an illiterate – was used to teach humility. The religious imagery notwithstanding, this kind of literature wasn't going to percolate through much of society; the conduct book for women came of age as a genre only when it ceased to be coloured by aristocratic imagery and ideals – and when a lot more women could read.

3

Lubricants and filters

'a kind of lesser morality'

It is hard to discuss manners for long without remembering certain sayings about them. The one that comes up most often is 'Manners maketh man'. When I told people that I was writing a book about manners, no response was more common than those three words, pronounced in an elliptical style that wasn't obviously either reverent or ironic. Spelled a little differently, they were the motto chosen in the fourteenth century by William of Wykeham, a rich bishop and artistic patron, when he founded Winchester College, a school for boys in Hampshire, and New College, part of the University of Oxford. I remember as a schoolchild being told that these words were inscribed above the entrances to both institutions, and on one occasion also being told that they should be inscribed outside every place of learning. Implicit in the motto was the idea that it was a man's mental and moral endowments, not the advantages of background, that were the measure of his worth.

William's motto may now strike us as archaic, in both its language and its content. Today the word *manners* is likely to make us think of qualities and behaviours different from those he had in mind. Some are visible: showing consideration for colleagues and neighbours, not leaving litter behind in public, driving considerately, helping an elderly person, offering one's seat to a pregnant woman, and so on. Others are not so visible: tact, for instance. Then there are the behaviours we identify as a failure of manners, as rudeness: loudness, spitting, swearing and name-calling, crass sexual advances, not listening, not returning a greeting, pushing and shoving, blocking other people's way, encroaching on their space. We arrive at a definition of manners as acts or gestures of avoidance and restraint.

Our glimpse of the medieval world has already suggested this: in the previous chapter we had John Russell pointing out the unsightliness of clawing at one's back, Petrus Alfonsi advising against lunging for the bread, and Daniel of Beccles counselling that one should not attack an enemy while he is at stool. That chapter set up two key themes of this book. First, as new forms of sociability develop, new manners develop too. Second, manners tend to serve as protection. They shield us from aggression, insults, contact with other people's bodily fluids (and those of their pets), exposure to others' rubbish, unpleasant details of their lives, and also often the truth. In those societies we are likely to think of as 'primitive', the situation is reversed: manners exist mainly so that the individual can keep others away from his or her germs and filth and grossness.

In the absence of good manners, the rawness of our primal urges bursts forth. Even when we maintain good manners, some of those urges may leak out in sublimated form, but by minimizing leakage we ensure that those around us do not feel anxious. We identify good manners as an aid to tranquillity; they are represented as something habitual and settled, and at the same time as a lubricant, preventing friction. Arguing that manners are 'a kind of lesser morality, calculated for the ease of company', the eighteenth-century philosopher David Hume wrote that 'every thing which promotes ease, without an indecent familiarity, is useful and laudable.' Good manners exist 'to facilitate the intercourse of minds, and an undisturbed commerce and conversation'. They are a 'companionable virtue'.[1]

This makes manners sound colourless. But an act of good manners can be accompanied by a bright pulse of feeling. The reward for treating another person well may seem to be no more than the pleasant consciousness of having done so, yet there are forces at work here that we cannot track. When we form an intimate bond with another person, the brain's reward centres are activated. Feelings of affiliation and attachment cause the hormone oxytocin to be released in the brain and secreted into the bloodstream, and oxytocin further promotes those feelings of affiliation and attachment. This happens when we look at a baby, when a mother breastfeeds her child, when we are shown a sign of trust, after taking MDMA, during sexual arousal, when we play a friendly game of table tennis (which I choose because it seems so much more plausible than a friendly game of squash or football) or when we deliberately extend a courtesy to someone who is not our kin. Stress blocks the release of oxytocin, and testosterone interferes with its reception. But when oxytocin is released and received, it causes dopamine to be released as well, heightening our sensitivity to pleasure. Affiliative or 'pro-social' behaviours start a virtuous circle in the chemical life of our brains.[2]

Hume's companionable virtue, with its chemical accompaniments, seems to be a fact of all human societies. When in 1945 the American anthropologist George P. Murdock noted the characteristics recorded in all cultures known to ethnographers, the list included cleanliness training, etiquette, greetings, hospitality, mealtimes and status differentiation.[3] The specific practices vary, but the basic principles appear to be universal.

What is more, the manners practised by humans echo some of the behaviours of other species. Chimpanzees selectively groom their intimates. They practise courtship. They innovate and use tools. When they develop a clever technique for doing something, they pass it on to others. After squabbling, they reconcile, kissing on the lips. This may not seem at all surprising. But consider ants, as the biologist Edward O. Wilson has done since the 1940s: their civilization contains practices equivalent to the human concern with cleanliness training, etiquette, greetings, hospitality and status differentiation, and it features caste laws, communal nurseries, courtship rituals, food taboos and rules of residence.

It is not the concept of manners that is unique to humans, but rather the ability to reason in a complex fashion about such behaviour, thinking and talking and indeed writing about it. The metaphors we use every day hint at submerged codes of manners. For instance, we often equate looking with touching: 'Their eyes met', 'Your eyes were glued to her performance', 'He totally eye-fucked me.' 'He can't take his eyes off me' expresses a shudder – perhaps of revulsion, perhaps of delight, but either way suggesting another person's projection of an interest that feels physically present though it is not. Being looked at can feel as invasive, intimate and even erotically charged as being touched.

To choose a different example: arguments, even when pursued in what we would regard as quite a civilized fashion, are warlike. Thus: 'She attacked all my main points', 'That's an indefensible position', 'This is one issue where you're not going to win', 'That's a weak strategy', 'His argument is unassailable.' It is normal to understand, conduct and discuss arguments as if they are small wars.[4] Clearly, arguments can be pursued with different levels of hostility. Yet the ordinary way of talking about them means that, even when they are pursued in a restrained and dignified way, the language of conflict remains. When we use manners in order to forestall arguments, their role is not to prevent thoughtful debate, but to reduce the chances of larger eruptions of violence. This suggests the way our metaphors disclose exactly what is at stake when we practise good manners.

Commenting on an encounter with a plausible young man who turned out to be a petty criminal, charity worker Janine says, 'His manners were disarming.' We are used to thinking that *disarming* means 'charming', but for most of its history the word has signified only the more military business of forcing a weapon from someone's hand or divesting him of armour. This is apt, for manners are a means of depriving other people of their weapons of attack, establishing a peaceful footing rather than a hostile one. They are part of our equipment for self-preservation.

Manners express power relationships. But while sometimes these are visible (as in the polite behaviour of a waiter towards a customer), often they are not. In the context of thinking about sex, the historian and philosopher Michel Foucault argued that 'Power is tolerable only on condition that it mask a substantial part of itself. Its success is proportional to its ability to hide its own mechanisms.'[5] Manners seem to bear out his point; they reinforce social similarities and dissimilarities while giving the appearance of taking no account of them.

Though easily construed as deference, mannerly behaviour tends to have an assertive undercurrent. Politeness can be strategic and egotistical even where it looks self-effacing or altruistic. The economist Thorstein Veblen in *The Theory of the Leisure Class* (1899) wrote of manners as a form of hangover from bygone rituals, a pantomime in which old gestures of mastery and subservience are symbolically revived. What, then, are we to make of the French philosopher Henri Bergson's statement, in a speech at a prize-giving in 1892, that '*Au fond de la vraie politesse vous trouverez un sentiment, qui est l'amour de l'égalité*'?[6] (This translates, approximately, as 'Deep down, you'll find that true politeness is a matter of loving equality.') At first blush, this seems to contradict everything else in this paragraph. But assiduously practising equality, displaying one's commitment to it, is itself an act of dominance. Whereas the *existence* of equality precludes dominance, making a show of equality amounts to confirmation that equality has not been achieved.

What, moreover, are we to make of the appearance here of the word *class*? So far I have used it only a handful of times. By convention, it is something we all know about but which decent folk do not discuss, something that is everywhere and yet nigh on impossible to treat with candour, a debatable matter but not one that often gets debated. Class is one of the things for which the English are famous; or rather, our concern with class is infamous. No outsider can reflect at length on England without attempting to unpick the peculiarities of its class system; meanwhile the English, even in the act of being hypersensitive about class, tend to profess themselves indifferent to it.

It was in the nineteenth century that the word *class* began to be used to signify a system. Since the seventeenth century people had spoken of classes – 'lower', 'higher', 'governing'. *Middle class* was established as a noun by around 1750; as an adjective it did not take off until about a hundred years later. We might interpret this as a sign that what we would call class distinctions were coming into sharper focus. But in its new sense the word *class*, rather than marking social differences precisely, did the reverse. It suggested the existence of a pattern of social divisions, yet created sketchiness where previously there had been the crisper demarcations of *rank, order, station* and *degree*. The old terms had connoted heredity, along with duties and ethical expectations. *Class* was not so bound up with the past, having no air of the feudal or the medieval, and was therefore easier to change. The business of changing it was spelled out in the Victorian period's innumerable etiquette books, which were aids to ambition. As social distinctions became less static, so defensiveness and rivalry increased, as did a fondness for playing detective, spotting differences that had been submerged.

To this day the language of class is neither consistent nor rigorous, and when inevitably it is used in discussions of social inequalities, it ensures that those discussions are vehemently general rather than usefully particular. In political debate, much is made of the need for a classless society, and all the major parties from time to time claim it as one of their goals. Yet people's notions of their own class provide them with security or with explanations for their disappointments and failures, and their class is something they reproduce – even in the act of trying to cover it up or deny its existence. The working class is alone in being licensed to extol its own culture publicly; other classes display what they think of as their virtues, rather than talking about them, and may even apologize as they display them (an English middle-class tic).

Our notions of class are piquant and likely to cause resentment, but are incapable of exact definition. The danger of examining class is that it is one of those subjects that disappear into thin air the moment you try to grasp hold of them. Jilly Cooper observes in her book *Class*, 'a view from middle England' published in 1979, that tackling the subject has been 'like trying to catalogue the sea'. When she tells acquaintances what she is doing, they reel from her in horror, as if she is trying to produce 'a standard work on coprophilia or child-molesting'. They pretend that class does not exist. The true aristocrat behaves as though ceremonies and boundaries have not been invented. Cooper cites the example of an earl who, at a stag party in a London club, urinates into a chamber pot in full view of the other guests. This kind of insouciance is noticeable even at upper-class weddings: 'As they are accustomed to giving and going to balls and big parties, the wedding is not such an event as it would be in a middle-class family.' She mentions 'one upper-class bride . . . so relaxed she spent her wedding morning washing her horse's tail'.[7]

What emerges from Jilly Cooper's assorted anecdotes is that it is the psychology of class that really matters – the presence of class in people's minds. One of the areas in which we see this most clearly is language. George Bernard Shaw famously remarked that 'it is impossible for an Englishman to open his mouth without making some other Englishman despise him.' The social anthropologist Kate Fox glosses this nicely: 'All English people, whether they admit it or not, are fitted with a sort of social Global Positioning Satellite computer that tells us a person's position on the class map as soon as he or she begins to speak.'[8] This GPS system is not unique to England, but the English version is an object of fascination to outsiders, a complicated feat of engineering that is heavy and built to last yet also highly sensitive, expensive to maintain and not known to travel well.

Once, when I was in my twenties, a mature guest at a friend's birthday party took exception to my relaxed posture (both my neighbours had gone walkabout), and asked, 'Where were you at school that they didn't teach you not to put your elbows on the table?' Some might say that such custodial questioning is worse than the behaviour it is designed to reprove. Certainly it doesn't help smooth out the wrinkles of social intercourse. What I remember most keenly, though, is the form of the question I was asked: 'Where were you at school . . . ?' This is a variant on a theme: What do your parents do? Whereabouts do you live? Where did you grow up? It's the GPS at work, the English appetite for 'placing' people. We know that Margaret Thatcher's father was a grocer in Grantham, and that her successor as Prime Minister, John Major, was the son of a one-time music-hall performer who manufactured garden gnomes. But how many Americans in the 1980s knew that Ronald Reagan's father had been a shoe salesman, and how many French citizens knew that the father of their president François Mitterrand had been a stationmaster and later the manager of a business that made vinegar? The English have long attached immense significance to the identity and origins of a person's father. Even though that preoccupation has receded a little, they remain alert to the minute particulars of other people's accents, habits, appearance and, of course, manners.

The insistence on placing people is a mark of unease. Kate Fox prefers the term 'dis-ease', which has connotations not only of extreme discomfort but also of perversely choosing to be uncomfortable. Sigmund Freud called it *Unbehagen*. This is conventionally translated as 'discontents', as in the title of his book *Civilization and Its Discontents* (in German *Das Unbehagen in der Kultur*), though 'discomfort' or 'malaise' would, along with 'unease', be appropriate. As Freud's title makes clear and the English version does not, the discontents are *in* civilization – its price – rather than a phenomenon separate from it. Social conformity, as we have already seen, thwarts our instincts, and we can feel frustrated when those instincts are not gratified. This existential malaise is something general, not something peculiarly English. But in English culture it manifests itself in a precise mapping of contours and other surface features, an analysis of positions and elevations. Tightly packed together, certainly when compared with most of the rest of Europe, the English are used to rubbing up against one another but, because so often obliged to do so, would prefer not to. By placing others, by putting them in particular compartments, we create more elbow room for ourselves.

I find it useful to think of society as if it is an apartment building. Residents feel a certain affinity with the others on their floor, even though in many ways they are a nuisance ('Why can't I have more considerate neighbours?'). Those on higher floors are admired or grudgingly respected, though it is more usual to think, 'I should be up there, too,' than to concede that 'The folks on the twenty-fifth floor really are a cut above'. People on lower floors are treated with a disdain that is carefully veiled – and may even hide behind a visor that looks like a smile. The grand folks at the very top appear unaware that the rest of the building contains much besides the lift shaft; occasionally they throw their trash off the balcony. Residents reserve their strongest reactions for those to whom they are proximate. Freud wrote about what he called the narcissism of small differences: the details that separate adjoining communities – or adjacent people – are exaggerated in order to italicize oppositions ('us and them', and so on).[9] A driver in a Mercedes E350 looks down on a driver in a Mercedes E250 more than one in a Ford Fiesta. In practice, observing the narcissism of small differences is crucial to an understanding of manners. We feel most strongly compelled to differentiate ourselves from those who are most like us.

4

Godspeed, babe

The greatest medieval English painting is the pair of oak panels known as the *Wilton Diptych*, created around 1395. A true English treasure, it is on show at the National Gallery in London. With its central hinge open, this portable masterpiece shows on the left-hand side Richard II, accompanied by the saints John the Baptist, Edward the Confessor and Edmund the Martyr; the right-hand panel shows the Virgin Mary, with Christ in her arms and a supporting cast of eleven angels. When the hinge is closed, we see a coat of arms and a white hart upon a grassy meadow, but it is the painting's open form that is relevant here, for it shows King Richard kneeling, backed by his patrons, waiting to make a delivery or more likely to receive something. Although the symbolism is open to interpretation, it seems that Richard is appealing to Mary to intercede on his behalf with Christ.

The *Wilton Diptych* is fascinating as an image of a medieval meeting. If it suggests the sacred nature of kingship, it also honours the idea of political alliance and the possibilities of art as religious propaganda. Enigmatic it may be, but it is a beautiful celebration of the significance of coming together.

Meeting new people is for most of us a common occurrence, not obviously fraught with danger, even if it can make us a little nervous. But in primitive societies it was a source of anxiety. First encounters were tentative and interrogative. Some of the modern rituals of greeting bear a trace of this: we assay a person by means of a handshake, perhaps, and with a conventional question ('How do you do?') that is a calcified form of what would once have been a genuine query.

Even when we present ourselves discreetly, we measure everyone we meet. The first time I encounter you, I will probably form a quick picture of your intelligence, education, attitudes, honesty, social and economic status, sexuality and emotional soundness. Some of my first impressions may well be incorrect; many will be right. I'm not making a claim here for my being outstandingly perceptive; as a species, we are adept at this rapid probing of strangers' key attributes. This ability is of immense practical use. For precisely this reason, we develop artful ways of deceiving others, manoeuvring in order to make our strengths look stronger and keep our vulnerabilities out of sight.

Greetings are routines, memorized performances of politeness. We learn them as children, and later they are refined. Think of what gets taught when you start learning a foreign language: it's all 'Hello', 'Good morning', 'How are you?', 'Where are you from?' The routines we use with strangers are acts of appeasement; those we use with more familiar people are means of asserting the continuity of our relationship – for instance, 'How are your mum and dad?' means 'I know your mum and dad. We've done this before.'

In other cultures, a meeting between two people may involve

waving, tongue-poking, rubbing noses or delicately patting each other on the bottom. Yet across cultures the essence of greetings is pairing: the structure is that of question-and-answer or call-and-response, a ritual of turn-taking that expresses recognition and the pleasure taken in recognition. When I greet someone, I am acknowledging that he or she is worth recognizing; when the greeting is returned, the value of being recognized by me is acknowledged. If this reciprocity is not achieved, offence is likely.

In some cultures this notion of pairing extends to forms of address. Anyone who speaks even a little French will be aware of the distinction between *tu* and *vous*: these are the singular and plural forms of 'you', but *vous* is also used when addressing just one person, either in formal situations or to mark politeness. Such a distinction does not exist in English, but it used to: *thou* was the singular form for intimate use, and *ye*, besides being the plural, was used in circumstances that demanded greater formality. The *thou/ye* distinction faded in the late sixteenth century; Shakespeare made dramatic use of it, but within a generation it had come to seem archaic, a fusty way of marking social differences, reminiscent of a feudal age. For a long time English has achieved something equivalent to the *tu/vous* distinction by other means: with nominals such as *mate* (the *tu* mode) and *sir* (the *vous* mode). Calling someone *dear* when she expects to be called *madam* will seem at best cheeky, and, again, not matching another person's formality – as by calling someone *bruv* when he has called you *sir* – will cause offence. It is generally expected that an invitation, which is a greeting and a call for participation, will be extended and answered in the same format. If it comes in the third person

('Mr and Mrs Leopold Bloom request the pleasure of your company . . .'), it is answered in the third person ('Henry Hitchings accepts with pleasure . . .').

Not all greetings are exactly paired; in some cases, the reciprocation takes the form of an acknowledgement rather than a duplication of the greeting. A bow, for instance, does not have to be answered with a bow, but it has to be recognized. Bowing is essentially an abbreviated form of the act of prostrating oneself before a superior. Prostration was common among the ancient Chinese (the word *kowtow*, literally 'knock the head', is a relic of this) and was encouraged by Alexander the Great. The Greek chronicler Plutarch records that his fellow historian Callisthenes would not make this servile gesture; the less demonstrative bow was his compromise.[1] In modern Japan there are distinct styles of bow such as the *eshaku*, which is a slight bending of the body, and the *saikeirei*, which is a slow, deep bow expressing great reverence; Buddhists when they bow make a gesture called *gassho*, in which the hands are held, palms together, in front of the heart, much like the Indian *namaste*.

The English bow is brief, short and masculine. The curtsy, which we now think of as a female gesture, achieves the same effect as the bow, but in a somewhat more expansive style that hints at the nimbleness of a dance move. The word itself is a variant of *courtesy*, and in the sixteenth century it was a general term for a gesture of obeisance (in Shakespeare the curtsying is often done by men). Up until the first half of the nineteenth century, it was usual to bow or curtsy when one entered or left a room where there were people of one's own or a higher status. One spoke not only of making a curtsy, but also of dropping one, and the choice of verb indicated both the necessary lowering of the body and the manner of one's doing so – lightly respectful rather than deeply reverent.

Today we are surprised if someone bows or curtsies. We are also unused to people wearing hats, except at occasions such as weddings, so the old practice of removing one's hat as a mark of respect is unfamiliar, and the one kind of hat we come across a lot, the baseball cap, is always resolutely kept on, a protection against the sun and the attentions of CCTV.

The formal greeting we experience most often is a handshake. This used to mark a pledge. There are handshakes in Homer, in both the *Iliad* and the *Odyssey*. In Britain, its significance changed from the middle of the seventeenth century, thanks to the Quakers. Trust and reciprocity were essential to Quaker business relationships, and they used the handshake as an egalitarian alternative to greetings that required any show of deference. The handshake did not fully establish itself in Britain until the late eighteenth century, but soon it was regarded as a distinctly British and indeed English custom. In Gustave Flaubert's *Madame Bovary*, published in 1856 with the subtitle '*Moeurs de province*' (Provincial Manners) and set a couple of decades earlier, a handshake is described as a greeting 'in the English fashion'.

People's handshakes often inadvertently convey an enthusiasm (or, more likely, lack of it) that they have carefully managed not to show in their facial expressions. But the handshake is in essence a gesture of openness: an act of physical engagement in which the two parties symbolically demonstrate that they are unarmed, a symmetrical expression of goodwill, and a form of touching that is exempt from the usual taboos about touching people with whom we are not intimate. Refusing to shake hands is understood as an insult. Incidentally, one of the reasons why young boys have traditionally been taught not to stand with their hands in their pockets is that there is something more than merely slovenly about concealing their hands: the attitude is one of closed defiance. In the 1820s a fashion for men walking with their hands in their pockets was noted with some alarm in the reference book *The Annual Register*, though it was apparently within a few years 'superseded by the general use of gloves'.[2]

The semiotics of the handshake are not especially subtle. A hand offered limply suggests weakness of character, while a hand clamped on yours with vice-like strength marks an assertiveness that may be a mark of psychotic competitiveness. A firm, sober shake projects an air of reasonableness and equability. A stranger's unfamiliar grip may be an attempt to see if you are a member of a secret society to which he belongs – perhaps the Freemasons. Slapping hands or touching fists (as famously done by Barack and Michelle Obama) can be an indication of spontaneous high spirits or of the desire to subvert the bourgeois nature of the handshake – something that also happened in Mussolini's Italy in the 1920s and 1930s, where the salute was preferred.

The handshake is, of course, tactile. For the most part touch is a channel for communication that we use in a rather guarded fashion. Our skin is a sensory system of vital importance, and the immediacy of touch makes it powerful, sometimes threateningly so. We cultivate the sense of touch less than our other senses. What do we touch the most, besides our own bodies and our loved ones? Among the first things that come to mind are keyboards, the screens of smartphones and similar devices, door handles, taps, cutlery, paper. But because we connect personal touch with affection and with sex, we are in many situations suspicious of it. We are encouraged to hug our children, yet mostly we are conditioned to avoid touching people, ourselves and objects that do not belong to us. Teachers are trained not to touch their students. It is not unusual for people who have been touched even in passing by a stranger or an authority figure to claim that this was an assault. When the English find themselves in more tactile cultures, they sometimes exult in the therapeutic and affective possibilities of touch, but a more common reaction is revulsion or at least a shiver of distaste. Although touch can be associated with comfort, nurture, pleasure and the breaking down of social and emotional distance, it is also associated with contamination, disruption, unwelcome influence and sexual intent, as well as with verification (as if in being touched you're being checked for signs of infirmity). The handshake is our most frequent form of public touching, but it is not sensorily rich.

One of the reasons why greetings have become less elaborate is that meeting new people has become a more common occurrence. Moreover, modern informality has eroded traditional formal greetings and replaced them with less predictable ones. Over a period of six months I noted the words with which I was greeted at the various coffee shops I patronize: 'Hi', 'Hiya', 'Hello', 'Hola', 'Hey, buddy', 'What can I get you?', 'Can I help you?', 'What you havin'?', 'What'll it be?', 'Yes, babe', 'My friend', 'Yes, boss', 'Yes, mate', 'Yes?', 'What can I do for you?', 'Who's next?', 'What do you fancy?', 'Next customer in line, please'. This freestyle approach is seen as authentic and spontaneous, but occasionally there can be confusion about how best to respond.

If greeting people has become more relaxed (and thus in fact more awkward), the language of parting remains comparatively clear-cut, despite the rise of alternatives to a straightforward 'goodbye'. We say goodbye – the word originally a contraction of 'God be with ye' – because it is a neat way of closing an encounter, but also out of some vestigial sense of the fragility of our existence and the possibility that this parting could be our last. 'God be with ye' was itself implicitly a contraction of 'God be with ye till we meet again'. Other phrases used at times of parting are similarly freighted with a sense of the hazards that life involves ('Take care', 'Godspeed', 'Be safe', 'Don't do anything I wouldn't do'), but then there are alternatives that, in their casualness, avoid any trace of such piety or solicitude ('See you around', 'Laters', 'Okay, then'). In other societies, the rituals of parting are more complicated. Chinese farewells are more painstaking than Chinese hellos, with the act of departure played out over an extended time and space.

The sociologist Erving Goffman has written of greetings and farewells as being like punctuation marks either side of a shared activity. They open and close a period of increased access to another person. He notes that when greetings are exchanged in passing, goodbyes are often dispensed with: we mark the end of not-being-in-touch, but we don't move on to a true state of being-in-touch, and the encounter's termination therefore doesn't require ritual comment.[3] In a more sustained encounter, mismatched punctuation can cause offence. Generally, a farewell is a more delicate matter than a greeting, because it lays the ground for one's next encounter with a person. Farewells are likely to be more effusive; a hugely enthusiastic greeting is unsettling compared with a similarly enthusiastic farewell – think of the different resonances of 'It's fantastic to see you' and 'It was fantastic to see you'.

Greeting people and bidding them farewell involve what we naturally think of as 'exchanges'. But in fact all inter-actions are exchanges. Sometimes the exchange is focused: there is mutual and sustained awareness of it, as when you're making love, having a tête-à-tête, or playing chess. Sometimes it is unwitting: it happens merely because people are in one another's presence. In both cases, though, we manage others' impressions of us. A lot of our managerial efforts happen below the threshold of consciousness. The elements of which we *are* conscious strike us as theatrical: learned lines and gestures, endlessly rehearsed, but, like all theatre, an illusion that, although it usually works (and because we know it usually works), is fragile.

Kissing has long played a part in greetings and farewells. The kiss has a complex history as a seal of trust, a gesture of peace, a sacred touch, a Judas-like portent of betrayal or disaster, and a magic charm, besides its simple uses as a token of greeting or affection – and its potential as something profane, invasive, outrageous. The Greek historian Herodotus records that among the ancient Persians one kissed an equal on the mouth and someone slightly one's inferior on the cheek. This contrasted with the restraint of the Egyptians, among whom one saluted another person in the street by letting one's hand fall down to one's knee. The English have in recent times been regarded as fairly unenthusiastic about greeting others with a kiss, but Erasmus, visiting England in 1499, was delighted to find that 'when you arrive anywhere, you are received with kisses on all sides, and when you take your leave they speed you on your way with kisses.'[4]

In 2011 the Knigge Society, a German etiquette watchdog that takes its name from the eighteenth-century moralist Adolph Knigge, declared that in the workplace a kiss on the cheek by way of greeting was an un-Teutonic aberration. Invited to comment on this, the president of an American 'etiquette consulting firm', Mannersmith, claimed that 'Kissing in greeting may be acceptable at the beginning of a business meeting or even possibly a job interview.'[5] But to accept the practice of greeting others with a kiss is not to dissolve all problems. How many kisses should one give? In Italy, two seems to be the norm; in Poland and the Netherlands, it's three; in most of France, it's two, though there are regions where the preferred number is three or even four. And in Britain? In England? Two seems normal now. *Mwah-mwah.* But while the use of kisses as a greeting is still widely derided as a rather superficial form of geniality, the immense amount of sensory information available to us when we exchange kisses – even air kisses – should not be ignored. Through the nerve endings in our lips, through our aroma and our sense of smell, and with our hands, we transmit and receive information that's useful, potentially empowering and potentially damaging. The line that 'It was just a kiss', usually mendacious, is also naïve.

Besides the encounters I've so far dealt with, there is another kind of meeting: a formal assembly. In the Middle Ages meetings were armed encounters: local disputes were settled by means of a 'moot', at which proposals were approved with a banging together of weapons – or dismissed with groans. These attempts to negotiate arguments gradually became less military in temper. During the Renaissance, urbanization and political centralization gave rise to a more parliamentary style of meeting, over which courtiers presided. Urbane discussion became the mechanism for resolving or curtailing differences and achieving solidarity. Yet even in the nineteenth century the word *meeting* was a euphemism for a duel – a hangover from a less bureaucratic age. And today *meeting* is associated with other ways of taking lives or at least sapping vitality.

The most celebrated meeting of the Tudor period is depicted in a painting not as remarkable as the *Wilton Diptych* but still of great historical significance: *The Field of the Cloth of Gold*, which today hangs at Hampton Court. In 1520 Henry VIII of England and Francis I of France staged an expensive jamboree in the vale between the villages of Ardres and Guines, a portion of neutral ground near Calais (a town then under English control). The two countries had concluded a treaty of 'perpetual friendship' in 1518. Now, for nearly three weeks in June, this Anglo-French accord – in truth a pretty hollow promise of peace – was sumptuously acted out. This extravagant performance was the brainchild of Thomas Wolsey, a master of alluring PR. The tents and pavilions in which much of it happened were decked with gold and silver cloth, thus providing posterity with a name to pin on this hybrid of tournament and festival, which combined diplomacy and pageantry with archery and jousting. There were feasts, processions, choral performances and displays of costume and jewellery. The two monarchs, both in their twenties, wrestled. The spirit was jubilant yet also suspicious and deeply competitive. The English contingent was more than 5,000 strong, with nearly 3,000 horses; the French contingent was of similar size and included 500 archers.

The encounter recorded in *The Field of the Cloth of Gold* was a giant charade, in which – no small irony – the making of peace was forcefully performed. For both parties, the weapon of choice was manners. It is fitting, then, that Henry was the dedicatee of Sir Thomas Elyot's *The Boke Named the Governour* (1531), a guide intended to equip men for positions of authority in public life. In the sixteenth century there was an increased self-consciousness about the processes by which identity was moulded.[6] *The Boke Named the Governour*, which encouraged its readers to develop an armoury of social skills, was a primer for aristocratic self-fashioning. It has a claim to be the first truly English book of this kind.

5

Of courtiers and codpieces

fashioning Renaissance identity

The *Lisle Letters*, which date from the years 1533 to 1540, allow us to eavesdrop on the daily business of the Tudor world. Lord Lisle, the illegitimate son of Edward IV, was Henry VIII's governor in Calais, and the letters sent by him and members of his family (and to them) reveal among other things the period's changing ideas about social hierarchy and education. They suggest a society freeing itself from medieval feudalism.

The letters are, to put it crudely, full of stuff: references to bonnets and caps, spaniels and mastiffs, wine and melons, damask and velvet, gold ornaments and rings. They illuminate the wealth and hedonism of the age, as well as the importance of gifts – and how rare it was for Tudor officials to admit that what they wanted was not wine or hawks or plump quails but ready money. For the most part, acts of generosity were large and formulaic. Yet sometimes the gifts could be disarmingly personal. When Honor, Lady Lisle, was a guest of the Elector Palatine at Calais, she was surprised to see that he picked his teeth with a pin, and later she sent him her own toothpick (which she had been using for seven years) by way of an improvement.

The *Lisle Letters* were written at a time when the population was rising and the gap between rich and poor was growing wider. Standards of personal comfort improved at this time, but plague, influenza and terrible harvests raised rates of mortality. There was upward social mobility, but also striking downward mobility. Of the families that rose, most owed their success to political office, legal careers or the City of London, rather than to the profits of owning land. England was becoming less agrarian. Education was expanding. Literature was being politicized. The monarch controlled who was admitted to the ranks of titled aristocracy. When Henry VIII died in 1547 there were just nine more peers than when he acceded to the throne in 1509. Queen Elizabeth created or revived only eighteen peerages across her reign (1558–1603); she seems to have thought of the peerage as a select caste, for men of august lineage.[1]

In the age of Henry and Elizabeth, manners were for courtiers. By the eighteenth century, they were for all enlightened men. This was a big change, and it began during the Renaissance. The word *courtesy* started to give way to *civility*. The transition was not smooth, but in the seventeenth century the words *civil* and *civility* – denoting concepts learned from Italy – became central to the vocabulary of good manners.[2] The distinction is this: *courtesy* is a quality, discussed using language that quickly becomes abstract, whereas *civility* implies a set of principles, an investment in a moral universe in which other people's dignity is respected and in which their desire for dignity is respected. Moreover, *courtesy* is a term associated with the court and the aristocracy, whereas *civility* is associated with 'civic' matters and the life of the town. Those who cultivated civility were not hostile to aristocracy, but they were concerned with social progress and harmonious living.

Across Europe, the doctrine of civility grew as the grip of Christianity, specifically Catholicism, weakened. This may sound counterintuitive, but the advance of civility was connected to the secularization of knowledge, the emancipation of subjective reason, and the particularization of truth. It became common during the Renaissance to think rationally about matters that would once have been dealt with intuitively. In England, the Reformation created a rivalry between different Christian groups, and that rivalry broke the moral unity of the people. Scepticism increased. As society grew more materialistic and mercantile, so it inevitably became more concerned with style and self-presentation. The Canadian scholar Benet Davetian makes the interesting point that the development in art of perspective (which began in Florence with Filippo Brunelleschi and Leon Battista Alberti in the fifteenth century) was an innovation with consequences for notions of personal identity: it replaced the symbolic representation of life with an undistorted, secular vision, allowing men and women to gaze upon art that showed the world 'as *they* saw it rather than ... the way they imagined God saw it'.[3]

None of this is to say that irrationality disappeared; we remain susceptible to intuitions, many of them flawed. Nor is it to say that all writings on manners at that time were devoid of Christian conviction. Far from it. William Fiston's *The School of Good Manners* (1595), based on a French translation of Erasmus and aimed squarely at children, opened with the words 'The fear of the Lord, is the beginning of wisdom, said

Solomon the wise most truly' – 'Let children therefore, first and principally learn to walk in this fear.'[4] Rhetoric of this kind was common, and to this day fear of divine judgement nourishes morality.

However, in the wake of the English Reformation, which had been catalysed by the growth of printing and literacy, there was a new emphasis on the faith of the individual – and indeed *on the individual*. Although religion continued to be understood as a great help in dealing with daily problems, it was a tenet of Protestantism that the individual had a personal relationship with God, rather than one mediated by a priest. For Protestants, faith was less corporate than it was for Roman Catholics; it was for the individual to achieve salvation. In time, an increasingly entrepreneurial streak would develop: ministers set up their own congregations, and worshippers shopped around for churches that suited their aspirations. Meanwhile individual believers, convinced of their personal accountability, were more likely to be critical of one another, engaging in 'mutual surveillance'.[5]

In the sixteenth century, visitors to England commented on the piety of the people they met, not on their scepticism. They also noted the freedom enjoyed by women, the abundance of silver in circulation, the absence of fortified towns, and the habit of sending children out to serve in other families. As for manners, it was usual for foreigners to assume that they were something quite new to the English. Typically the English had been represented as a barbarous island race, heartless and destructive, although there was also a tradition of regarding the English as unusually good-natured and free from vindictiveness.

Meanwhile the English who ventured abroad were a source

of concern to their compatriots. Allegedly they were quick to fall for new fashions and glittering trinkets, and it was common for critics of foreign travel to claim that it exacerbated English 'inconstancy' and posed a threat to the political and moral character of the nation. The poet-soldier Sir Philip Sidney was praised for rejecting 'foreign toys' during his travels; by implication, others were more susceptible to novelties.

One of the more insightful travellers was Thomas Hoby. Born in 1530, Hoby began his studies in 1545 at Cambridge and continued them in Strasbourg and Padua. In the summer of 1549 he toured around Italy, venturing to other university cities such as Florence and Bologna before heading south to Naples and then on to Sicily. He later wrote up his experiences. The authenticity of his account is open to question; he drew heavily on a book by Leandro Alberti, which provided details with which he could embellish his picture of Italy. Still, his knowledge of Italian culture was deep, and it enabled him to translate Baldassare Castiglione's *Il Libro del Cortegiano* (*The Book of the Courtier*), a key work in establishing the importance of the arts in shaping the identity of the social elite.

Hoby was a shrewd participant in all areas of aristocratic life. Knighted for his diplomatic services, he died aged thirty-six, before he could fulfil his potential. But he is representative of a certain kind of sixteenth-century Englishman: cultivated and proud, well-connected and adventurous. In the royal courts of the sixteenth and seventeenth centuries, taste and learning were highly valued. This was especially true in the reign of Elizabeth. She savoured ceremony and creativity, and the Elizabethan courtier was a glittering all-rounder, a man of thought and of action, ornamented with accomplishments. The model for such figures was Italian, and the most prized skills included a mastery of poetry, dancing and music. Hence our calling a polymath a 'Renaissance man'. Jacob Burckhardt in *The Civilization of the Renaissance in Italy* distinguished between 'many-sided men' and the remarkable few who were 'all-sided': a society full of the latter resembled not a corporation but 'a matter of art'.[6] Cosmopolitan men such as Hoby and Sir Philip Sidney wanted to reproduce these conditions.

All the while much of Elizabethan England was delighting in cruel amusements: public executions, bear-baiting, cock-fighting. This is a side of Englishness that we are likely to recognize: a quickness to drop all pretence of decorous restraint and collapse delightedly into brawling pugnacity.

Imagine then that you are an Elizabethan living in a town, familiar with cruel amusements yet also with the sight of the occasional glittering all-rounder. What does your world feel like? In the street there are dogs and pigs, noisy as well as filthy. Unless you are rich, you are unlikely to be insulated from the din of musicians, traffic and your neighbours. You rely on casual scavengers and gunge-farmers to keep the streets free from the worst kinds of grime. Your property is narrow, sooty, dusty and probably also musty. You are certainly able to sleep in a bed – and regard the bedstead as your main domestic asset, though it is likely to smell and be riddled with fleas. Washing your linen is a great chore, and when you clean your body it is usually without water – a brush will do to dislodge lice. You are nevertheless sensitive to bad smells, especially the stink of cesspits and latrines; you use soap and perfume to mask your own odours, aniseed or cumin to freshen your breath. Light is a valuable resource; in the houses of all but the rich, there is a choice between having enough light and having enough warmth.

You live in a home without upholstery, in which the model for furniture is that of the church, where comfort does not matter. In fact, you probably have nothing better to sit on than a stool. Before the eighteenth century, not many chairs were upholstered or provided with cushions, and the kind of sprung padding we might expect of an armchair or sofa was not common until the Victorian era. The historian Keith Thomas writes that 'People unused to upholstered furniture do not have a desire for it.' But people who are used to it think un-upholstered furniture looks naked, spartan and primitive – or painfully fashionable. Certainly your Elizabethan surroundings will seem, to twenty-first-century eyes, alarmingly stark. Thomas provides a list of goods that were rare or non-existent in the early sixteenth century but common by the middle of the eighteenth. It includes sugar, tobacco, books, newspapers, clocks, pictures, curtains and glass drinking vessels.[7]

Yet there were luxuries on show. The best houses contained handsome carvings and tapestries, and at the richest tables the food was spread out in a thick carpet, coloured here and there with saffron or even gold leaf, washed down with wines from Gascony or the Rhineland. One's person was to be similarly bedecked: some of the clothes worn by aristocrats were made of sable and cloth of gold, while velvet, satin and taffeta were all reserved for affluent folk.[8] Fine dress was the sign of fine feelings, and clothes were used strategically, to heighten the authority of men (think of the familiar images of Henry VIII, for instance) and emphasize the most appealing physical traits of women (hence Henry's displeasure when his bride-to-be Anne of Cleves wore a high-cut German dress). One historian says of the codpiece that it might 'somewhat frivolously . . . be called the Renaissance man's Wonderbra'.[9] Inspiration for personal adornment could be drawn from far afield. Costume books began to circulate in the 1560s, providing images of people in their best outfits; a Venetian, Cesare Vecellio, produced a volume that contained 500 woodcuts showing forms of attire from all around the world.

For the courtly elite, the nature of excellence was presented in conduct books. Castiglione's was one such work. In *The Boke Named the Governour*, his home-grown recipe for domestic and public competence, Sir Thomas Elyot suggested that prospective members of the ruling class should cultivate self-lessness and dedicate themselves to personal development. He recommended chess, condemned games involving dice, and applauded the refreshing powers of music. Elyot's ideal courtier is an impersonal figure, whose qualities include affability and mercy, courage and temperance – the last of these not always popular in the reign of Henry VIII. His later *The Castle of Health* provided further details about the correct diet and exercise regimen for a young nobleman; it includes surprising information, such as that all fruits are 'noyfull' (noxious) and often cause 'putrified fevers'.

The written history of manners, inasmuch as it exists at all, tends to be the history of such books. The genre survives to this day. Classics in the field include *The Whole Duty of Man*, a collection of lessons about personal duties published in 1658 by the clergyman Richard Allestree, and the Scottish moralist James Fordyce's *Sermons to Young Women* (1766). Going further back, one might mention the educational treatise *De Civilitate*

Morum Puerilium (published in 1530 and translated into English two years later), in which Erasmus preached piety and 'outward bodily propriety', and Stefano Guazzo's *La Civil Conversazione* (1574), which emphasized that civility was not a matter of status but one of spiritual qualities expressed through habits. Guazzo's book was not a guide to chitchat, whatever its title may suggest. He had in mind not merely talk, but the whole business of human interactions. Educated English readers latched on to his style, which mixed seriousness with an appetite for witty proverbs, and English authors pilfered his wisdom.

In between Erasmus and Guazzo came Giovanni della Casa's *Galateo* (1558). Della Casa was a churchman but also worldly-wise, a patrician Florentine writing for an audience of public, active individuals. He advised his readers that when in company they should not clean their fingernails, read letters or fall asleep (the last for fear of waking up covered in sweat and slobber). He also counselled that one ought never to present a friend with something pungent and say, 'Please smell how this stinks'; one's impulse should instead to be to say, 'Don't smell this, because it stinks.' Nor should you look in your handkerchief after blowing your nose, 'as if pearls or rubies might have descended from your brain'.[10] Della Casa's main concern was how to avoid giving offence: don't suck your teeth, hum when you have company, discuss at table wounds or disease, or point out to your friends disgusting things by the roadside.

None of these three works was written in English, but the ideas contained in them found significant English-speaking audiences. They offered a guide to life in broad terms, rather than just to some small corner of it. These conduct books' modern counterparts are self-help guides, volumes such as *The Rules* (1995), in which Ellen Fein and Sherrie Schneider proffer 'time-tested secrets for capturing the heart of Mr Right' (for instance, 'Be honest but mysterious' and 'Don't rush into sex, wait at least three dates'). There is a difference between the two genres: conduct books are concerned with teaching norms of behaviour, whereas self-help, besides its obvious accent on improving performance, is more concerned with psychological norms – with eradicating existing patterns of thought and replacing them with more affirmative or tactically cunning ones. The audience for *The Rules* is plainly different from the audience for a book called *La Civil Conversazione*. Yet while the modern self-help guide may be less dignified and more ruthlessly pragmatic than the conduct books used by previous generations, the two kinds of writing share an instructional approach to personal development and achieve-ment, as well as emphasizing individuality and the importance of appearances.

There are essentially two kinds of book in this whole field. There are books of practical advice: 'Do this', 'Don't do that'. And there are books that set out a theory of how we should behave. The former have tended to be written for a narrow audience (there is a tradition of parents producing works of this kind to aid their children), whereas the latter have tended to reach larger constituencies. The more abstract works of instruction can be philosophically profound, but mostly they appeal because their message is affirmative and banal.

In sixteenth-century England one of the more assertively practical programmes was Thomas Wolsey's Eltham Ordinance of 1526. An attempt to reform the court of Henry VIII, its provisions were minute. For instance, the king's barber was expected to be in attendance every day when he rose, with all his equipment ready – water, cloths, knives, combs, scissors – and was strictly instructed to avoid the company 'of vile persons, or of misguided women'. Those in attendance in the king's privy chamber were to be 'loving together, and of good unity and accord'; if the king was absent when they expected him, they were not to ask why and should avoid 'mumbling or talking of the King's pastime'. Leftover candles were to be collected by nine o'clock in the morning, and failure to do so would be punished by the withholding of a week's wages.

Impromptu guides to manners also passed around, and could be of great use to traders. Richard Chancellor, who commanded the first expedition of the Muscovy Company in 1555, explained the rituals of the Russian tsar's court in a series of handwritten notes; these were an indispensable guide to the ins and outs of doing business in Russia. With their details of toasts and correct form at table, as well as their remarks about the importance of oaths and letters of introduction, Chancellor's jottings are an early example of the notion that manners can be a business tool. But the deepest influence was exerted by writers who proposed philosophies of personal excellence. The two that stood out were Erasmus and Castiglione, and it is to them that we now turn.

6

But who was the Renaissance man?

Modern notions of civility begin with Erasmus. His writings, elegant and accessible, preached the idea that training and practice were essential to making the most of one's natural gifts. *De Civilitate Morum Puerilium*, published in 1530 and translated into English two years later, was aimed at young boys – and not just noble ones.[1] It systematically explained how to do the right thing: how to stand and sit, bow, wear one's hair (neat, but not shiny like a girl's), behave in church (small talk is out of the question), lie in bed with a male companion (no stealing all the blankets) and project an air of modesty. Running through all this was an obvious concern with outward bodily propriety.

Erasmus's guidelines were adopted by schools and widely copied. Much of what he wrote remains interesting, not least because it is often informed by an acute understanding of the relationship between behaviour and image. He advises against certain facial expressions: staring is a sign of inertia, a wide-eyed gaze indicates stupidity, furrowing the eyebrows makes you look cruel, puffing your cheeks out suggests disdain. The soul expresses itself through the eyes, so it is important to regulate the way you use them. Don't neigh when you laugh, and avoid giggling at private jokes. Don't intersperse your speech with little coughs, which hint at deceitfulness. Don't stroke your face as if trying to wipe away your shame.

He also talks about matters that don't tend to be publicly discussed any more. Ideally, you should expel snot into a cloth rather than wiping your nose on your clothes; if no cloth is to hand and you blow your nose using only your fingers, you should tread the snot into the ground rather than simply leaving it in open view. He suggests that if you sneeze when others are around you should turn aside – and remember that the sneeze may have temporarily impaired your hearing. If someone else sneezes, everyone should bless him scrupulously. At the time the usual response in polite English circles was immediately and quietly to say 'Christ help' (a forerunner of the still common 'Bless you'); this type of practice had been around at least since ancient Greek society, in which sneezes were regarded as ominous, and stemmed from the belief that any interruption of the breath of life was dangerous, posing a threat to the sanctity of the head and its precious contents.

To a modern audience, the pleasures of Erasmus lie in such details. He is dismissive of people who snort and trumpet like elephants, but makes the point that one should not suppress natural, necessary bodily noises out of prissiness. He advises that a boy should keep his penis out of sight: 'Revealing without need those parts of the body which nature has covered with modesty is to be completely avoided.' Conversation at mealtimes is recommended; vomiting is regarded as much less offensive than elaborately trying to choke back vomit; one should cough to mask the passing of wind; and one should not greet others while they are urinating or defecating. Here there is a mixture of plain-spokenness and repugnance. Erasmus urges delicacy, yet also seems unsqueamish, as when he suggests that it is foolish (and dangerous) to try to hold back a fart. Above all, one should ignore other people's faults, and 'if a friend does something wrong without realizing it, and it seems important, then it's polite to inform him of it gently and in private.'[2]

Castiglione is a different sort of guide, writing for a different audience. He is suave where Erasmus is sober. He concentrates on life outside the home, picturing a readership that is outgoing and – as his book's title makes plain – courtly. This is not to say that *The Book of the Courtier* is a terribly good guide to the specifics of behaviour. Rather, it functions as a motivational work, urging the reader to sharpen his social intelligence. It was not enough to know how to behave; the correct forms of behaviour should be absorbed into the courtier's being.

It was while serving as a courtier in Urbino, a community aglow with cultural activity, that Castiglione wrote *The Book of the Courtier*. It was published in 1528 in Venice, in an edition that today looks small: 1,030 copies. But there were almost sixty editions before 1600, as well as numerous imitations. Its reputation reached far; the prestige of Italian culture was percolating westward. Many foreigners read Castiglione in Italian, and there were soon versions in French, Spanish and German. In the eighteenth century *The Book of the Courtier* could be found in the libraries of gentlemen as far afield as Philadelphia. On its travels the text was often supplemented with generous notes, which helped make it seem more practically useful. Elements were cut, too; the historian Peter

Burke mentions that the Polish version did away with all discussion of the arts, as the subject struck the translator as wholly irrelevant to his audience.

Although interpreted as a handbook and a moral treatise, *The Book of the Courtier* was also regarded as a work of nostalgic escapism and a defence of aristocratic values. The context in which Castiglione had written it was soon forgotten; he drafted a first version between 1513 and 1518, and then rewrote it in the 1520s, recalling as he did so a time closer to the start of the century, when Urbino had been peaceful rather than caught up in war. Castiglione, who had aspired to a life of happy and contemplative tranquillity, had instead found himself in a precarious society where diplomacy was essential to survival.

The book is set in Urbino, which is presented as a harmonious place. Organized in the form of a stylized discussion that takes place over four successive evenings, it idealizes gracious talk and its deft give and take. This structure allows Castiglione to present a variety of points of view; it makes the pursuit of truth feel like a game. Dexterity in speech is the mark of the accomplished courtier. We gather that a society in which social skills are the norm will be an oasis of calm in an otherwise vicious world. But those skills equip a man for a life beyond the oasis, where he will be surrounded by ambitious rivals scrambling for office and influence, and even in Castiglione's Urbino there are traces of paradox, suspicion and duplicity. Opportunists get everywhere.

Castiglione builds up a picture of the courtier as a man of the world, multi-talented and scholarly, an athlete and a warrior, politically astute and self-reliant. Among the qualities he prescribes are affability, charm, honesty and modesty. A man with these traits is likely to be able to please his master and make him receptive to ideas. The perfect courtier is one whose accomplishment means he can always approach his master with confidence and be sure that even his most candid words are accepted and heeded. He is a manager, good at handling other people's hubris. Granted, much of what Castiglione says makes this ideal figure sound glib. But crucially, although Castiglione emphasizes the value of being well-born, he says that education matters more than background. A person may be considered noble on account of some accident of birth, but true nobility is a state of mind – something that can be learned and indeed taught. Its distinguishing features have to be *performed*.

The basic message is one that still resonates: the need to control one's social space. Castiglione has often been accused of shallowness, but his appreciation of the importance of surfaces seems modern rather than merely desultory. He is alive to the way other people use one's physical characteristics to form a view of one's character and even of what one is likely to think. In this he seems prescient, for it was at the end of the eighteenth century, under the influence of the Swiss writer Johann Kaspar Lavater, that the doctrine of physiognomy became popular, allowing disciples to persuade themselves that they could determine a person's temperament and trustworthiness from the form of his or her face.

At the same time, Castiglione thinks in broader terms about self-presentation. It is not enough to do things well; one must also be seen to do them well. He introduces a truly psychological dimension to the discussion and practice of manners. One of his key realizations is that, in appraising others, we take a part for the whole: some perfect little touch of elegance or refinement will be interpreted as a sign of vast unseen continents of sophistication. Displaying some wondrous part of ourselves is a way of suggesting that we are wondrous through and through. This is the art of 'less is more': to make a good impression we disclose only a few sparkling details.

Castiglione thinks of public life as theatre. A man's construction of his identity is a feat of acting, and he should be intent on pleasing his audience. This idea does not originate with him; he probably took it over from Cicero. Yet Castiglione is supremely alert to the layers that make up a good performance. He emphasizes the physical aspect of manners. There was an established idea of how one should comport oneself in church, based on monastic principles: no shuffling from foot to foot, no slouching or leaning, no leg-crossing or foot-pointing, a fundamental quietness and restraint. But Castiglione expounds a code of physical manners for a secular audience. The preoccupation with the physical bearing of the courtly man has many times been reproduced. John Ruskin could assert in *Modern Painters* (its final volume, in 1860) that 'A gentleman's first characteristic is that fineness of structure in the body, which renders it capable of the most delicate sensation.'[3] For Castiglione, 'grace' is paramount. He admires the 'quiet gravity' of the Spanish and prefers it to the French 'quick liveliness'. Skill should be cultivated as a habit, but this self-fashioning should never turn into pedantry. At the same time he exalts skill in horsemanship as the loftiest of accomplishments; it connects the courtier to the chivalric past. Castiglione thinks of grace almost as a technology; it is an adornment that multiplies itself, because one's own grace begets grace in others.

There are real limitations in Castiglione's worldview. Even though lying is condemned, there are notes of hypocrisy – and of naïvety. We may balk, too, at the lengthy discussion of jokes. 'A very entertaining source of practical jokes, as well as of jests, is to be found in the pretence that one understands that a man wishes to do something which he most certainly does not.' Put thus, it sounds about as entertaining as an enema. Women have a mainly decorative role in *The Book of the Courtier*; they are assets, icons, listeners or unreasoning chatterers. Yet while the guidance for women tends not to be of a practical bent, there are some intriguing specifics. For instance, in the presence of people talking immodestly or with undue familiarity, a lady should 'listen . . . with a slight blush of shame', and when besieged with presumptuously amorous talk by a man she should refuse to believe a word of his spiel.

In the England where Castiglione's ideas held sway, ladies were expected to be more rigid than men, though sobriety was not to be confused with dullness. Of particular importance was making sure that their clothes were securely fastened. A handkerchief was a useful accessory, but, when it was tucked into the sleeve, only half of it should be visible; otherwise there was a risk of its falling out and causing a commotion. A lady could invite a man to dance by means of a curtsy, but not by gesturing or using his name. When a woman sat down, she was expected to nudge her gown close to her chair, like a cat tucking away its tail. Once seated, she should be still without resembling a statue, making some small movement from time to time – perhaps with her fan.

Some of the principles of the period feel familiar; others seem alien in being so schematic. Among men rich attire was desirable, a mark of wealth and liberality. A lady should never be offered a gloved hand. One shouldn't walk with one's hand on one's hip, for fear of looking like a peacock. Even sitting was an art: in a chair with arms, one should rest one's own left arm and cock one's right arm so that the elbow touched the arm of the chair and the hand was free to display items such as gloves or a flower. Haven't we all seen that posture and thought it a touch arrogant or coquettish? In Renaissance portraits, a cocked elbow was a sign of self-possession and even of provocative aggression.[4]

Castiglione urges that gestures should be subtle, not affected. Other writers on this theme can seem negative, itemizing all the things you shouldn't do with your hands and feet, but Castiglione makes gesture seem an art. He differentiates two kinds of body language: one is grave and closely regulated, the other flamboyant – the former Spanish, the latter French. For the true sophisticate, there has to be a middle way. We get a sense of the English interest in the matter that followed the translation of Castiglione by turning to the second (1609) edition of Robert Cawdrey's *A Table Alphabetical*, a primitive dictionary. There Cawdrey provides an entry for the newly adopted verb *gesticulate*, which he explains as '[to] use much or foolish gesture'. *Gesticulation* was also a vogue word at this time; a rival dictionary defines it as 'a moving of the fingers, hands, or other parts, either in idle wantonness, or to express some matter'.

The English have tended not to think of themselves as gesticulators. We leave all that arm-waving, finger-wagging and grimacing to others. Or so we imagine, perhaps aware of the ancient Roman distinction: slaves gesticulated broadly, free men didn't. The great eighteenth-century moralist Samuel Johnson would grab and restrain a man who gesticulated to add force to an argument, thereby ironically adding the force of gesture to his campaign against gesticulation. This kind of behaviour is familiar: a regulation of other people's expressiveness that is itself a robust expression of self. The English penchant for modesty is pushily upheld.

More appealing than artful body language, at least to those who could read Castiglione in Italian, was the notion of *sprezzatura*. The word has half crept into English; I have seen it used of Miles Davis, Joe DiMaggio and Edward Cullen in Stephenie Meyer's *Twilight* novels. Castiglione's *sprezzatura* is effortless excellence, an ability to mask one's desires, a nonchalant artfulness or studied carelessness. It is the opposite of vulgarity. Alexis de Tocqueville would some 300 years later discern the 'aroma of aristocracy' among the easy, nonchalant, unpompous members of the House of Lords, and attempts to define gentlemanliness have tended to include confidence, coolness and an unaffected air of disengagement. An easy, unassertive self-possession was valued by Castiglione, who mocked the kind of man who kept a comb up his sleeve in case he rumpled his hair. He was dismissive of those who exaggerated the ceremonies of politeness, as if proposing to 'keep a book and a reckoning of it'. The most important thing was not to look like you were trying: *sprezzatura* carried no whiff of pretentiousness and was contrasted with *affettazione*, a word I hardly need gloss. Yet *sprezzatura* was an act of simulation, and Castiglione's critics suggested that his advocacy of social strategy was suspect on religious grounds.

Castiglione was not cynical in the manner of Niccolò

Machiavelli, whose doctrine laid the grounds for the ruthless, crafty and risk-taking behaviour of the modern executive. It is Machiavelli, not Castiglione, whose work gets wonkily referenced by Tony Soprano (he calls him Prince Matchabelli). Whereas Machiavelli was prepared to separate the good from the useful, Castiglione insisted on maintaining a link between them. Castiglione's elegant *sprezzatura* differs from Machiavelli's celebrated concept of *virtù* – a mixture of masculine forceful-ness, foresight and flexibility. Castiglione's approach was less foxy and charismatic. Yet both were seeking to equip young men with the skills for survival and success in a highly competitive world.

The first English translation of Castiglione was published in 1561. Interest in Italian culture was intense, and Thomas Hoby's version capitalized on this. Although he closely followed the sense of the original, Hoby was concerned to write what he considered pure English. His prose is often rough where the original appears refined. He certainly wasn't about to bring the glossy word *sprezzatura* into English and his two renderings of it, 'disgracing' and 'recklessness', look wayward. The former may strike us as especially odd; it seems that Hoby was trying to convey something along the lines of 'negligence' or 'inelegance'.

As a prose stylist Hoby deliberately set himself at odds with the exhibitionism of so many of his contemporaries. They dealt in strange imported terms; the vogue for them led to the creation of the first English dictionaries, such as Robert Cawdrey's, which were glossaries of 'hard' words. Hoby prom-ised to express himself plainly and without any borrowed 'counterfeitness'. Nevertheless, his version of Castiglione introduced English readers to the words *self-liking* and *youthful*, and there we have an apt summary of *The Book of the Courtier*.

Annotated for ease of use, Hoby's translation was like a study guide. He included appendices which were of great use to lazy readers, providing a summary of the qualities required in courtiers and gentlewomen. The outline of ladylike 'conditions' was succinct yet demanding. A lady should have 'a sweetness in language', as well as skill in drawing, painting and music. She should be a good dancer but should need to be asked before showing this (and should not use 'too swift measures'). Her style of dress should not be 'fond and fantastical'; her clothes should be becoming, yet she should make it look as though she did not expend much effort on achieving this. Her sober, quiet manners should not preclude 'a lively quickness of wit'; and she should at all times present herself gracefully but also discreetly.[5]

Shakespeare's plays demonstrate his familiarity with Castiglione's ideas, though it is not clear whether he came to them via Hoby. Benedick in *Much Ado About Nothing* is an example of a character who, though worried at first about how he is perceived by his male companions, adapts rapidly, refashioning himself in a way that evinces the courtly qualities praised by Castiglione. His sparring partner Beatrice is not impressed by the flexibility and sophistication of men's manners, and says that 'manhood is melted into courtesies, valour into compliment, and men are only turned into tongue'. She means that men have become slick orators, and masculinity has been debased.

For precisely this reason, there was hostility to Castiglione's values. Castiglione himself recognized that Italians had a reputation for vanity and dissolute behaviour, and this ill repute drew negative comment from, among others, the educational theorist Roger Ascham, sometime tutor to the future Queen Elizabeth. In Castiglione's praise of grace Ascham saw a weakness for empty sophistication. He thought that reading Castiglione was less harmful than travelling to Italy, which was sure to encourage lust and other vices. But Italianate Englishmen, however they were formed, seemed dangerous in their ambition. Ascham's attitudes were influential, and he reduced upper-class enthusiasm for foreign travel, which would not fully recover from his opprobrium until the eighteenth century. Interestingly, he thought the key period during which young men should be imbued with moral discipline was between the ages of seventeen and twenty-seven; this was therefore the worst possible time for them to go gadding about abroad.

The courtier Edward de Vere, seventeenth Earl of Oxford, was a notable example of an Englishman steeped in Italian manners. Effeminate and erratic, with a great aptitude for dance, he was among Queen Elizabeth's favourites. The gossipy biographer John Aubrey tells the story of how Oxford, making a deep bow before Elizabeth, 'happened to let a fart'. He was so ashamed that he left the country – Aubrey says for seven years, though his spell abroad was in fact much shorter – and it is alleged that on his return Elizabeth greeted him with the words 'My lord, I had forgot the fart.'

It is not uniquely Elizabethan to draw attention to some past embarrassment while claiming to have lost sight (or scent) of it. This is teasing passing itself off as magnanimity. But we are accustomed to think of farting as unwelcome when involuntary and crass when intentional; we may therefore be surprised to find Elizabeth feeling otherwise. Before Elizabeth, though, farting had even enjoyed royal favour. In the reign of Henry II a man known as Roland le Pettour (Roland the Farter) was granted thirty acres of land in Suffolk on condition of annually at Christmas performing – all at once – a leap, a whistle and a fart; in the reign of Henry III he was obliged to switch to paying rent instead. Before we discern in Elizabeth's quip a return to royal indulgence of farting, we should be aware that the Earl of Oxford was a cruel and violent sexual omnivore who preferred the company of a Venetian choirboy to that of his wife, killed an unarmed cook while practising with his sword, and may have plotted the murder of Sir Philip Sidney, but kept himself in royal favour with gifts of perfumed gloves. Ostensibly forgetting the fart, Elizabeth was really overlooking all his other outbursts.

For Elizabethans negotiating a world full of posturing and counterfeitness, a word of particular significance was *gentleman*. The term has been employed since the thirteenth century. Originally it was a social grade, signifying someone who, though not a nobleman, was entitled to bear arms. It was not a badge of great distinction: a gentleman was the dependant of a man of higher grade (that is, a lord). The word became common in a less specific sense, denoting someone capable of fine feelings and virtuous behaviour, around 1400. In 1434 Nicholas Upton, a cleric who wrote on heraldic and military subjects, remarked that of late many 'poor' men had come to be considered gentlemen because of their 'grace, favour, labour or deserving'. The nature of gentlemanliness was blurry. But the name was still valued. The previous year at Bayeux, a man called William Packington, a one-time haberdasher and now the controller of the local English garrison, stabbed to death an acquaintance, Thomas Souderne, for pronouncing him 'no sort of gentleman'.[6]

In Elizabethan England, as now, *gentleman* was a term defined in a variety of ways. A volume dating from 1555 and bearing the title *Institucion of a Gentleman* argued that 'No man becometh gentle without virtue.' The gentleman was a person of high social and economic standing – anyone who had to labour for his livelihood was automatically no gentleman – but he also had to possess certain intellectual attributes and moral qualities, and commentators stressed the importance of these. Definitions were mainly philosophical, but there were practical instructions too. A gentleman should not walk with his feet splayed, should keep both feet on the ground when sitting, and should on no account run in the street. He should also rehearse perfection in his mind. Roger Ascham's *Toxophilus* of 1545, addressed 'to all gentlemen and yeomen of England', is a key work in the field, ostensibly about archery but really a guide to 'hitting the mark' in all departments of gentlemanly thought and conduct. A word Ascham likes to use in this context is *comely*, which at that time suggested a blend of sobriety and quiet decorousness. Composed and therefore able to be subtly perceptive, the comely man could see the wind before he felt it, and his aesthetic faculties had been tuned to assist his powers of reason.

There was hostility to both the word *gentleman* and the thing it denoted. This was strongest among Puritans, who, beginning around 1560, attempted to bring about moral reform. Some Puritans objected to good manners on the grounds that they were little more than flattery and ingratiating slipperiness – what the poet Nicholas Breton in a treatise of 1618 called 'wily-beguily'.[7] Richard Brathwait's *The English Gentleman* (1630) used the contested term in its title but distanced gentlemanliness from the courtly habit of chameleon-like mutability. He emphasized the need for men 'of selecter rank and quality' to pursue an active life: 'A crest displays his house, but his own actions express himself,' and 'He holds idleness to be the very moth of man's time.'[8] This work was followed soon afterwards by the rather shorter *The English Gentlewoman*, which we have already encountered. Brathwait was at pains to try to reintroduce Christian values into the conception of virtue, which by the 1630s had become largely secular. After Brathwait, most Puritan literature simply stated that Christianity and the profession of gentlemanliness were at odds.

All the while, though, there were new conduct books that gave prominence to the word *gentleman*, which gradually replaced *courtier.* Henry Peacham's *The Compleat Gentleman* (1622, with an enlarged edition in 1634) outlined 'the most necessary and commendable qualities concerning mind or body'. It made familiar claims for the benefits of learning to swim and shoot, but also attached great importance to the study of heraldry: a gentleman should be able to describe and depict not only his own coat of arms, but also those of his friends. Peacham had travelled on the Continent and felt that the education of young Englishmen lagged behind that given to their counterparts abroad. He pictured an oligarchy of virtuous noblemen, well-informed and physically fit (he recommends some leaping in the morning, but not wrestling).

In *The Art of Living in London* (1642) he presents a more prosaic vision of the particular needs of a gentleman in a modern city: a private chamber, thrift, patience and wariness, especially where the enticements of golden harlots are concerned.

The plural *gentlemen* grew common, as a form of address for a group of men of any rank, in the age of Shakespeare. Although for much of the seventeenth century there remained a tendency to think of a gentleman as a superior type who had both money and ample leisure, by 1700 the term was applied vaguely to anyone found to be socially respectable. Moreover, it was not unusual to apply it humorously to those who were deeply unrespectable. Writing in 1729, Daniel Defoe distinguished between the 'born gentleman' and the 'bred gentleman', and in doing so highlighted the word's ambiguity.[9] We can detect the same slipperiness – masquerading as certainty – in the legendary banker John Pierpont Morgan's line that 'you can do business with anyone but you can only sail a boat with a gentleman.'[10] In 1601 Thomas Wilson reckoned that there were 500 knights and 16,000 gentlemen in England. More than four centuries on, there can be certainty about the number of knights, but none at all about the number of gentlemen.

To foreigners the word has long been synonymous with Englishness, never mind the statistics. To them the 'English gentleman' is a notion of character more than of class, though he is often associated with the public schools that in Victorian England became factories for producing this type. He is a creature at once a little laughable and thoroughly wholesome, dignified, reserved, perhaps a bit sporty, certainly masculine but also somewhat repressed, brave rather than courageous, closely concerned with 'the not doing of the things which are not done' – in short, a myth that has not been deflated.[11]

Among the English, the term *gentleman* remains double-edged. It conveys images of both honour and humour, notes of respect but also jocularity. We may well associate it with the anti-democratic spirit of a leisured elite, the deliberate uselessness of the dandy, though also with sobriety and even a smooth sort of modesty. Many people find it hard to use the word *gentleman* with any degree of seriousness; others employ it apologetically; and then there are others who cannot utter it without a tingling of the blood. In the 1950s Evelyn Waugh could observe, in a letter to his fellow novelist Nancy Mitford, that 'the basic principle of English social life is that *everyone . . . thinks he is a gentleman*. There is a second principle of almost equal importance: *everyone draws the line of demarcation immediately below his own heels.*'[12] The first of these statements no longer holds true. In fact, it wasn't true when Waugh made it. The English gentleman was really a Victorian obsession, an ideal inherited from the age of Elizabeth, moulded in the eighteenth century by the essayists Richard Steele and Joseph Addison and the novelist Samuel Richardson, and given a special significance as the middle classes consolidated their status in the nineteenth century. In the twentieth century he gradually slipped from view, his disappearance an effect of the inflation of the middle class.[13]

7

Table manners

or, how to eat a cobra's heart

Visiting Italy in 1608, almost sixty years after Hoby's tour of the country, the traveller Thomas Coryat saw forks being used — by individuals, rather than as a shared implement for hoicking food from a common dish. To be precise: 'The Italian and also most strangers that are commorant [i.e. resident] in Italy, do always at their meals use a little fork when they cut their meat . . . because the Italian cannot by any means endure to have his dish touched with fingers, seeing all men's fingers are not alike clean.'[1] This was novel. Erasmus had counselled that meat should be picked up with three fingers, not with the whole hand. But Coryat had stumbled on a neat alternative. Forks of this kind had been adopted in Venice and then in Italy more generally in the previous century. Tickled by the existence of an accessory that seemed almost scandalously luxurious, Coryat decided to bring one home. He was mocked for using it. Yet forks caught on, becoming popular initially because they made it possible to eat berries without staining one's fingers. There were other benefits: using a fork made eating seem less lascivious, and later, as knives and forks were used together, it became easy to indicate when one had finished eating.

Thomas Coryat could hardly have imagined how many kinds of fork there would eventually be, with distinct forms of this little implement for dealing with pickles, oysters, chips, cheese and pastry. Nor could he have foreseen the differences of fork etiquette, principally today the disparity between the European and American styles, the latter involving the repeated 'zig-zag' switching of the fork from the left hand to the right. The first table fork reached America in 1633. It was a gift sent from England to John Winthrop, the governor of the Massachusetts Bay Colony. The sender left the item's 'useful application . . . to your discretion'; there is no evidence that any such useful application was achieved.[2]

The arrival of the fork is a significant moment in the development of table manners, for the adoption of eating utensils changed the nature of communal eating. Having one's own implements inevitably made the process of eating a more delicate one, an act of revulsion disguised as a rational act of hygiene. It influenced not only what went into one's mouth, but also, more surprisingly, what came out of it. A greater physical sensitivity and delicacy at table were matched by greater delicacy and sensitivity in speech, a sense of 'verbal hygiene' and correct expression. This was heightened as awareness grew that there were other places, far from England, where savagery was the norm. The English delighted in contrasting themselves with the barbarous peoples of the New World (and, closer to home, the reputedly barbarous Irish).

Nightclothes and bathing clothes became common at around the same time as this, and Norbert Elias suggests that, as it grew less usual to see other people naked, so artistic depictions of nudity felt like images from the dreamworld, fulfilments of wishfulness. Similarly, 'naked' eating – using the hands rather than utensils – would come to seem, for all its connections with barbarity, something fun, a sensuous experience akin to, say, walking barefoot through lush grass. In both cases, nudity is liberating because it is recognized as temporary, a departure from the formal norm.

We cannot survive without food, and the sharing of food is an essential feature of civilization – a prerequisite for it. Table manners express our awareness of the importance of sharing food; they are rituals shaped by the need to eat in a way that is hygienic, efficient, reverential and predictable, and they reinforce social connections by allowing us, at table, to perform rather like musicians – a duo or quartet or orchestra, as the case may be. Someone whose table manners differ from our own is someone we may find a little unnerving: 'If he eats a tomato like that, what else is he capable of . . .?'

Families have taken meals together for tens of thousands of years. Anyone who has much experience of eating with others will know all about the power games and bickering it can entail, but the communal taking of meals is a symbolic act, suggesting unity. It may be festive or spiritual (for some, an anticipation of the great banquet that is the afterlife), or it may simply be companionable and economical. Eating alone, which is stigmatized in many cultures, can feel pleasantly free, but it also affords an opportunity for eating badly – eating too fast or without regard for hygiene or nutritional value. Part of a child's socialization is learning to eat with others, in an acceptably adult fashion, and later the child learns about conversational turn-taking at table.

Yet eating and drinking are today a less critical part of social life than they have been traditionally. In the age of the micro-wave oven, we often do eat alone and rapidly, and as we fill ourselves with convenience foods, mealtime seems less important. We love our consumer durables, and the kitchen is full of labour-saving devices that reflect a desire to get food ready fast. The TV dinner, the snatched sandwich, the salad in a bag, the nutritionally turbocharged 'meal replacement', the cheeky takeaway, the guilty fast food pit-stop – all provide evidence of haste, multitasking and antisocial eating. Even eating out, which tends to be thought of as happily sociable, can be regarded as antisocial, in that it absolves us of respon-sibility for sourcing and preparing our food, allowing us simply to be blithe consumers, eating alongside others but not eating *with* them. And even if you are an expert cook and prepare everything you eat from scratch, insisting on sit-down family meals, you will have been affected by the general trend towards speedy, unsociable meals. An incidental point, only half flip-pant: the more expensive a person's kitchen, the less likely it is that a lot of cooking happens there, and the modern English kitchen, splendid with steel and granite, may well set back its owner more than a car or a wedding.

English eating habits have become markedly less predictable. When we look back at medieval dining practices, we glimpse an array of attempts to limit uncertainty and improvisation. John Russell's fifteenth-century *Boke of Nurture* issues instruc-tions about how to lay the table: salt within reach of the lord's right hand, and to his left a napkin (a newish contrivance, replacing the communal cloths known as the *doublier* and the *longière*) with a spoon folded inside it. There is also guidance on how to carve different meats and fish: the nape of a rabbit's neck should be cut out and discarded; peacock should be carved with its feet on; cod should be split up and spread out on the plate; and eels should be boned before being seasoned with vinegar. Until the seventeenth century, knowing how to carve meat was an essential skill for upper-class men – highlighted by Erasmus among others. In medieval households cooked animals were brought to the table whole, and cutting them up was a source of pleasure, but, as society became more refined, so the association between the whole animal and the food derived from it became uncomfortable, and squeamishness dictated that carving should be performed by experts, in kitchens or shops. This is part of a larger pattern whereby things that are considered distasteful are removed from view. Today we are not prim about carving, but, for want of practice, we are mostly not very good at it.

The space in which we eat has changed, too. The dining room became a discrete area within the English house only in the eighteenth century. Although grand ceremony was uncommon, a smart eighteenth-century dinner involved each course being brought to the table by handsomely liveried footmen; the butler remained by the sideboard, in charge of the wine. Turning to *The Habits of Good Society*, published in 1859, we get a taste of Victorian dining arrangements: 'The dining room must be, of course, carpeted even in the heat of summer, to deaden the noise of the servants' feet', 'Each person should be provided with a footstool', 'A little green tea is necessary after wine.'[3] It all sounds so sedate. Now, even at a chic dinner party, we are likely to see and hear the hosts fussing over the preparations.

For most readers of this book, service will be something

experienced in hotels and restaurants, not at home. So it is worth calling to mind how large a part of society until quite recently had servants at its disposal and how many people were in service. Perhaps we think here of *Upstairs, Downstairs* or *Downton Abbey*, in which we see again and again the protocols about who can access certain parts of a house. The juxtaposition of the servants and those they serve is most striking at mealtimes. In the nineteenth century few guides to household management even allowed time for servants' meals in the schedules they set out: more important than when they ate was their not exceeding their allowance.[4]

Imagine the effects on your behaviour of having a retinue of domestic servants and the consequences of not having to dress yourself or make your own bed, clean your own clothes or comb your own hair. In the medieval period domestic servants tended to be male, and the senior roles were taken by the sons of what would later be thought of as gentlemen. By the end of the seventeenth century, the majority of domestic servants were women, and it was rare for the sons of gentlemen to go into service. Whether the work is done by men or women, though, being served at table puts distance between food and the means of its preparation, and this is corrupting, for it suggests that food is something that is always abundant and appears on our plates as if by the magic of our desire. In a house with servants, meals can be elaborate; without them, and with the labour palpable as well as visible, meals are likely to be more simple, and the intricate manners of formal dining melt away.

The ways in which we behave at mealtimes, especially with regard to the people who prepare the food and serve it, bear unsettlingly intimate witness to how we feel about ourselves. But then so does the nature of the things we consume. You are what you eat, as the old proverb has it. It is better in German: *Der Mensch ist was er isst.* The English are adept at nabbing bits of other people's cuisines (and their words), but are apt to bastardize them: chicken tikka masala has the reputation of being one of the essential Anglo improvisations, though possibly originating in Glasgow. They have also, notoriously, tended to insist on eating 'proper English food' when abroad. This is a blend of imperialism, insensitivity, incuriosity and fear, passed off as justifiable caution. It is not so very far removed from the practice, when trying to make oneself understood to people who speak little or no English, of repeating oneself at ever increasing volume.

We accept that people's diet varies. We may even exult in the details. In Bali roasted dragonflies are a popular snack; among Aboriginal Australians the larvae known as witchetty grubs are a delicacy; in Vietnam and Thailand cobra is eaten, and the chef Anthony Bourdain reports being offered a cobra's heart in Saigon, 'a Chiclet-sized oysterlike organ' which he gulps down while it is still beating. Wilfred Thesiger writes in *Arabian Sands* about seeing a man in the desert drinking camel's urine to ease a stomach pain. Sir Walter Scott records in *Tales of a Grandfather* the story of a woman and her daughter, tried for witchcraft as a result of looking 'fresh and fair' during a period of famine; their secret was a diet of salted snails.[5] But the English, even those who think of themselves as cosmopolitan, recoil from unfamiliar food, often without considering the possibility of its virtues. For instance, there are dietary and environmental arguments in favour of eating insects (entomophagy), yet few readers of this book would contemplate chowing down on a bowl of termites or crickets, however nutrient-rich. In many cases, the technique required to consume such alien food seems to cause more consternation than the nature of the food itself: gourmets unfazed by the idea of eating an ortolan that has been drowned in Armagnac will balk at having to munch through the little bird's ribcage with their heads shrouded beneath napkins.

Although this particular convention is beyond the ken of most diners, we can be quick, where everyday table manners are concerned, to assume that our way is the best way. The hazards of denying variation were well illustrated by an episode in Canada in 2006: seven-year-old Luc Cagadoc, a boy of Filipino heritage, was disciplined at his school in Montreal for using a fork to break up his food, which he then ate from a spoon. His behaviour was at odds with Canadian norms. The harsh manner in which he was treated caused uproar and became a ferociously contested issue of human rights. A tribunal eventually ruled that the school should pay damages of $17,000 to Cagadoc's family. I don't know of a comparable incident in Britain, but I can recall that when I was eight or nine a left-handed boy at my school was beaten for insisting on eating with his knife in his left hand and his fork in his right. When he questioned why this was considered so terrible, he was told, not obviously in jest, that if necessary a fork could be strapped or glued to his left hand. This happening in a less litigious time and place, he acquiesced.

In Korea belching after a meal is interpreted as a compliment to the chef. Some tribes in Nigeria forbid men to talk about food. Germans do not cut potatoes; to cut them is to suggest that they have not been properly cooked. The French believe that one should not cut through salad with a knife; lettuce should be folded rather than sliced. There is also a French convention of not praising the culinary efforts of one's host, because to do so sounds like a veiled request for an extra helping. In ancient Greece children ate with their parents, but were seated rather than recumbent like the adults. In ancient Rome, nine was regarded as the ideal number for a dinner party; in the formal dining room known as a *triclinium* there were three couches, each of which could seat three diners. There, as in Greece, it was normal to recline while eating. All guests would have two napkins: one to stop food getting on their clothes, the other for wiping their fingers. The usual English response to foreign practices of this kind is to assume that everyone is merely waiting to learn a better way of doing things, namely the English way.

At a Chinese dinner party you are expected to leave some of your food; if you finish everything on your plate, your host will give you another serving. There is much about Chinese eating habits that appals outsiders, the insensitive and the hypersensitive alike. If a Chinese diner encounters a bone in a mouthful of food, he spits it out on to the tablecloth. Burping is not considered offensive. An English friend of mine who has spent an extended spell living in Chongqing reports seeing a child allowed to pee on the floor in a fast food restaurant; when the foreign diners fled from the next table in disgust, the child's parents plundered their leftover food. Reporting for *Vanity Fair* in October 2011 on the new high-speed train line between Shanghai and Beijing, Simon Winchester wrote: 'Cultural attitudes toward personal space – litter, chicken bones, soda cans – which may be fine on a country line in Yunnan, where you share with goats and chickens and pay just a handful of dollars for the privilege, may not be entirely acceptable on high-speed expresses between China's major cities.'[6] Yet while visitors are shocked by this behaviour, Chinese diners are often puzzled by the lack of deference those visitors show to their elders at table.

Among the foreign eating habits of which the English are most aware is the tendency in many cultures for the use of the left hand to be forbidden at mealtimes. In modern Muslim society, the left hand is little used at table because it is under-stood to be reserved for unclean acts; one should not put one's left hand near one's mouth or into a shared dish, though it is acceptable to use it for peeling fruit. This makes sense. Yet some English people believe that the left hand has a specific role to play in conveying food to one's mouth. I can remember being told off – as an adult, and certainly not by either of my parents – for holding a sandwich in my right hand. 'Is there something the matter with your left hand?' came the question. I offered reassurances that my left hand was fine. These met with three words: 'How peculiar, then.' When I pointed out, rather gauchely, that in some parts of the world the left hand was reserved for baser functions, I was sharply told that this subject was not 'suitable for discussion'.

For the scholar of table manners, Japan has long been a source of fascination. A Portuguese visitor to Japan in the sixteenth century claimed that the Ainu people used little wooden moustache-lifters at mealtimes so as not to sully their facial hair. In fact, he had misidentified sticks designed to carry the Ainu's prayers heavenwards. Later accounts found other things to marvel at. In nineteenth-century Japan dinner was a male affair; if women were invited, they were expected to keep to themselves, confined to one corner of the room. Spatially at least, this was not so far from medieval European practices, where noblemen would feast while women watched them from a gallery, but to a nineteenth-century observer it seemed archaic.

Visiting Japan myself, I was surprised to find that the family with whom I stayed in Hiroshima slurped enthusiastically while eating and regarded my lack of slurping as a sign of not enjoying the food they served me (which was superb). I noted, too, that the size and shape of the vessels from which I ate varied far more than in Europe. Japanese tourists in Europe have long been bemused by how little interest Europeans show in such matters. The French philosopher and literary theorist Roland Barthes applauded Japanese cuisine because none of its dishes had a centre; one was free, he sensed, to use one's chopsticks to pluck and peck as one pleased, the approach to eating thus being fragmented rather than hierarchical.

Using chopsticks, one makes selections rather than incisions. There are seven kinds of offence possible with chopsticks in Japan. *Komi-bashi* involves stuffing several things into your mouth at one time. *Neburi-bashi* is the act of licking chopsticks, while *mogi-kui* consists of using the mouth to remove rice that is stuck to them. *Sora-bashi* is using chopsticks to put aside food you had earlier intended to eat. *Utsuri-bashi* is a violation of the principle that between every two bites of meat, fish or vegetables you must consume some rice. *Saguri-bashi* is using your chopsticks to probe your dish to see if there is any more of what you want. *Hashi-namari* is a hesitation over what to select with your chopsticks. The etiquette is different in China, Korea and Vietnam. But even quite competent English users of chopsticks manifest some of the bewilderment of the nineteenth-century observer who spoke of them as 'curious implements' and 'little rods'.[7]

Part of the attraction of chopsticks, wherever they are used, is that they are more like an extension of one's fingers than a set of miniature weapons. This removes one of the hazards of the table. (Or usually does; in Takeshi Kitano's film *Brother* a character is killed when chopsticks are speared up his nose.) The implements we use at table can be turned to aggressive ends; table manners ensure that violence is kept at bay.[8] In the days when it was normal to keep a knife about one's person, no one was terribly fussy about how knives were passed at table, but once knives had become less common as personal accessories, the knife at table seemed more threatening and it became important to pass it carefully, with the point not facing the recipient.

As well as having an air of not-quite-allayed violence, eating has some sexual connotations, and there is plenty of research linking eating disorders to sexual trauma or abuse. It seems likely that in the early stages of human evolution the need for food and the urge to procreate were the two main drives that brought us into contact. Eating is our first strong experience of sensual pleasure. Accordingly, we are taught to do it in moderation. As with sex, qualms about food stem from a fear of infection or pollution. The materials from which our cutlery and dishes and drinking vessels are made have been selected because they can be kept clean and will look clean, as well as because they will impart as little unwanted flavour as possible to what we consume. An irony, though: to create food that looks clean, producers use pesticides, preservatives and colouring agents, which compromise its integrity. In the eighteenth century food was adulterated so as to look more desirable: alum and chalk were added to bread to whiten it, and tea was darkened using lead. There persists an English preference for 'clean' food that looks the 'right' colour, and it is still achieved using dodgy additives.

When we are consuming food, clean or not, we are expected to regulate our mouths. But in truth the regulation of the mouth is a fundamental of good manners: both physically and metaphorically, for we are told not to gawp, pout or yawn unguardedly, and also not to swear, spread scandal, talk too volubly or dwell on certain subjects (politics, religion). 'Are you a Jewish?' asks a workman carrying out a job in my home. I reply that I am not 'a Jewish', and he follows up with 'Are you a gay?' By way of explanation he adds, 'Because when you talk you make, a lot, faces with your mouth.'

One of the fundamental facts of human behaviour is our bodies' natural expressiveness. There is a constant tension between this expressiveness and the need to regulate it, between doing what comes naturally and striving to avoid giving offence. The body is sacred but also shameful, truthful but also treacherous.

When we experience an emotion, it has what are known as somatic accompaniments. Some of these are physiological and objective: secretions in our glands, a surge of activity in the brain. Others are 'felt' and subjective: we are aware of our heart racing or of the sensation often referred to as 'having butterflies'. The emotion is expressed in behaviours: some of these are involuntary but can be controlled to a degree (crying, groaning, smiling), and there are others over which we have no control whatsoever – sweating, for instance. In general, we are suspicious of physical overproductiveness: exhibitionism, extravagant gestures, logorrhoea and other sudden broadcasts of so-called nervous energy. We associate other people's most expressive moments with the risk of physical and psychological injury. Some actions that appear really unusual may be the result of neurological disorders, but it requires less time and empathy to dismiss them as rudeness.

Table manners can seem not only a discouragement of expressiveness, but also an obstruction of enjoyment. Marek, a plasterer with whom I share a table in a diner one blustery April afternoon, explains that he doesn't stand on ceremony when eating because 'I don't worry what other people think. I just want to eat.' He pretty much inhales his lunch. 'If I am less time eating, I am more time working' – a sentiment many readers will find admirable and un-English. Yet delaying self-gratification can increase pleasure rather than prevent it. Instant satisfaction is disappointing. People complain about waiting, but, when we wait for something we really want, the delay can be delicious. What frustrates us is having to wait to complete some piffling intermediate transaction – checking in at the airport, perhaps – which feels as though it could be dealt with quickly yet ends up forcing upon us the sensation that time, rather than being an element through which we pass, is something to be endured.

Part of the point of table manners is to make us wait. They have an equalizing effect, defusing the risk of unseemly competition. We judge people on their table manners because we understand these manners as an index of their selfishness, potential for violence, tolerance of ugliness, and wider personal hygiene. In an adult, bad table manners suggest childishness: a lack of education, a chaotic or overindulgent upbringing, even the likelihood of a guzzling or ham-fisted approach to sex. Table manners are a means of managing disgust; they keep us from thinking about what the philosopher Colin McGinn calls 'the unseemly reality of digestion'. Someone who gapes while eating reminds us that there is a 'mass of organic pulp on the brink of descent into the bilious hell of the stomach'. The art of dining 'keeps the underlying process as hidden as possible, so that it can be publicly performed'.[9]

English table manners, though once disparaged as slovenly (by the linguist John Florio, for instance, in the reign of Elizabeth I), have the reputation of being meticulous. The care we are believed to take over how we put food into our bodies is matched by a concern about how the resulting waste products are expelled. The English have tended to swing between abhorrence of bodily functions and a delight in them. Both are reflected in a large and inventive lavatorial vocabulary, in which something is held back yet made poetic: 'passing water' is also a 'minor function' or 'making room for my tea', and a 'bowel movement' can be 'night soil' or a matter of attending to 'the demands of nature'. It seems an eloquent detail that at the court of Henry VIII the person who carried the king's portable loo and wiped his bottom was not a grubby underling but a high-ranking courtier: here there are notes of the proprietorial, the fastidious and the absurd, as a monarch not wanting to dirty his hands prizes the intimacy of his relationship with the man who saves him from doing so.

As for the English diet, I'm struck by its realities while sitting next to a group of smartly dressed cricket fans of both sexes at Lord's, the spiritual home of the game. They chew with their mouths open, belying the good reputation mentioned above. Consequently I get to see their elevenses, lunch and tea at close quarters. *Munch, munch, squelch, gulp.* The English think of food as fuel. Copiousness is important. So is value for money. The popularity of the 'all you can eat' offering is a symptom of this, and it seems to throw down a challenge, inviting feats of gastronomic bravado: we're to eat not as much as we want, but as much as possible. Related to this is an obsession with choice: a menu with a lot of different things on it is good, whereas one that promises a small number of dishes is seen as unreasonably restrictive, and the perceived appeal of a shop selling food is commonly related to the number of lines it stocks. We love a 'buy one, get one free' offer, even if we throw away the item that's free – or both. So it is no surprise that at the end of the day the smartly dressed group leaves behind three half-consumed Cornish pasties, some untouched sausage rolls and a pot of unidentifiable sweet goo. Nor is it surprising that their conversation as they go is about where nearby they can pick up 'a cheap bite'.

There are many champions and purveyors of superb English produce and cooking, much of it far from cheap. They have to work hard, because the default setting is so stodgily unambitious. Traditionally, foreigners visiting England have remarked on the natives' consumption of meat, and it has been the quantity consumed, not the quality, that has attracted comment. Meat and especially beef, often accompanied by tangy condiments, is associated in English minds with honesty, freedom, bullish patriotism and a resistance to foreign artifice. In Henry Fielding's novel *Tom Jones* (1749), the hero's special qualities are evidenced by a meal at which 'Three pounds at least of that flesh which formerly had contributed to the composition of an ox, was now honoured with becoming part of the individual Mr Jones.' The comic evasiveness with which the process is presented suggests the need to draw a veil over Tom's very English and very gluttonous performance.

8

The Clothes Show

'When in doubt, opt for navy'

Table manners seem to invite assessment. As we observe other people at table, they are like caged specimens, trapped inside a narrow event. But people spend only some of their time eating, so their table manners are only some of the time available for evaluation. Away from the table, we can place them according to their appearance. In a variation of Lavater's principles of physiognomy, we like to think that we can tell a lot about someone's background from his or her face. Or perhaps we dislike thinking this, but do it all the same.

Clothes, too, enable us to place people, and clothes seem easy to 'read'. In the early eighteenth century the third Earl of Shaftesbury, a philosopher whose central concern was politeness, drew a connection between morality and aesthetics, arguing that in our acts and achievements symmetry is crucially important, a guarantee of mental order and a sense of moral proportion. But while easy to recognize in people's dress and possessions, symmetry was harder to see in their character. As a result, an assessment of Mr and Mrs X's dress and possessions was often used to determine what sort of people they were.

Whether we like it or not, we do this a great deal, interpreting clothing as an extension of personality. As far as dress is concerned, good manners are a matter of conformism. The English like wearing uniforms, except school uniforms; they also like to customize them in the most tiny ways (a hint of red socks under a dark suit). Clothes that can be described as 'extreme' may be appropriate at a fancy-dress party or in a fetish club, but they are unsettling in the workplace and other everyday situations. Overdressing is still widely considered worse than being underdressed: the latter can suggest an innocent ignorance or confident self-containment, whereas the former is interpreted as the behaviour of parvenus and narcissists. We often hear someone condemned for wearing too much jewellery, having too deep a tan, or favouring bold colours and fabrics. 'Her heels are too high,' says a guest sitting next to me at a wedding, of the bride, 'and her dress looks too expensive.' We may sometimes make judgements about people not adorning themselves enough, but they are articulated differently. It's rare to hear anyone say 'Her heels aren't high enough' or 'That outfit needs more jewellery', because the disapproval will be less specifically expressed: 'She could make a bit more of herself', 'He doesn't have a clue about clothes', 'She's sending out all the wrong signals.'

Where clothes are concerned, the word *appropriate* usually means 'appropriately modest': we are expected to avoid both coquetry and austerity. For most people, sartorial conspicuousness causes embarrassment rather than boosting self-esteem; if you appear to enjoy conspicuousness, you are condemned in much the same terms as you would be for talking too loud, and the censure may come with an extra shot of moral indignation. When I was at university I sometimes wore a pair of plum-coloured suede loafers. These provoked a lot of comment, much of it hostile: 'Why are you wearing women's shoes?', 'Are you a faggot or something?' The most extreme reaction was that of a man who stopped his car on a busy street to confront me, saying, 'It's people like you who are bringing this country to her knees.'

It was my choice of colour that caused offence. The colour of a person's attire has long had a role as an indicator of status. In imperial China only the emperor's heir could wear apricot yellow; the other sons wore orange. Purple has traditionally been a colour for emperors and popes. Bold colour has also been a way of marking bold character. The intrepid eighteenth-century politician Charles James Fox was noted for his blue hair powder and red-heeled shoes. But such boldness has tended to be associated with mere ostentation. Erasmus thought that striped or multicoloured clothes made one look like either a charlatan or a monkey. Even today, in an age of sartorial freedom, wearing certain colours (gold, bright red, bright pink) or only clothes of one colour (brilliant white, jet black) is interpreted as contentious or belligerent, and superfluity in dress is associated not just with vanity, but with depravity.

Footwear provokes especially strong reactions. Fundamentally, it exists to protect us. But it does much more than that. According to the designer Christian Louboutin, whose shoes are known for their lacquered red soles, 'The shoe is very much an X-ray of social comportment.'[1] Wearing the wrong thing on one's feet can seem the most grotesque of faux pas. The symbolism of shoes is social – our footwear says something about what we do – yet is also sexual.

The Cinderella story illustrates the erotic potential of footwear. The foot slipping snugly into the shoe evokes an image of other intimate conjunctions. The story's most famous version is the one used in the 1950 Walt Disney film, in which the slipper is made of glass, Cinderella's slipper thus being a symbol of her fragile and irreparable virginity. Vulnerability is central to the sexual experience of the foot. Either the foot is a soft plaything, to be nuzzled and caressed, or it is armoured (with a stiletto, for instance) and becomes a weapon, suitable for use in trampling or penetration. Feet can telegraph sexual attraction. Their flexibility is essential to the sensuality of the human gait: every person's footsteps sound slightly different, and we know our lover by his or her approach. The shoe at once embellishes and conceals the foot; the effect can be beguiling, though the widespread and understandable preference for comfy footwear means it often isn't.

In his classic work *The Psychology of Clothes*, J. C. Flügel observes the ways in which clothes arouse sexual interest and even tacitly symbolize the sexual organs. Clothing enables us to augment ourselves, as for instance when a skirt 'adds to the human form certain qualities with which nature has failed to endow it' and enables the wearer to create 'an impression of bodily power and grace which could not possibly be achieved by the naked body, beautiful as this may sometimes be'. Reflecting on the changing nature of fashion (this in 1930), Flügel notes that even the most outré outfit offends us less than the sight in public of the naked body. Successive trends are 'minor disturbances and readjustments of the equilibrium'; they amount to changes in the relative moral and aesthetic weight we give to modesty and display.[2]

It is tempting to see scanty or revealing dress (be it a bikini, a skirt that's little more than a belt, a low-cut top, or under-pants that seem to accentuate a man's assets) as a mark of moral laxity. But it can also be interpreted as a sign of a society that has developed a great deal of confidence about its powers of self-restraint. Either way, it indicates that clothes are no longer, as they once were, mainly a form of covering, for purposes of protection and modesty.

Fashion is an extension of social and sexual competition. For precisely this reason, it is perpetually in a state of 'double movement': 'one from the lower social ranks in the direction of those who stand higher in the scale, and another from these latter away from their own former position, which has now become . . . untenable'.[3] This commentary by Flügel may be couched in language that now seems too class-ridden, but fashion is undoubtedly always in retreat from its own success. The moment something is actually 'in fashion', it is likely to seem abominable to the people who started the fashion.

English fashions have had their political and economic aspects, with royal favour often a factor. In 1765 the London peruke-makers, appalled by how many people were 'wearing their own hair', petitioned George III to discourage this prac-tice. That year Queen Charlotte asked the ladies at court to wear only Spitalfields silk, to encourage the London weavers and curtail imports. There was also at this time a brief mania for shoe-buckles, which George was expected to sport when he returned to public life after his first illness. But he wore shoe-laces on his first public appearance, and the town of Walsall, a buckle-making centre, allegedly came close to ruin. Gold-laced hats had a brief vogue, in 1778, among men trying to give themselves an air of military distinction or avoid the attentions of press gangs. The use of hair powder by women dropped off after it was abandoned by Queen Charlotte in 1793; along with dogs and armorial bearings, it was an item on which William Pitt imposed a special tax during the revolutionary war with France. Queen Charlotte's influence was not always positive. The huge, impractical hoop petticoat, very probably an English invention and most popular around 1750, had largely disappeared by 1780, but she encouraged the continued use of the hoop in public life – with the intention of supporting the many people who made a living out of its elaborate construction.[4]

The hoop petticoat was expensive, uncomfortable and inconvenient – which some might say is a definition of fashion. The anxieties bound up with voguishness are today discernible in the strange double meaning of the phrase 'too fashionable': once a criticism, this is now sometimes a plaudit, and it can be hard to tell which is the desired sense. Here we return to the question of sartorial good manners, which involves careful judgement about colours, shapes and materials. Making the most of oneself can be a matter of spreading one's plumage in imitation of a peacock. Mostly, though, it is a case of wearing the right uniform (in many cases the uniform not of an organization, but of a social group). While this may be inventively accessorized, even gently subverted, we strike a balance between expression and repression. Clothes do not just add to our appearance; often they *are* our appearance. In fashion, features that at first serve some useful purpose are later retained as ornaments: this is true of manners and, much more broadly, of life.

Dress codes exist to regulate appearances. They tend to be designed to curb the excesses of fashion, but sometimes they enforce them, as in the case of the club Torture Garden, where the code is 'Fantasy, Fetish, Latex, SM, Body Art, Drag, Burlesque, Moulin Rouge, Medical, Uniform, Militaria, Vegas Showgirl, Kit Kat Cabaret, Venice Carnival, Circus Freak Show, Boudoir, Top Hat & Tails, Electro Freak, Porno Punk etc.'.[5] In the workplace a dress code will probably signify the status of employees; it may also present a company's brand and serve a practical purpose in relation to safety or hygiene. Generally, a dress code works like a screening device, a means of preserving standards. 'Standards', it should be said, doesn't always mean 'high standards'. I have been refused entry to a bar because I wasn't wearing a jacket, but have also been refused entry to a bar because I was wearing one.

Failing to observe a dress code, whether prescribed or implicit, is considered at best gauche and at worst a sort of vandalism. Observing the code is a passport into a realm in which the code can (sometimes) be dropped: once we have shown an understanding of context, we are granted more latitude. The most tightly specified dress codes are ephemeral ones: what you're expected to wear to a party, for instance. Then there are broad codes that may not even be explicitly set out, such as what's appropriate in a particular office; these are likely to be absorbed, as if by osmosis. The broadest codes might be called 'general principles of dress': men's attire and women's are different, clothes protect the skin and keep certain delicate parts of the body out of sight, and our garments exist perhaps not so much to protect our modesty as to create it. But these principles are not rock-solid, and plenty has altered that once seemed immutable. Women no longer expect to have to put on gloves before leaving the house. Jeans are not associated with protest or even that often with the utilitarian needs of cowboys. Nor do we associate striped garments with ignominy, whereas in the medieval world they marked a person as an outsider: juggler, fool, prostitute, executioner.[6]

For a common-sense view of what to wear, I like Laurie Graham's five rules for the wardrobe door: 'Studied perfection should be ruffled before use', 'All attention-seeking items should be donated to Oxfam', 'When in doubt, opt for navy', 'When in navy, use a clothes brush', 'Always check your rear-view mirror.'[7] The pragmatism here is something we may well regard as redoubtably English. The grandest statements of English fashion are the result of a dialogue with French style, in which the English influence is a moderating one. Even the most consistently outrageous of English fashion designers, Vivienne Westwood, blends her swagger and punk sensibility with nostalgia. A surprising number of her inspirations are seventeenth-century: the enthusiasm for slashed hose, the baroque theatricality of Anthony van Dyck's portraits, the coquettish wit and style of the courtesan Ninon de l'Enclos. Having digressed into table manners and matters sartorial, it is time to return to that period.

9

Mr Sex

On New Year's Day in 1660 a twenty-something Londoner, the son of a tailor, starts keeping a diary in a fat notebook. He maintains it with enthusiasm. In the first month he records that he eats a delicious slice of brawn but has a poor night's sleep afterwards, suffers a swollen nose and is told by his doctor that it is due to nothing more serious than a cold, shares his financial anxieties with his wife in bed, goes to what he describes as a coffee club where he enjoys a debate about Roman government, expresses his shame at not dining more often with his father, observes his wife's difficulties with an uncomfortable new pair of shoes, and stays up one evening to create pegs from which to hang his hats and cloaks.

The twenty-something Londoner is of course Samuel Pepys. His diaries, which eventually cover a period up to the middle of 1669, illuminate the life of seventeenth-century England. He also turns a great deal of attention on himself. He is a useful guide to the manners of his age, three and a half centuries remote from our own, but he is more than that: his experience has a timelessness, and there is a tremendous amount that we can recognize and savour in his depiction of a world full of indulgences, smart manoeuvres, come-ons and brush-offs.

The year Pepys began the diaries was a watershed: in May the twenty-nine-year-old Charles II arrived in England; he had been the lawful monarch since the death of his father Charles I in 1649, but had spent the 1650s in exile on the Continent, where he had learned French tastes and manners. In Thomas Shadwell's play *The Humorists* (1671), a character complains that there is no corner of town 'without French tailors, weavers, milliners, strong water-men, perfumers and surgeons'.[1] With Charles's return came a fashion for wigs (Pepys acquired his first in 1664), expensive combs and silk handkerchiefs. Courtiers adorned themselves with ribbons and velvet, and sported ostrich feathers in their beaver hats. Heels were high; trousers were wide.

The poet John Wilmot, second Earl of Rochester, embodied the new spirit of dandyism. Intent on breaking taboos, he delighted in pranks and 'the free use of wine and women'. Unless it was dangerous to others or to his own health, pleasure 'was to be indulged as the gratification of our natural appetites'.[2] Rochester took hedonism to an extreme matched by few others, and repented only when he was on his deathbed, aged thirty-three, ravaged by syphilis. He was a divisive figure, and a symbolic one: his extravagance and individualism will strike us as modern.

Rather than being self-indulgent like Rochester, Charles II was strategic. He was ambitious to match the dazzle of Louis XIV and his court. Louis had transformed Versailles from a hunting lodge into a palace containing a 240-foot-long Hall of Mirrors. The noblemen he chose to elevate were made to understand that they were tame, obedient and under surveillance. Rochester portrayed Louis as 'the French fool who wanders up and down / Starving his people'.[3] Lest we imagine him a creature more soigné than any star of *MTV Cribs*, it is worth noting that at his court a bath was taken only in exceptional circumstances. But Louis instituted rituals that inspired awe in his subjects: all his actions, from getting up and dressing to receiving courtiers, were tightly regulated and accompanied by ceremony. These routines were means of dramatizing his power and his subjects' subordination.

There were similarly precise rules about the conduct of Charles's royal household. For instance, it was decreed that when Charles was out walking, 'a gentleman usher daily waiter and a gentleman usher assistant shall go before us, and a gentleman usher daily waiter, or gentleman usher assistant and a gentleman usher quarter waiter shall go behind us, unless there be no gentleman usher daily waiter or gentleman usher assistant'.[4] The language here, repetitious and pedantic, sounds like that of a legal contract. Charles had twelve Grooms of the Bedchamber, supporting the First Gentleman and Groom of the Stool, and six pages as well. His everyday life was crammed with ceremony. But this was hardly the same thing as civility, and Charles's palace at Whitehall was a scene of open exuberance. Pepys's fellow diarist John Evelyn, though intent on finding favour at court, characterized it as a profane place, aswarm with lackeys and packed with gamblers. Profligacy, artificiality and the pursuit of sensual pleasure were rife. A mid-nineteenth-century historian wrote: 'It is . . . to the wanton and lascivious court of Charles the Second that we must look for the origin of that general demoralization which tainted the manners of the fashionable world during great part of the last century.'[5]

Ceremony is an edifice we construct: it consumes our time and shields from us the fact that we have a lot of time on our hands. Charles made himself more accessible to his subjects than his predecessors had done, but ceremony ensured that the nature of his relationship with them was unambiguous. Processions were a means of advertising both his openness and his regal bearing. The practice of touching his subjects to alleviate their ailments – specifically the tubercular disease known as scrofula – was a means of capitalizing on their awe, investing him, like Louis, with a mystique that bordered on the magical.

The culture of Charles's court differed from that of Versailles in being less driven by a theory of domination. The circulation of the Sun King's image (on medals, in prints) was a carefully managed form of propaganda. Portraits of Louis identified him with Alexander the Great, the Good Shepherd and Hercules, and it was an offence not only to turn one's back on the king, but even to turn one's back on a picture of him. Critics of Louis's policy noted its use of *divertissement*, entertainment that served to distract attention from hardship, drugging the people with spectacle.[6] Charles's publicity campaigns were more haphazard and impromptu. An aversion to political theory would in the following century become an emblem of anti-French sentiment and English self-confidence. Something of that remains, as in the joke about a French politician who listens to an English official's sage proposal and says, 'I can see that it will work in practice. But will it work in theory?'

For an immediate sense of the atmosphere of Charles's rule, we can turn to Pepys. He observes with pleasure the pageantry attending Charles's coronation and later his enthusiasm for church music and good sermons. He notices how busy the king keeps himself, finding time for real tennis only at five o'clock in the morning. Yet he is appalled by Charles's unconcealed adultery ('a poor thing for a prince to do') and by his inability to address parliament without a written text in front of him. Charles's speeches can be silly, suggesting restlessness. In time we see Pepys come to be valued by Charles, who shares his interest in naval matters. When the Great Fire of London rips through the city in September 1666, it is Pepys who receives Charles's orders about the need for houses to be torn down to create firebreaks.

Pepys's narrative is studded with lovely detail. There are revelations about his own conduct (as the fire rages, he packs his valuables off to Bethnal Green and buries his Parmesan cheese in the garden), but also insights into the more general currents of behaviour. He remarks on curious ideas that circulate among people he knows, be they the prophecies of Nostradamus or the claim by a sea captain that 'negroes drowned look white and lose their blackness'. His frequent trips to the theatre bring him into contact with a wide range of people. In 1663 he notes that it has recently become fashionable for ladies to keep their faces masked in public places such as the theatre. A couple of years earlier, a woman at the theatre spits and the saliva hits him; rather than being appalled, Pepys regards this merely as a mistake and 'after seeing her to be a very pretty lady, I was not troubled at it at all'. With hindsight, he can be seen as representative of a new age in which ideas about manners were no longer based on what happened at court.

The court was still important, but politeness was less specifically rooted in its rituals.

One feature of Pepys's diary is his system of moral accountancy, in which acts of self-indulgence are balanced by gifts and charity. Thus, the day after dallying with an unexpectedly obliging young woman, he buys his wife Elizabeth an expensive pearl necklace. Pepys appears affectionate but also practical, pleasure-seeking but also orderly, and benevolent but also stingy; he often has the look of a magistrate surveying his own lapses.

Where might Pepys have picked up his ideas about how to conduct himself? Although in his youth he had been a Puritan and a republican, in adulthood his convictions relaxed. He turned to religion only in moments of crisis. In the diary, when he thanks God for some pleasing development, the gratitude seems a reflex. In the England of Charles II, there were more immediately practical guides to behaviour. One of these was Francis Osborne's *Advice to a Son* (1656–8), remarkable for preaching a form of good manners that had little to do with other kinds of goodness. Osborne's 'good manners' were useful, and they enabled whoever had them to carve a passage through the corruption and confusions of society. Osborne advised his son to learn about medicine, for instance, on the grounds that it would make him a welcome guest in many places – and especially among women, who treated physicians with reverence. Presenting marriage as a trap, at best a necessary evil, he described it as 'a clog fastened to the neck of Liberty' and a means of providing life's 'general necessities' rather than its 'particular conveniences'. One of his fundamental principles was that self-preservation mattered more than great displays of honour: after all, he said with a nod to the Old Testament book of Ecclesiastes, 'a living dog is better than a dead lion'.[7]

Pepys knew Osborne's book and reported that it was among the works his contemporaries were most likely to praise as a fund of wit. Its cynical, conceited worldliness impressed readers who thought of society as a treacherous place full of bribable officials and grasping relatives. Osborne's shrewdness did not prevent his ending up poor, as a result of a property dispute; his atheism and sour attitude to women led to proposals that his books be banned and even publicly burned. He represented a new turn in discussions of English manners: towards insiderish and disillusioned counsel, smacking of opportunism. He is the precursor of the advice columns in modern men's magazines, preaching ruthlessness and avoidance of commitment.

At the opposite end of the moral scale was the clergyman Richard Allestree, whose sober writings urged a blemishless earthly existence as the only means to guarantee happiness in the hereafter. Allestree wearily observed that his contemporaries did not give as much attention to religious duties as they did to observing codes of politeness. In 1668 Pepys had Allestree's recently published *The Causes of the Decay of Christian Piety* urged on him at a dinner in Lincoln's Inn. Allestree described the ruinous consequences of lust, wealth and an interest in fashion. He might have been writing with Pepys in mind. Yet although Pepys in his diaries is candid about his own shortcomings, in a way that proves endearing, we recognize him not as a disciple of the sober Allestree, but as a hedonistic inhabitant of the worldly sphere Osborne depicted. When Pepys refers to him as 'my father Osborne', his chosen form of words is only mildly surprising.

Like many cultivated men of his time, Pepys thought that hard work and business had a civilizing effect. But he was easily diverted. It was fashionable among his contemporaries to show contempt for the cautious middle orders by posing as a libertine – Rochester being an extreme example. The morality of a patrician man could be called into question without dark consequences for his social standing. In 1696 the bookseller John Dunton published a work with the splendid title *The Night-walker: or, Evening Rambles in Search of Lewd Women*. Dunton recorded his conversations with prostitutes, noting that it was young women's desire for 'honour' that led them to behave in unchaste ways; to consort with a man of breeding, no matter how immoral the connection, was a sure means of boosting their chances in life. Something of this remains, in the co-ordinated uproariousness of a certain very small, privileged section of England, drunk on a sense of its entitlement. These people's rivalry (over sex, drinking, drugs, possessions and their rampages), matched by that of the frolicking admirers who cling to them, is a flaunting of resources and also of power.[8]

Pepys's sexual behaviour often involves some kind of barter: a small gift or loan, or helping a mistress's husband advance professionally. He is opportunistic, too. On one occasion he is caught by Elizabeth in a compromising embrace with one of her companions, seventeen-year-old Deborah Willet, known as Deb. It is a Sunday, and the episode 'occasioned the greatest sorrow to me that ever I knew in this world', for 'indeed I was with my main [i.e. hand] in her cunny. I was at a wonderful loss upon it and the girl also.' It is worth picturing this exactly. What could Pepys have said to account for the obvious physical intimacy? You can be sure that it was not very convincing. Readers of the diary have by this stage seen him brought to orgasm in a moving coach by a married, pregnant acquaintance, so they know what to expect. But this was the first time that Elizabeth had got wind of his infidelity. She pulled her husband's hair and threatened to slit Deb's nose.

It is clear that Pepys loved Elizabeth, even if he was intrigued by the idea of her more than he was satisfied by the reality. They married two weeks before her fifteenth birthday; the union, bedevilled early on by arguments, seems to have matured into a largely characteristic mixture of jealousies, intimacies and periods of indifference. They had no children, which meant Elizabeth was able to enjoy a much fuller life of leisure than most of her female contemporaries. Pepys paid for her to have dance lessons; he was jealous when she appeared to enjoy a special rapport with her teacher Pembleton, and even listened at the door during their private sessions.

It is worth emphasizing that in the seventeenth and eighteenth centuries dance was considered the best means of developing skills in the use of one's body. Of particular importance was what one did with one's head. The art of gracefulness began with mastering how to stand still; then movements could be added to a person's repertoire. In his treatise *Some Thoughts Concerning Education* John Locke argued that little children should not be 'much tormented about . . . niceties of breeding', but felt that dance endowed them with confidence and that 'they should be taught to dance, as soon as they are capable of learning it'. Even in 1822 William Hazlitt in his essay 'On the Conduct of Life', presented as a letter of advice to a schoolboy, busily advised the study of Latin,

French and dancing, and wrote: 'I would insist upon the last more particularly'.[9]

For men of Pepys's generation, the standard work in the field was John Playford's *The English Dancing Master* (1651). Pepys himself had had no early instruction in dance, and a diary entry in 1661 suggests that he did not even try to dance until he was in his late twenties. In due course he bought a copy of Playford's book. There he could read that the ability to dance was 'a commendable and rare quality fit for young gentlemen' and had the effect of 'making the body active and strong, graceful in deportment'.[10] For Pepys and his contemporaries, dance was a means of engaging entertainingly with the question of deportment (a word first used around 1600). Experts in this area, concerned with their subjects' carriage and bearing, paid close attention to the positioning of the legs, which were to be turned a little outward – not at the ankle, but from the hip. Women for their part were encouraged to take small steps and concentrate on walking in a straight line.

Even sitting was taught, and its importance increased with the rise in tea-drinking, a sedentary practice. Tea was brought to England in 1644 by East India Company traders. The first shop where the public could obtain it was run by Thomas Garway; it opened in 1657, and Garway publicized the drink's virtues. Pepys records consuming tea – 'a China drink' – for the first time in September 1660. This was an early hint of what would develop into an upper- and middle-class mania for chinoiserie, a lust for Chinese silks, screens, lacquerware, jars and delicate figurines. Within a few years Elizabeth was consuming tea for its alleged medicinal properties.

Reflecting on a century of tea-drinking, Jonas Hanway in 1756 published a scathing attack on the habit. A merchant and philanthropist, Hanway was the first Englishman to make regular use of an umbrella, for which he was ridiculed and also resented (mainly by the men who protected rich folk from the elements by carrying them around in sedan chairs). In addition, he was a production-line writer specializing in moralizing manuals. In his treatise of 1756 he claimed that tea was 'prejudicial' to commerce, 'pernicious . . . with regard to domestic industry and labour' and 'very injurious to health', causing men to become effeminate. 'This many-headed monster . . . devours so great a part of the best fruits of this land,' he wrote. 'Were they the sons of tea-sippers, who won the fields of Crécy and Agincourt, or dyed the Danube's streams with Gallic blood?'[11] Hanway felt about tea the way a modern commentator might feel about, say, crack cocaine.

Yet even a less partisan observer could grasp that as tea grew more popular, overtaking coffee by around 1730, social life changed. Tea was drunk mainly at home, whereas coffee was drunk outside the home. Both were stimulants, though, and encouraged a busy, sober sociability different from that produced by alcohol. Furniture changed as well; it had to be lighter so that it could be moved around more easily, and the tea table became a crucial marker of its owner's aspirations. The ritual serving of tea was a female activity: the taking of tea gave women the chance to assert themselves socially, and the whole business of tea-drinking reinforced domesticity. I hardly need say that tea has become the English national drink, though there are other countries (Morocco, Turkey) where it is more liberally consumed. It continues to be associated with alertness but also with calmness and meditation. Appropriated from the far-flung outposts of Empire, it has been transformed into something completely dissociated from its origins in China, India and Burma: a tonic, a necessity, a suitable beverage for a phlegmatic people.

It is apt that Pepys should provide this early sighting of tea, for he is alert to novelty. In 1663 he buys Elizabeth what he refers to as a 'Chinke' – a painted calico for lining the walls of her study, which later generations would call a chintz. The previous year he records going to Gray's Inn with her to see what the latest fashions are, to be sure of getting the right outfits for spring. Visiting his bookseller, he is impressed by some modish French pornography; after sampling it extensively, he buys a copy. He is struck by the well-equipped shops set up during the rebuilding that follows the Great Fire. He is excited by a new vintage of French wine and has his crest stamped on bottles that are to be served at table. All the while he uses his diary to make sense of his daily activities and their relationship to the world at large; he is clarifying the structure of his life. He glories in his ego, too, in a way that seems thoroughly modern. Pepys is the earliest diarist whose writings in this vein are well-known today; the genre would later be applauded by etiquette experts as an extension of the author's mind and a history of his or her development, a place to grow and to make plans, and a moral instrument, a nightly 'stomach-pill of self-examination'.[12]

In Pepys's England, there were also new ideas of fashionable womanhood, adopted from France. The refined lady was a creature of the French salons, a poised and luminous woman addicted to luxury and intrigue, wit and scepticism.

The type is memorably presented by Marie de Rabutin-Chantal, marquise de Sévigné, whose letters, meant for sharing rather than the exclusive consumption of individual recipients, were admired for their apparent naturalness. In reality they were artful, but to readers outside her coterie their gossip and intimacy seemed shockingly open.

The word *politesse* became current in the age of Mme de Sévigné, and another theorist of salon life, Madeleine de Scudéry, defined it as '*savoir vivre*'. English readers of the period did not pick up this language from the *salonnières*, but learned the principles thanks to a new French literature of upward mobility. In 1671 the diplomat Antoine de Courtin published a work entitled *Nouveau traité de la civilité qui se pratique en France parmi les honnêtes gens* (which roughly translates as 'A new treatise on civility as it is practised in France among honourable [i.e. upper-class] people'). He wrote for an audience of young, well-bred individuals who did not have the means or opportunity to travel to Paris and see how things were done there, and his *Nouveau traité* soon appeared in English, as *The Rules of Civility*. De Courtin's use of the word *honnête* was loaded. Nicolas Faret had in 1630 published a guide to the art of pleasing at court; this had offered a picture of the ideal royal servant, whose loyal service was the thing that made it possible to call him *honnête*. By the time de Courtin produced his treatise, the *honnête* individual was not a devoted subject of the monarch, but someone versed in deft sociability. His contemporary Antoine Gombaud wrote about this new kind of *honnête* conduct, claiming as its defining feature an elegant '*je ne sais quoi*'.[13]

To exalt *je ne sais quoi* is to exalt the fleeting and the

insubstantial, the deliciousness of uncertainty. It is also a sign of a much less precisely defined class structure. Less precisely defined – and therefore more debatable. Previously, the '*quoi*' of good manners had been exactly identified and understood. As we move into the eighteenth century, discussion of manners grows more abstract. The practical aspects of manners become a separate affair: etiquette. Meanwhile snobbishness is rampant: to speak of *je ne sais quoi* is to say '*tu ne sais quoi*' – 'The secret is mine, and I can't put it into words you'll understand.'

De Courtin is more helpfully specific than many of the writers who follow. He is clear about the physical side of mannerly behaviour, saying for instance that one should scratch rather than knock on a bedroom door to gain admission. He states that olives must be taken from a dish with a spoon, not a fork, and that it is impolite to announce one's dietary preferences. Bowing must be done without extravagance. In the sixteenth century one had stepped back before bowing; in the seventeenth, one stepped forward, which necessitated more caution. This was what de Courtin counselled as he explained the mechanics of the bow: 'neither throwing ourselves hastily upon our nose, nor rising up again too suddenly, but gently by degrees, lest the person saluted . . . might have his teeth beaten out'.[14]

English moralists recoiled from this kind of writing. In *The Ladies Calling* (1673) Richard Allestree spoke out against modish pleasures; he wanted to 'awaken some ladies from their stupid dreams' and convince them that they had been sent into the world 'for nobler purposes, than only to make a little glittering in it'. (Tellingly, he defines female modesty not by explaining what it is, but by spending twenty-seven pages on the various ways in which it can be violated.) Mary Astell, in *A Serious Proposal to the Ladies* (1694), urged women to give up frivolous activities such as reading romances; instead they should broaden their attainments. She also attacked the dissolute fashionable men of the day, who trivialized religion and were guilty of 'brutish appetite'.[15] Both writers worried about the way so many contemporary works of literature placed an emphasis on flirtation and ideas of love that were voguish rather than solidly Christian. For Astell, the obsession with refined manners prevented women from getting a useful education. The cult of politesse elevated external values at the expense of internal ones – a preference that would eventually pollute the entire literature of manners.

Astell and Allestree were trying to resist forces that were much bigger than them. Pepys was more representative of the age's inclinations: pliable, politically sophisticated, attuned to the minute business of science and finance (and of the self), frequently content to let aesthetics outshine morals. He was also a Londoner, and in the seventeenth century London was associated with opportunity and mobility; by its end, the city's population was close to 600,000, while the second largest city in England was Bristol, with a population of just 30,000.[16] The influence of London was felt all over England, and the city was a honeypot for people with ambition.

For an insight into a much less exalted form of life at this time, Richard Gough's *The History of Myddle* is invaluable. It is an account of a Shropshire parish, written around 1700. As he introduces us to the parishioners, Gough frequently describes their 'vicious' actions: one is 'addicted to idleness' and consorts with 'ugly nasty bawds', and another is reputed to have 'had no guts in his brains, but it seemed he had gear in his britches, for he got one of his uncle's servant maids with child'. Among Gough's common terms of approval for women is 'modest', while a favourite term of approval for their housekeeping is 'orderly'. For men, the equivalent is 'sober'. In Gough's vignettes social deficiency is strongly associated among women with sexual brazenness (he calls it lewdness) and domestic laxity, and among men with drunkenness.

One of the themes of Gough's writing is the capacity of drink to ruin decent men. For instance, he tells of a farmer who went daily with his wife to the alehouse, 'and soon after the cows went thither also'. Gough is appalled that a man should have to sell his herd to pay for his drinking, but he is not surprised by it. Drunkenness is a state that has long been associated with the English, by foreigners and by the English themselves. The chronicler John of Salisbury recorded this perception in the twelfth century, and commentators have since then frequently spoken of the joyless, violent inebriation of Englishmen. In the age Gough documents, around 15 per cent of total income was spent on drink.[17]

In Myddle, the church is at the centre of the locals' lives. Gough classifies people according to where they sit in church, and this is how they would have seen themselves: church seating was a visible expression of hierarchy, often disputed. But Gough was writing from memory, and the world he depicted was being swept away. Farms were disappearing, rural communities were shrinking, improved education was gradually broadening local people's horizons, and as the smaller farms were bought up by bigger landowners, the divisions between rich and poor became more palpable.

Four events at the end of the century changed the texture of social life in England: the Glorious Revolution of 1688, which boosted both law and liberty; the Act of Toleration in 1689, which reduced religious persecution; the financial revolution of the 1690s, which included the establishment of the Bank of England in 1694; and the failure in 1695 to renew the Licensing Act, which ended arbitrary government censorship and resulted in a proliferation of printed material, not least a tide of partisan journalism. The result was a noisy pluralism. As society altered, there was a new relish for artistic, political and philosophical debate. At the same time, courtly models of behaviour were superseded. An example of this was the increasing hostility to duelling; once seen as romantic and honourable, it was in the eighteenth century widely deplored (not least for being a French affectation), and by around 1730 the badge of a gentleman was not a sword but instead a Malacca cane.[18] The philosopher David Hume, writing about duels in the 1740s, was unusual in thinking them modern.

A new urban middle-class value system was emerging: people were mobile, money was mobile, aspiration was bound up with ownership of objects more than with qualities, and transactions were the stuff of life. Manners were increasingly associated with fashionable goods and fashionable places. Indeed, manners were one of these fashionable goods – something to be marketed. But before we see this, we need to look more closely at one of Pepys's favourite subjects, a matter eternally fraught with perils, confusions and complications, even if also with pleasures.

10

Not Mr Sex

There is an episode of *Seinfeld* in which George Costanza, the show's resident neurotic, is invited back to a woman's apartment for coffee. He declines, explaining that the caffeine would keep him awake all night. Later he realizes his mistake: '"Coffee" doesn't mean coffee; "coffee" means sex!'

Readers of this book do not need to be told why it is unusual for someone to say, 'Would you like to come back to my place for sex?' Coffee stands in for sex because it is a post-prandial staple. It is an unembarrassing euphemism, although to some it suggests darker pleasures. Yet really what we see in George Constanza's misreading is the way fuzziness is an important part of sexual behaviour. We are socially and sexually selective, and this involves competition. Fuzziness exists to mask our impulses. But it is also a filter for screening out of our sex lives people like George Costanza, who on one occasion tells his girlfriend that he loves her while they're listening to a hockey game on the radio, is bemused by her failure to reciprocate, then delightedly discovers that she is deaf in one ear, and when he next sees her bellows the words 'I love you' into her good ear — which elicits the response, 'I know. I heard you the first time.'

In essence, sexual manners are about saying 'coffee' rather than 'sex'. But I should add here that a brief survey of friends revealed differences between men and women regarding the fundamentals of sexual manners. Men seemed to think they were a matter of, for instance, not falling asleep straight after intercourse. Women thought they were mainly concerned with the preamble, the preamble's preamble or the larger issues: can you sleep with someone on the first date or should you wait till the third, and when do you discuss contraception or exclusivity? I can't be sure that these findings are normal. I can report, however, that George Costanza's misunderstanding elicited responses every bit as divergent, with men saying, 'I've been there, too,' and women saying, 'Ah, but "coffee" really can mean just "coffee".' The charades that are assumed to be universally understood can in practice be ambiguous.

George Costanza may be a native of Brooklyn (and a fictional figure, largely based on his Brooklyn-born creator Larry David), but his problems resonate with an English audience, for whom sex is traditionally a subject mired in hypocrisy, mostly handled with either prudery or prurience, and often treated in a manner that seems a mixture of the furtive and the fetishistic.

The history of English sexuality tends to focus on outliers: the rakes of the Regency period, the gay brothels known as molly houses, the addicts of flagellation who have earned sexual beating its nickname 'the English vice', and the exploits of individuals such as the eighteenth-century diarist (and Scot)

James Boswell, who was repeatedly struck down by venereal disease, and 'Walter', the author of a Victorian diary that is a monument to his encounters with more than 1,000 women (among whom, he regretfully tells us, there has never been a Laplander). When foreigners think of sex and the English, they think of self-deprecatory remarks rather than of crimson passion, but they may also think of archaic deviancy, which is likely to be much concerned with bottoms. The French call spanking *le vice anglais*. They like to label bad habits in this way, and we return the compliment: what they call *filer à l'anglaise*, we call French leave.

But there is another image of English sexuality – summed up in the humorist George Mikes's line that 'continental people have sex life; the English have hot-water bottles.'[1] And there is another, more humdrum story of fumbling initiations and cautious abstinence, repression, folklore and the skulking sharing of information.

In other cultures, sex has been at the heart of medicine. In Han Dynasty China, roughly 2,000 years ago, Taoist doctrine regarding health and hygiene emphasized the benefits of sex and the possibility of achieving longevity or even immortality through the diligent pursuit of *fang zhong shu* (the art of the bedchamber). The *Kama Sutra*, a Sanskrit text compiled at about the same time, weaves a web of philosophy around matters that the English tend to treat with either trepidation or humour. For the record, the *Kama Sutra* isn't a sex manual and doesn't contain saucy illustrations, though it does mount a defence of the important role sex plays in civilized existence.

That may strike us as a modern attitude. It is fashionable to say that in Britain modern attitudes to sex were born in the eighteenth century. It was a feature of that period that men, who had long been assumed to be no more sexually excitable than women, were represented as more libidinous and less able to control their amorous urges. Libertinism was a way of life for many, and could be an asset for a man with political ambitions (like the radical John Wilkes) or a philosophical commitment to pleasure (in fact best embodied by Rochester in the previous century). Furthermore, at that time homosexuality began to be thought about in terms that we would now recognize. Sex was openly discussed and often celebrated.

Yet attitudes to sex have always tended to oscillate, with each surge in sexual self-expression answered by an attempt to smother it. The historian Lawrence Stone, examining the records of sex offences in sixteenth-century Essex, found a society that was sexually lax and decidedly inquisitorial. There was a great deal of extramarital sex, but at the same time a great readiness to denounce other people's transgressions.[2] The eighteenth century differed from the sixteenth not so much with regard to sexual attitudes as with regard to the media through which those attitudes could be broadcast. In the later period there was a large, inexpensive literature of sexual pleasure, which included erotic prints; previously, works of that kind had circulated in manuscript and had been consumed in secret.

The movement to smother sexuality is most famously embodied by those zealous busybodies the Puritans. Sustained movements of this kind had been launched before and would be revived many times. But Puritanism was strikingly intolerant and coercive. Its agenda was at once religious and economic.

The Puritan spirit persists in the desire – often understandable, but in many cases reeking of paranoia – to interfere in the behaviour of our neighbours.

A notable Puritan tract of the 1580s was Philip Stubbes's *Anatomie of Abuses*. Stubbes complained of the prevalence of earrings, dyed hair and make-up. Instead of going to church, citizens went in for dicing, bear-baiting and football ('a friendly kind of fight'). They visited banqueting houses and descended into filthy amusement, living beyond their means and sporting silly hats and expensive shirts with curious stitching. Dancing stirred up lust. Women dressed like men and as a result resembled hermaphrodites. Of all the things that corrupted people, Stubbes thought none worse than the theatre; he worried that the relaxed socializing that happened there was likely to send people home on unusually friendly terms to 'play the sodomites, or worse'. The productions his contemporaries watched were either tragedies stuffed with 'cruelty, injury, incest, murder, and such like' or comedies full of 'flattery, whoredom, adultery'.[3]

Stubbes's attitudes were echoed by many commentators in the century that followed. The clergyman Thomas Tuke published in 1616 an entire treatise against the wearing of make-up, and William Prynne in 1628 published one that damned women's 'mannish' and 'unchristian' hairstyles, before moving on to write a pamphlet denouncing actors – especially female ones, who were in the table of contents described as 'notorious whores'. Sexual legislation abounded. Bills requiring stricter punishment of sexual offences were passed in 1601, 1604, 1606–7, 1614, 1621, 1626, 1628 and 1629.[4] At this time it was common to use the word *folly* as a euphemism for immoral sexual behaviour, and the records of church courts often used *uncivil* and *rude* as terms to connote gross sexual offences. Sexual misconduct was associated with low intelligence and even madness.

The campaign against vice was invigorated at the end of the century by the Society for the Reformation of Manners. Founded in London in 1690, and backed by the new king and queen William and Mary, it vigorously prosecuted brothel-keepers and homosexuals as well as insufficiently moralistic playwrights. Related societies sprang up in other parts of the country: not just in cities, but in towns such as Alnwick, Shepton Mallet, Kidderminster and Tamworth. Crucially, they did not address crimes that had victims (such as burglary), preferring to focus on the causes of crime. Up till 1738, when all such societies were formally disbanded, their influence was strong – and unpopular. In the 1750s they resurfaced, and the spirit of the original society has since been revived at intervals under different names, from the National Vigilance Association, established in 1885 to monitor the 'moral welfare' of young women, to Mary Whitehouse's National Viewers' and Listeners' Association, set up in 1965 and still active under the name Mediawatch-uk.

All the while, there were countercurrents of rebellion. Sex manuals proved essential to this, informing readers about techniques and necessary precautions, albeit without exactly dispelling their worries. One of the most notable was *Aristotle's Masterpiece*, a guide to reproduction published in 1684 and popular well into the nineteenth century. It celebrates sex as something natural and pleasurable, and is in many respects surprisingly accurate, but there is room for folk wisdom and

odd ideas: the notion that the size of a man's nose is an indication of the size of his penis; the assertion that pubescent
girls, 'desirous of copulation', exhibit a 'weasel colour' and 'short
breathings, tremblings, and pantings of the heart'; and the
claim that women who live 'near the seaside, being restless
and troubled in copulation, bring forth misshapen embryos'.[5]

Today information about sex is far more scientific. It is
plentiful, too, and sex education is provided in schools. But
strange ideas persist, and so does ignorance. Practical knowledge of sex – what goes where – is often treated as if it is
a subject devoid of emotional, moral and ethical implications.
Sexual liberation is acclaimed. But really one kind of angst
has replaced another: instead of feeling guilty about having
or wanting sex, we are now made to feel guilty if we aren't
at it like polecats.

Changes in behaviour have been brought about by the
contraceptive Pill, improved rights for women and widespread
internet access. The last of these has enabled new ways of
locating a partner, and with them come new problems. A
piece in the *Guardian* in January 2009 noted that 'for the
resolutely polite, searching for a partner online can become
very time-consuming', and as a result there is 'an unwritten
rule in the internet dating world that it is acceptable to ignore
mail from people who don't interest you'.[6] This is the discreet
end of what internet daters consider 'necessary rudeness'.
Veterans of the online romantic and sexual marketplace
complain that its much vaunted efficiencies are offset by new
forms of anxiety and a new rhetoric of rejection.

The abundance of free internet pornography also means that
many young people embarking on sex lives have seen footage

of sex acts that previous generations might never have imagined. Notions of what's sexually orthodox and of polite sexual behaviour have relaxed. Yet there are still many conservative ideas about codes of courtship, acceptable forms of flirtation, same-sex relationships and the virtues of abstinence. Tunde, a thirty-two-year-old street sweeper in Camden, speaks for many when he says that 'Respectfulness is important. Sometimes that means not doing what you want to do – waiting, or never doing it.' Teenage skateboarders Connor and Ben, whom I meet on London's South Bank, agree. Connor says that you 'can't have sex with a girl straightaway. She's got to make you wait.' Ben explains, 'That's why people get married. It's like saying in public that you're ready to play by the rules.'

The persistence of conservatism is noticeable in the way most of us talk about sex. It is not just a case of the kind of façade that throws George Constanza off the scent; except when telling jokes, we find sexual frankness unsettling. Although this isn't peculiarly English, sex is an area in which we deploy a wealth of euphemisms, some of them very obscure. Among those I heard, when I canvassed examples for this book, there were many familiar ones ('They were getting down to it', 'Oh, he's been doing it with her for a while'), but also many that struck me as bizarre and not entirely successful ('He got a bit of jam', 'They've been making feet for children's shoes'). We are accustomed to the way the words *inappropriate* and *unfortunate* stand in for *odious* or *terrible* ('His joke about disabled children was inappropriate', 'The defendant made some unfortunate choices'), yet one acquaintance surprised me, in the context of talking about her sex life, with the information that a lover had been 'good at first – enjoyably . . . inappropriate –

but then he seemed to lose interest and was just a little unfortunate'.

The evasive ways in which we refer to sex are often
delightful, examples of verbal play at its most dextrous. In
Shakespeare's *Othello*, for instance, Iago says that the lovers
Othello and Desdemona 'are now making the beast with two
backs', and in a dictionary of slang dating from 1811 we learn
that two overweight people who have been doing the same
thing might be said to have savoured 'melting moments'.
Such inventive phrasing is a reminder of the anxieties that
surround sexual pleasure, sexuality and sexual effluvia. Even
banal conversation can resemble a diplomatic tête-à-tête: the
parties involved are negotiating their levels of power, intimacy
and entitlement, and may well be exploring ways of saving
face and indemnifying themselves against liabilities.[7] But it
is in our sexual relationships, and especially in those inchoate
relationships we would like to become more sexual, that we
are most likely to simulate feelings, feign curiosity, compliment what we consider average, solicit agreement and
sympathy, make gestures of deference and delicately phrase
our requests, while also going to elaborate lengths to make
it look as though we are doing none of these things.

Few writers have tapped into the male side of this experience more successfully than Neil Strauss, whose book *The
Game* is an investigation of the techniques used by men who
dedicate themselves to the art of the sexual pick-up. Strauss's
chapter titles are sufficient evidence of the nature of their
behaviour: 'Disarm the Obstacles', 'Isolate the Target', 'Blast
Last-Minute Resistance'. There is something comically
un-English about this. Yet if the language Strauss uses is military,

the techniques are more in line with the book's title: playful, manipulative, evasive and conducive to a certain amount of immature cliquiness among those who practise them. Even in the realm of the pick-up artist, sexual intent comes cloaked.

Neil Strauss's antecedents include Francis Osborne, the man Samuel Pepys called 'my father Osborne'. In *Advice to a Son* Osborne portrays monogamy as the result of law, custom and man's 'stupendous folly'. The real business of a man, he suggests, is his own pleasure. He advises against consorting with notable women, who may even make 'your desires subject to theirs', and against celebrated beauties, 'unless you are ambitious of rendering your house as populous as a confectioner's shop'. He equates love with 'whining'. Lust promises nothing 'beyond the repetition of the same again, which after a few enjoyments grows tedious'. Children are dismissed, too; at their worst they are the product of 'the tedious commerce and loathsome sheets of a silly woman', and in any case they are 'no more ours, than the curls of our hair, or the parings of our nails'.[8] For Osborne, sex is a game and relationships are pitfalls; one must learn to be a master strategist.

11

The elephant and the bad baby

the everyday language of manners

Euphemism, so disconcerting for *Seinfeld*'s George Costanza, masks not just real filth but also matters we consider filthy or indecent, matters that we would prefer others to think we condemn, and matters that we know others consider taboo. It is a species of good manners, hardly unique to English. Chinese thrill-seekers can buy *qingqu yongpin*, 'interesting love products', while in France an *autodidacte* is someone who did not have the benefit of higher education. In Portugal someone who is fat will be described as *forte* ('strong'); in Poland the equivalent is *puszysty*, which means something more like 'fluffy' or 'puffy'. But English euphemisms seem to be everywhere, and many of the words we feel the need to avoid were euphemisms in their time – *vagina* and *excrement*, for instance. What's more, many English euphemisms speak loudly of the conspiracy into which they are urging us. Obituarists make bold use of their favourites: someone who did not suffer fools gladly in fact had a volcanic temper, a person described as convivial was a heavy drinker, and someone said to have been a raconteur was really a bore.

Propriety influences plenty of other linguistic choices. It

can take the form of inclusiveness ('Let's get something to drink', meaning 'I want something to drink, and you're coming'), forewarning ('I'm afraid this is going to be a touch dull, but let's go over the details again'), asserting common ground or shared experience ('Yes, isn't it terrible the way that always happens!') and moderating one's complaints or criticisms ('You're sort of not with it today, aren't you?', 'That's not technically true'). Deference, which should stop short of servility, is another such choice. So is avoiding language that feels coercive. 'Is it me, or is it cold in here?' will often softly do the work of a less gentle 'Shut the door, please.'

The desire to find common ground is interesting. English has an unusually rich vocabulary with which we can establish rapport. When I was a student, a friend of mine, while being mugged, managed to allay the violence by pointing out to his attacker that they were wearing the same brand of trainers – 'but I think yours are a bit newer than mine'. Where else in the world would this happen? That almost parenthetical 'I think' is an example of a quirk of English that native English-speakers are not necessarily able to recognize: the prevalence, when compared with other languages, of little phrases (epistemic phrases) that show my stance in relation to what I am saying – 'I think', 'I gather', 'I imagine', 'I would suggest', 'I would have guessed', 'I take it', and so on. These can be used to express caution about opinions, but also to express caution about facts – a reluctance to declare what can instead be put more discreetly and with a stronger air of the personal. Many adverbs do the same: *presumably, conceivably, arguably, probably*. Of these the last is the most common, suggesting measured thought and reflectiveness even when neither has been practised.[1] *Probably* is a word of genial, reasonable, unintellectual hue, and is far more common than its foreign equivalents such as the German *wahrscheinlich* or the Spanish *probablemente*.

Hints, hesitation and vagueness can all be strategies for avoiding rudeness – for showing sensitivity to another person's vulnerabilities, or perhaps for shielding from view one's awareness of such vulnerabilities. Yet we tend to recognize them as such, and the rudeness is thus not fully out of sight. Hinting can be a test rather than a tactful indication. I can remember as a child discovering that when a glacial relative asked me if I wanted some more salad (the answer was definitely 'No'), what she really meant was that she would like some more. I was supposed to infer this and give her a second helping. When I didn't, my error was explained to me at length. Then there is the propriety of apology: 'I'm sorry to be a nuisance, but could you turn your music down?', 'I wouldn't normally ask this, but have you got change for a pound?' That *but* only pretends to be deflective and smothering; the substance of the sentence is what follows it.

Polite language can be an attempt to have (and show) consideration for others, or it can be a form of self-interested display. Obviously, vulgar or profane language is also a display: people object to it because it smacks of excitability, pain or menace, and because it seems an attempt to force an unpalatable thought upon them. But often deeper offence is caused by poor choices of language that are inadvertent. Verbal gaffes can spark diplomatic incidents. In 2010, offering thanks for Germany's help in the rescue of a group of trapped Chilean miners, President Sebastián Piñera wrote in the German President's official guestbook the words '*Deutschland Über Alles*', a slogan strongly associated with Nazism. The verbal slips of George W. Bush were condemned by his critics as insults to the American electorate. Sometimes they slid into other kinds of faux pas. In May 2007 Bush appeared to suggest that Queen Elizabeth II had visited his country in 1776; he tried to compensate for this by winking at her, a gesture received frostily. The Queen's husband, Prince Philip, has plenty of form in this area: observing of the Nigerian President's national dress, 'You look like you're ready for bed'; saying that a poorly installed fuse box looked 'as if it was put in by an Indian'; and enquiring of Cayman Islanders, 'Aren't most of you descended from pirates?' Such blunders are perceived as failures of restraint and sensitivity, and in Prince Philip's case especially they are at odds with the putative dignity of his position. In some cases, they are the result of too much clarity, of people saying precisely what is on their minds, rather than self-editing.

In conversation, clarity is generally desirable, as are relevance and succinctness. But when clarity and politeness are in conflict, politeness usually wins. Consider, for instance, the difference between the following: 'If you don't start a pension now, you'll be poor when you're old,' and 'You know, a lot of people would say that making a monthly pension contribution is a very tax-efficient way of saving for retirement.'

Prince Philip notwithstanding, the English have an international reputation for not saying what they mean. Often they are characterized as inarticulate; in French and Italian theatre, the stock Englishman is traditionally a bungler who struggles to form a coherent sentence. The English, it's said, are silent because they are inept with words – or fearful of the consequences of speech. James Salgado, a refugee from Spain in the 1670s, commented that an Englishman usually spoke as if afraid of his mouth catching cold: a small number of words were pushed out through a small opening. How ironic that that great English saying 'Brevity is the soul of wit' first came from the busy mouth of Shakespeare's Polonius. As we have seen, the English affection for reticent brevity is proverbial; the word *understatement* is traced back no further than 1799 by the *OED*, but it seems likely to have emerged earlier in that century as the art of conversation was cultivated, with the aid of guides by writers such as Henry Fielding. In English conversation, understatement has been prized on account of its cushioning effect.

Also common, though, is the image of the English as gossips, whose garrulity is a means of avoiding serious talk. When they rise above casual, rumour-laden chat, they are debaters or aphorists – not conversationalists, but specialists in speechifying, uninterested in replies. Eighteenth-century observers noted that English orators, especially in parliamentary debates, were formal and impressive but lacked social skill: this was eloquence of an uneasy kind. To have a real conversation was to risk interfering in the business of one's companions. The English have often been criticized (and sometimes applauded) for their directness, but such directness is typically a means of closing down the dynamic possibilities of conversation, rather than of subtly opening them up.

Practising good manners can also involve saying things we do not mean. Many would diagnose this as a peculiarly English affliction. It is not so much a matter of euphemism as of strategic misrepresentation. Foreigners learn to translate this idiom, in which something described as *interesting* is regarded as tedious nonsense, a *brave* plan is an insane one, and *quite good* means 'disappointing' (*not bad* is better than *quite good*). A more extreme form of this, in which evasiveness shades into unreliability, is the phrase *I shall bear that in mind*, which equates to 'I'm going to forget about it immediately'. Perhaps the most laughable examples are *by the way*, which, in common with *incidentally*, translates as 'this is the main thing I want to say'; *it's my fault*, meaning 'it's your fault'; and *with all due respect*, which means something closer to 'Now listen to *me*'. A further, puzzling example: 'We must have lunch', or an equivalent such as 'We really ought to go for a drink some time', is not an invitation to be followed up, but instead a way of indicating that one's feelings towards a person, while they may be mildly favourable, do not extend as far as making definite plans. Words such as *must* and *ought*, which appear to suggest necessity, here put a matter vaguely in the present tense rather than precisely in the future ('We'll have coffee on Tuesday'). The elasticity of the present tense is convenient; it can give the impression of a future commitment without actually cementing that commitment, the words 'I love you' being an example of a statement in the present that implies futurity without assuring it.

The philosopher Bertrand Russell addresses the question of strategic misrepresentation (my words, not his) in a short essay on 'Good Manners and Hypocrisy'. In it he recalls 'my perplexity at the age of five when a man gave me a picture-book I had already and I was reproached for not expressing a pleasure I did not feel'.[2] In the interests of politeness, he reflects, one must sometimes embroider or slant one's feelings, simulating enthusiasm to avoid giving offence. Generosity, even if its cargo is not ambrosial, requires pleasant acknowledgement.

As the ethicist Karen Stohr maintains, this acknowledgement is not a 'current status report' of the kind that might be spewed out by a computer; it is a signal that one believes that gratitude is morally appropriate.

We nevertheless understand that we should avoid great displays of simulated enthusiasm. For instance, if I have lunch at a friend's house and she serves me overcooked salmon I will cause offence if I say I disliked it. But while it would be transparently sycophantic to pretend that it was the best salmon I have ever had, I can say that I quite like my salmon well-done. By finessing the truth, I keep my friend from feeling bad. Of course, some people see no difference between this and telling a lie – which they condemn. The philosopher Immanuel Kant argued that when we lie we violate our self-respect, the dignity of the person to whom we lie, and our duty to humanity as a whole. No less influential, though, is the notion of the 'useful lie', set out by the thirteenth-century theologian Thomas Aquinas. According to Aquinas, a lie is useful if it prevents another person from coming to harm. The intention is not to deceive, but to reserve part of the truth (it stays in my head): thus I say only some of the sentence 'I quite like my salmon well-done, although I prefer it less well-done than this.' The danger of reserving part of the truth is that my friend may feel patronized. In such a situation the real skill lies in finding something about which I can tell the truth, and in building on that: 'The beans are perfect. Where are they from?'[3]

While we are probing the language that is exploited in the interests of politeness, it is worth examining a little more closely the development of the English vocabulary used to *denote* manners, for the changing functions of its most basic terms reveal changing attitudes. Inevitably, we begin with the word *manners* itself, which derives via French from the Latin *manuaria*, a term that signified actions done with the hand and methods of handling things. (The Latin for *hand* was *manus*.) The singular *manner* began to be used of people's habitual behaviour – with a distinctly moral hue – in the thirteenth century. Late in the century that followed, people started to use it to designate rules of behaviour or what we might label 'proper conduct'; this sense became more frequent in the fifteenth century. The plural *manners* is employed with something close to its modern sense in the age of Chaucer. In the Elizabethan period the word's moral weight seems to have been accentuated, and by the time Shakespeare writes *Othello*, around 1604, the plural *manners* is common enough that he can put it in the mouths of three different characters.

The adjective *mannerly*, meaning 'well-mannered', never caught on in the same way. It strikes me as useful, but has an air of tweeness, captured in the title of the romance novel *Thoroughly Mannerly Millicent*. The word appears in texts 600 years ago; in *Sir Gawain and the Green Knight*, written no later than 1400, there is reference to 'mannerly mirth'. *Mannerliness* appears not long after this, and never quite sheds an image of stuffy overnicety. The noun *form* (as in Ophelia's description of Hamlet as 'The glass of fashion, and the mould of form') is also found at that time, but is not common before the eighteenth century. No one referred to 'good form' and 'bad form' till the second half of the nineteenth century; an article in the *Spectator* in June 1890 states that 'It is not good intellectual form to grow angry in discussion.'

It was only in the eighteenth century that *polite*, which originally meant 'polished' or 'burnished', became a term used of manners rather than to signify cultural refinement and elegance. In that era of commerce and enlightenment, one looked at somebody else and saw one's reflection in his or her polished, shining exterior, and this was aesthetically and psychologically gratifying. The smooth word *politesse* was a borrowing of the Restoration period, when Charles II returned from exile with a taste for all things French, but as late as the 1770s the novelist Fanny Burney was using it in her journal with a touch of uncertainty (and in the plural). *Politeness* was used early in the seventeenth century to signify elegance, refinement and smoothness; it was employed not just of people, but of stones and glass. As a term for courtesy and respect-fulness, it gained currency during the Restoration, being popularized by the philosopher John Locke in *Some Thoughts Concerning Education* (1693), where he deemed politeness an essential quality in a tutor.

The language of politeness has long been saturated with French. Following the Norman Conquest of England, Norman French was the language not only of power and administra-tion, but also of prestige. This French influence would never go away. It is perhaps most obvious in the realm of food, where it tends to have connotations of sophisticated dining rather than piggish troughing-down: *restaurant, gourmet, chef, cuisine, patisserie, menu*. But the range of borrowings from French is wide. Thus in Charles II's England, new words included *clique, caprice, faux pas, nonchalance, ennui, carte blanche* and *double-entendre*, all redolent of the competitive, gossipy and suavely sociable nature of the court. English-speakers have often discerned in such borrowings evidence of French playfulness and effervescence – and also loucheness.

We can pick out cultural trends by looking at the different frequency with which relevant words appear in printed texts. It seems, for instance, that the popularity of the word *politesse* peaked between 1820 and 1850. *Impolite* has been becoming steadily more common since around 1800, whereas the word *polite* has become a little less frequent over the last 200 years, and *politeness* has been declining. This does not necessarily mean that there has been less politeness and more impoliteness; rather, it has become less common to remark upon the former and more common to discuss the latter.

Civility was a popular word from the 1660s to the 1680s, and became popular again in the last decades of the eighteenth century. In the first of these periods it denoted in particular a cessation of the disorderliness of the Civil Wars; in the second it more broadly signified a concern, not motivated by religion, for the good of society as a whole. The peak years for *incivility* stretch from about 1770 to 1850. *Unmannerly* was especially popular in the late seventeenth century, as were *mannerly* and *good manners*. In the 1770s there was much talk of *rude manners*. *Rudeness* itself took off around 1800. But references to *bad manners* grew steadily through the nineteenth century and reached a peak in the 1940s, dropping off in the 1950s, only to prove resurgent in the last couple of decades.

Manners and language have a lot in common: they are means of communication, which we can use to represent our selves; we take them for granted; both are responsive to wider social and cultural changes; the ways in which they change are unpredictable and not immediately recognized (because cumulative and gradual), and change is a consequence of their purposeful use; one of the forms of change is borrowing elements from other cultures; and change is the aspect of them we are most likely to comment on, often with the conviction that it is catastrophic.

Language is also a medium through which we show, be it wittingly or not, our manners and our status. We are back with George Bernard Shaw's line that 'it is impossible for an Englishman to open his mouth without making some other Englishman despise him.' Discussion of the relationship between language and manners goes back long before Shaw. In the sixteenth century, for instance, there was fierce debate about whether the use in English of words imported from other languages (French, Italian, Latin) was a mark of civility and polish, or a graceless retreat from Anglo-Saxon simplicity. Early in the eighteenth century Jonathan Swift issued *A Proposal for Correcting, Improving and Ascertaining the English Tongue*, in which he suggested that the imperfect state of the language was a sign of his contemporaries' corrupt manners, licentiousness and conceit. He saw a connection between good manners and the art of rhetoric; both were formal means of pleasing and persuading others.

Most of us are quick to penalize others' use of language without being adept at explaining what is correct, and, in much the same way, we are better at identifying impoliteness than we are at precisely defining what is polite. Attempts to locate politeness tend to involve our noting that certain routine formulae have been observed: the result is that we come to think that politeness consists of those formulae *and nothing else*. Deference and indirectness are to the fore here. The essentially negative way we think about politeness is reflected in the fact that polite behaviour often causes resentment.

Good manners are like the principles of grammar: we make use of them all the time but also violate them frequently; we tend to believe we are getting them right but would struggle to explain clearly what they are or how exactly we came by them; and occasionally we worry that we are getting them wrong, and look around rather hopelessly for a lucid, authoritative, realistic account of what we ought to be doing. Manners can be thought of as the syntax of the social self.

In common with many linguistic principles that we think of as 'rules', manners are conventions. They make up a system of expectations. Across the history of manners, there is a pattern of particular behaviours being cultivated by the social elite in order to distinguish them from everyone else – and of those behaviours being modified or dropped once the lower ranks of society have started to imitate them successfully.

We touch here on the idea that manners are not obligatory. Over the course of our lives we internalize rules and principles of behaviour. These rules are not like those of algebra, permanent and universal laws. Although other people may make us feel as if they are just that, manners have meaning because they have been performed voluntarily. At least, this is true in Britain and America; it is not the case in Japan, where in a great many social situations *wakimae* (discernment) counts for more than volition. *Wakimae* involves a strict, automatic conformity to an almost feudal set of expectations in which the individual's tastes and opinions are suppressed. It thus embodies the arguments of the French thinker Pierre Bourdieu, who spoke of manners as symbolic taxes. Bourdieu believed that just as material taxes are exacted by the elite, so these symbolic ones are paid – in the form of deference and humility – as a tribute to rulers and the status quo. When they aren't paid, the status quo trembles.

In a society that is not so rigid, manners are less like taxes than habits. Rather than being enforced, they are exalted by tradition. Their acquisition is gradual, and after a time, as they are repeated, they become automatic. This may seem a humdrum observation, yet it leads to an important point, because habits don't have a good name. The Victorian manual *The Habits of Good Society* sounds not just antique but also a little suspect. The word we are most likely to associate with *habits* is *bad*. Discussion of manners-as-habits tends, inevitably, to dwell on the failure of the habits to become ingrained.

There has also been a pattern of equating manners and morals – or of suggesting that the former mature into the latter. As we shall see, this is an appealing notion rather than a secure one. There is something quaintly satisfying in Thomas Hobbes's reference in *Leviathan*, a masterpiece of political philosophy, to manners being 'small morals'.[4] But the tendency to present manners as small – 'It's the little things that count' – is a rhetorical dodge. Whoever says that manners are 'only' little is invariably attaching a huge amount of significance to them. One of the most common politely misleading statements takes the form 'It's only a small thing, but would you mind not doing X?' Translated into guileless speech, this is 'I absolutely hate it when you do X.'

We have got used to manners being treated as a small subject. It is therefore worth noticing how many of the most influential thinkers have examined manners: not just Hobbes, but also the philosophers John Locke, David Hume and Immanuel Kant as well as their ancient predecessors Plato, Aristotle and Seneca. For instance, Kant thought of manners as by-products of a virtuous disposition; they were virtue in miniature.

Where manners are concerned, we think that our way is the right way. This is true at a personal level ('The way I do this is just so obviously *the* way to do it') and in much broader terms ('The only proper way is the English way'). Asked to explain, we fall back on fuzzy notions that we call logic or common sense. The latter means something different from its supposed equivalents in other languages, such as the French *sens commun* and *bon sens* or the Italian *senso comune* and *buon senso*. In English, common sense is mainly diagnosed as absent: it is not the presence of common sense that is remarked on, but rather the need to introduce common sense into a discussion from which it has been missing. Even when common sense is more positively invoked, the term is often buttressed by adjectives such as *simple, plain* and *basic*, which betray exasperation: someone who says that X is a matter of basic common sense has got fed up with X not being understood or appreciated. Often English common sense is represented as a tool ('Use common sense'), and its bluntness is reassuring. I think of it as being less like a rapier than a gardener's trowel.

The English set great store by reasonableness. This is not a philosophical concept, but something much folksier: a preference for proverb over theory, for conventions (preferably unspoken) rather than boldly stated rules. *Reasonableness* is not the same as *reason*, but is a watered-down version of it.

We are used to hearing or reading statements that begin 'It is reasonable to . . .', and in these cases what comes next is usually thinking, asking, supposing, assuming. This is tentativeness couched as shrewd judgement. In other sentences, where we come across terms such as 'reasonable doubt', 'reasonable time' or 'reasonable force', the word *reasonable* swabs away thoughts about unreasonableness – or its user at least hopes it will swab them away. It appears that we are being invited to think about a matter with crisp rationality, but really we are being nudged towards suspending any grievance or anxiety we may feel.

Reasonableness can manifest itself as the most dreadful pomposity or philistinism. It is part of the English love of empiricism, apparent in an aversion to abstract thinking and elevated theories ('Come off it!'), a preference for the testimony of our own experience ('Seeing is believing'), and a sense that true experience is a social phenomenon more than a psychological one (something consensual, not internal). The word *experience*, a more crucial one for the English than is usually recognized, suggests accumulated wisdom – the lessons of the past – but also a good deal of faith in transient perceptions. Rather than being suspicious of these, we exalt them: 'First impressions count.' Related to this are two other forms of English reasonableness: one that smacks of unreason yet is treated as if incontrovertible, namely gut instinct; and another, the preoccupation with evidence, that seems more secure. However, in English *evidence* is not the same as *proof*, and when we speak of 'hard evidence' we signal not absolute certainty but an impression of certainty, which we want to beef up.[5] English manners are pervaded by what I'll call unreasoned reasonableness. This is the attempt to pass off opinions (which may of course be valid) as facts.

The cult of the reasonable is also expressed in the English notion of fair play, which is less about real fairness (fairness to all) than about my getting what I think is mine. The words *fair* and *fairness*, distinct from *just* and *justness* (or *justice*), do not have direct equivalents in other languages. The strong association between *fair* and *play* hints at the English-speaker's tendency to think of interactions as if they are games.[6] Reasonableness and fairness form a trio with the notion of 'good faith', which has a particular sense in law but which we tend to come across when someone is protesting (or professing) that a colossal balls-up was achieved without malice.

My use of *we* illustrates the slippery nature of the first person plural: a writer or orator will use it to suggest, if not universals, at least broad similarities of feelings, interests and experiences, but the affinity it implies is really a fiction. Throughout this book I speak of *we* and *us* for the sake of convenience, rather than because I think I can be sure of your views or because I am trying to conscript you in my arguments. When I speak of the English and *their* manners, it is not because I want to dissociate myself from Englishness or manners, but because I want to maintain a degree of dispassionate distance. Still, I can say with confidence that we care about manners. Why else would you – or we – be here?

When the *Daily Mail* in 2008 reported the study claiming that bad manners were the biggest problem facing society, one theme was the reduced use of *please* and *thank you*. It is striking that the report homed in on language. Complaints about manners often come down to just this: the absence of these so-called magic words. Their alleged disappearance is today used as an index of social decline. Certain media commentators revel in stories of such decline, and plenty of those who respond to their comments fantasize about painful ways of underscoring the words' importance.

In childhood we are taught that giving and receiving are fundamental features of life, and that, as the five-year-old Bertrand Russell found out, receiving must be accompanied by gratitude. This behaviour has to be instilled; small children do not spontaneously express gratitude. Thanking people is a form of mindfulness. Its expression can be full of humility. We are grateful *to* people and *for* things; thanks are directional, and tell us about the source of the things for which we are grateful. The words *gratitude* and *ingratitude* emerged when feudal loyalties were replaced by chosen loyalties. *Ingratitude* is found in the thirteenth century, but with a highly specific sense, to do with forgetting God and his gifts; its current sense caught on in the sixteenth century (Shakespeare uses the word in twelve of his plays), at the same time that *gratitude* became common.

I remember that when I was a child my mother read me a book called *The Elephant and the Bad Baby*.[7] It depicts an elephant, which is out for a walk one day and meets a baby; together they embark on a shoplifting spree, with the elephant going '*rumpeta-rumpeta-rumpeta*' an awful lot. Eventually the elephant, noticing that the baby isn't polite, sits down suddenly and tumbles him from his back. Never mind the shoplifting, the baby's offence lies in not saying 'please'.

The use of *please* as an adverb ('Please do not feed the right-wing commentators') is more recent than we might imagine. The first citation in the *OED* is from 1771. Its use as an interjection ('Oh, please, the right-wing commentators can look after themselves') seems to be a twentieth-century development; the *OED*'s first citation is from E. M. Forster's *A Room with a View*, published in 1908. *Thank you* is older than *please*, but the *OED* has only one citation – an obscure one – earlier than 1631. It is not as if politeness in framing requests and courteous acknowledgement of their being met were invented after the Renaissance; rather, these things were expressed in different ways. Today we can be hung up on whether *please* and *thank you* are being said, at the expense of a more thoughtful attention to the ways in which we ask and acknowledge. *Please* and *thank you* are useful, and people who omit them appear guilty of an ugly sense of entitlement, but there is a lot more to manners than these not-so-magic words, just as there is a lot more to love than saying 'I love you'.

Many performances of gratitude are hollow. It is not always possible or indeed wise to infuse our words of thanks with sensuous originality, and saying 'thank you' may often be a way of acknowledging another person's presence rather than an expression of profound appreciation – a nod, not a bow. Still, words of thanks can be uttered with a reflexivity that is graceless, and they can be received with similar numbness. In Britain there is no standard equivalent for the Italian *prego* or the German *bitte*, routine responses to thanks; although 'You're welcome' has gained ground, it is still viewed as an Americanism and even a sham. Traditionally, silence has sufficed. However, in the last couple of decades it has become common for shop assistants and waiting staff to respond to the words 'Thank you' with 'No problem'. This causes offence to some, because it presents service as the avoidance of nuisance rather than as a pleasure.

'It's only words,' says a barista at my favourite coffee shop, when I ask why he has responded to my request for a black filter coffee with a clipped 'Don't worry about it'. But because we use language to project ourselves into the world, and because we use other people's language to inform judgements about their character, it's never 'only' words. We attach great importance to them; they seem to act as summaries of attitudes. Where the language of thanks is concerned, the attitude we look for is one that preserves the fiction of solidarity.

The Stoic philosopher Seneca, active in the first century AD, discussed in his *De beneficiis* ('On favours') how and why we express gratitude. He argued that acts of generosity deserve no thanks if they have to be screwed out of their givers or just fall from them casually: 'A gift is much more welcome from a ready than from a full hand.' He also believed that 'The mind is frayed and crushed by continual reminders of service rendered . . . Your service, if I recall it at my pleasure, is life to me. If I do so at yours, it is death.'[8] Gratitude, he thought, can only be properly expressed when gifts and benefits are properly conveyed. The trouble with 'No problem' is that it raises the possibility that we have in fact caused a problem; it makes our thanks seem misplaced, as if they should have been framed as an apology, and hollows out the experience of gratefulness.

12

Spectators and stratagems

In 1709 Richard Steele founded the *Tatler*, a thrice-weekly magazine intended 'to expose the false arts of life, to pull off the disguises of cunning, vanity, and affectation, and to recommend a general simplicity in our dress, our discourse, and our behaviour'. When it folded, he launched another magazine, the *Spectator*, with Joseph Addison.

The *Tatler* and the *Spectator* were two of the many new papers and journals to emerge in the early part of the eighteenth century. As print culture burgeoned, there developed a public space in which it was possible to exchange arguments and opinions. Newspapers and magazines provoked debate. They invited questions from readers, who were able to air thoughts for which they would previously have found only a small audience. A great range of views found their way into print; the norms of conduct were up for discussion, and writers set themselves up as arbiters of behaviour. Publications such as the *Athenian Mercury* raised certain issues repeatedly: could a man and a woman simply be friends, and was adultery ever justifiable? Questions of virtue were dealt with in secular terms.[1]

From its debut in 1711, the *Spectator* aimed to bring 'philosophy out of closets and libraries, schools and colleges, to dwell in clubs and assemblies, at tea tables and in coffee houses'. It promoted an idea of politeness that consisted mainly of gracious conversation and sociability. This had to appear smooth and natural, yet was cultivated. Addison noticed a change from the ceremonial encumbrances of the Restoration period. 'Our manners sit more loose upon us,' he wrote in an issue dating from July of that year. 'Nothing is so modish as an agreeable negligence,' he claimed, and 'good breeding shows itself most where to an ordinary eye it appears the least.'[2]

Addison and Steele were presenting, in a quirky way, the notion that the world could be improved through a greater openness, a less showy personal style. They announced their distance from the frivolity and wastefulness of the reign of Charles II, and argued instead for a model of society embodied in Steele's dictum that 'equality is the life of conversation.'

In fact, the previous century had seen a new recognition, among scholars in particular, of the need for just this kind of equal conversation. Harmonious, genial talk was a feature of the Royal Society, founded in 1660; genteel debate replaced the quibbling of previous generations as learned men pursued what they called natural philosophy (we would call it science) in a manner that avoided confrontation and instead favoured diligence and agreement. Fellows of the society assumed that those with whom they conversed were competent and sincere, and that their reports of what they had seen and heard could be relied on. At the same time, it was considered proper to make claims (scientific or otherwise) in a manner that was modest and not pedantic.[3] In the eighteenth century, this civil approach became more common.

The authors of the *Spectator* also argued that society was inherently a good thing: that to be sociable was a virtue (and a secular virtue), and that cultural refinement was a mark of politeness, which could be discerned in a person's devotion to reading, though this should never seem overly fastidious. A balance had to be struck between seriousness and a too urgent fervour, between friendliness and over-familiarity. The *Spectator* celebrated variety, curiosity, imagination, commerce and new ideas. Unsurprisingly, given the recent political upheavals, it also quietly commended social cohesion. Its authors saw knowledge as something to be shared, rather than as something to be cloaked in exclusivity, and the fluent, conversational style in which the *Spectator* was written embodied the qualities that Addison and Steele applauded.

In the 1770s Samuel Johnson approvingly mentioned a proposed edition of the *Spectator* that was to include explanatory notes. He apparently observed that 'all works which describe manners, require notes in sixty or seventy years, or less.'[4] While it is true that a lot of the *Spectator* must have seemed dated by the 1770s, it is an indication of the essays' lasting influence that they were still being cited, commended and imitated, as well as being deprecated, in the early decades of the nineteenth century. In 1945 C. S. Lewis felt able to claim that the code of manners under which he and his contemporaries lived was to a large degree a legacy of the *Tatler* and the *Spectator*.[5] Lewis's conviction might be mistaken for mouldy traditionalism, but really it was an honest assessment of the long perspectives that manners afford us – links to worlds that for the most part seem lost.

The *Spectator* did not have a large circulation; each issue sold about 3,000 copies. But copies were read aloud, often in places far removed from fashionable London. Urging the widest possible consumption, Addison recommended that the *Spectator* be served to its readers at teatime, 'as a part of the tea equipage'.[6] The magazine benefited from the social circumstances it diagnosed. One of Richard Steele's subjects was the recent growth of nightlife. Street lighting arrived in London in the 1680s; Paris had had it since 1667, Amsterdam since 1669. There was also better domestic lighting. The development of coffee houses, which were hubs of sociability by day but came into their own once night fell, meant that there was an increase in nocturnal activity.

There was thus a new polite and enlightened nightlife, based around clubs, salons and theatres. The historian Craig Koslofsky has written incisively of the expansion of the social uses of the night, a revolution he calls 'nocturnalization'. Night was seen as a time for leisure rather than inertia, and traditional fears of the night diminished. Criminals, though they did not disappear from the urban streets, had fewer dark corners in which to lurk. In towns, the authorities concerned themselves less with bad smells and infections and more with getting rid of obstacles; by the middle of the eighteenth century the aesthetics of urban space were being urgently and intelligently debated.[7] But while the night became a new scene of consumer activity in towns and the boundary between the private and public spheres became less clear, in rural communities the night remained dark and impenetrable. The question of whether one lived in the town or in the country significantly influenced what time one rose, ate and slept.

The new nocturnal, urban sociability was at once exciting and problematic. The city authorities found that the night became an opportunity for the limits of their control to be tested. This meant that they ended up imposing restraints on the very phenomenon they had made possible.[8] The character of this sociability was reflective: you didn't go hunting at night; instead you played cards or exchanged refined chat. The preferred activities were less physical and more accessible to women. In retrospect, the changes that came about would look like a process of 'feminization'. The people one met in the new urban spaces could not be placed immediately; as society became more fluid, social rank was less immediately discernible, and politeness became an important marker of one's personal qualities, while also moderating extremes of political opinion.

All this was prime material for satire. A leading exponent of the form was Ned Ward, whose targets included bent lawyers, maladroit doctors, astrologers and cheating wine merchants. He mocked the cult of politesse, especially as developed within private clubs. *Politesse* was defined by Abel Boyer, a journalist and lexicographer active around 1700, as 'a dextrous management of our words and actions, whereby we make other people have better opinion of us and themselves'. Boyer's definition suggests the lubriciousness of this simulated felicity. Ward for his part emphasized fakery and emptiness. In *The History of the London Clubs* (1709) he depicted fashionable men who 'fancy themselves women' and mimic female behaviour, as well as a group of fine gentlemen who get together each week for a farting contest – a noxious variant on the hot air that was apt to circulate in such places.

Politeness was effeminate, hypocritical and theatrical. The satirist Nicholas Amhurst in *Terrae-filius*, a collection of essays begun in 1721, gave an account of the manners of students and scholars at Oxford University. At first this work could not be bought in Oxford, and those interested in reading it – of whom there were many – had to obtain it from an ironmonger's shop in nearby Abingdon. The world Amhurst depicted was shallow, corrupt and politically hazardous. He made much of the special privileges accorded to the richest students, who frittered away their time by drinking and womanizing, and he noted the extent to which superficial punctiliousness prevailed at the expense of real decency.

At the same time as politesse was proliferating in ways that lent themselves to satire, there was a different kind of politeness, not just in the mould of Addison and Steele, but with a philo-sophical foundation. This owed a good deal to John Locke, the previous century's pre-eminent British philosopher. For those who mocked the trumpery of contemporary conduct, his consideration of human error was valuable; one of the subjects Locke dealt with in detail was the potential for communication to fail, for our expressive gestures to go awry. At the core of Locke's thinking was an understanding that knowledge is grounded in experience; individuals, rather than just accepting the views of authority, should seek the truth using their powers of reason. In the later eighteenth century Locke's arguments played a part in revolutions on both sides of the Atlantic; more immediately, they shaped new ideas of personal responsibility.

Locke believed that conscious beings are aware of themselves as agents or actors in the world. One is a witness to one's own thoughts and is responsible for their consequences. In the process of discussing accountability and personal identity, Locke used the word *self-consciousness*. He did not coin the term, but it was new and he popularized it. The Earl of Shaftesbury, who as a boy was taught by Locke, would elaborate on this in the essays collected under the title *Characteristics of Men, Manners, Opinions, Times* (1711). Shaftesbury's writings promoted the idea that every individual possesses a 'moral sense'. He did not think this was an innate faculty. Rather, it was through education and sociability that one's potential for moral thinking was activated. Shaftesbury believed that politeness, essentially the deft management of one's words and deeds, stemmed from the ability to socialize freely, and that all people were improved by contact with others: 'All politeness is owing to liberty. We polish one another and rub off our corners and rough sides by a sort of amicable collision.'[9]

Shaftesbury's image of amicable collision is pleasing. It seems to suggest a society in perpetual, useful, gratifying motion. His view of man struck many of his contemporaries as refreshingly positive. Yet negativity persisted, and among his notable antagonists was Bernard Mandeville, a doctor who specialized in treating hysteria and hypochondria and had a sideline in apparently facetious yet morally trenchant literature. Mandeville's *The Fable of the Bees* (1714) was mainly concerned with economic ideas, but touched on 'the doctrine of good manners', suggesting that what passed for politeness, benevolence and sociability were really just by-products of self-interest. They were the mechanisms by which one made one's hateful impulses more acceptable.

To a twenty-first-century reader, it may seem strange to

give so much weight to the writings of philosophers. We tend to think of philosophers as the inhabitants of ivory towers, or at any rate of book-lined studies; they are caricatured as unable to poach an egg or drive a car, and as incapable of saying anything decipherable. But English philosophy is woven into English history (and vice versa). Hobbes, Locke and Shaftesbury were widely read by their contemporaries and by succeeding generations, who did not regard them as obscure, but thought their writings essential and exciting. It is only in the nineteenth century that discussions of manners and behaviour detach themselves from philosophy. Up till then, philosophy was not seen as a dry academic specialism and the literature of civility was not seen as pedantic.

Even as Shaftesbury and Mandeville were hammering out their different arguments, picturing a distinctly masculine world, others besides Addison and Steele were constructing a new ideal of politeness, more relaxed and much less assertively male. On a practical level, an important figure in these developments was Richard 'Beau' Nash. A generous and extravagant showman, who had toyed with a legal career in London, Nash was elected Master of Ceremonies by the Corporation of Bath shortly after his arrival there in 1705. Bath was at that time an increasingly fashionable spa town, a symbol of the leisured classes and their aspirations. (The health-giving properties of water, so long regarded with doubt, had been talked up by John Locke and in Sir John Floyer's 1701 *The History of Cold Bathing*.) Encouraging easy sociability in place of Bath's existing culture of haughty elitism, Nash laid down rules for public behaviour. Men were forbidden to carry swords; now manners, rather than sharp blades, were the means of protecting honour.

He moved to curb drunkenness, specified that evening enter-tainment should end punctually at eleven o'clock, and ventured public criticism of those who flouted his rules. From 1716 until about 1740 he wielded authority on a regal scale. The ideals of polite behaviour that obtained in Bath – and also at Tunbridge Wells, which in the late 1730s Nash helped turn into a smart destination – were reproduced throughout fash-ionable society.

Programmes such as Nash's attracted the satirical attentions of Jonathan Swift, a writer temperamentally inclined to be suspicious of anyone who pretended to be the saviour of the art of sociability. In Swift's view, 'good sense is the principal foundation of good manners.' However, because good sense is in short supply, 'all the civilized nations of the world have agreed upon fixing some rules for common behaviour . . . as a kind of artificial good sense.'[10] In the trio of dialogues he published in 1738 as *Polite Conversation* – the title of which resonates today, though it would have struck his contempor-aries as bizarre – he draws attention to this artificiality.

It is not easy to be sure whether *Polite Conversation* is a record of eighteenth-century speech, a satire on upper-class idiocy, an extended bad joke or a lament for the passing of conversational skill. Perhaps it is all these things. But there is something painful in Swift's exposition of the mechanical inanity that passes for respectable chatter: 'May you live all the days of your life', 'There's none so blind as they that won't see', 'That's as well said, as if I had said it myself.'[11] Swift suggests that you cannot learn by rote how to talk. He sees what he thinks is the decay of conversation and notes the degree to which, for modish folk, conversation has become an end it itself. Here, as in so many of his works, Swift contrasts skin-deep refinement with all the brute impulses that lurk beneath it.

Five years after Swift published *Polite Conversation*, Henry Fielding's 'An Essay on Conversation' appeared. Fielding explained how to please others with one's talk. His approach was philosophical rather than closely detailed. He provided guidance about subjects to be avoided: general reflections on countries, religions and professions; other people's physical blemishes and past accidents; anything obscene, including obscene jokes (jokes as a whole being regarded as the preserve of fools). When he speaks of 'The end of conversation being the happiness of mankind', we feel we ought to be a long way from Swift's examples, but may wonder how far from them we really are.[12]

It is Swift who is most alive to the ironies, discontents and delusions of eighteenth-century English society. It helped, no doubt, that he was an outsider: born and brought up in Ireland; drawn to England but always a visitor there, even if a well-connected one; and, back in Ireland, conscious of being 'a stranger in a strange land' or merely 'a poisoned rat in a hole'. He was perceptive about inequalities. We see this in his *Directions to Servants* (posthumously published in 1745, begun thirty years earlier), which pictures servants and their masters engaged in something akin to guerrilla warfare. He advises a manservant, if he happens to be good-looking, 'whenever you whisper [to] your mistress at the table, run your nose full in her cheek; or, if your breath be good, breathe full in her face.'[13] *Directions to Servants* was not read by servants, but by people accustomed to receiving poor service. After digesting Swift's observations, they were probably grateful that they had not been even worse served.

Swift was spoofing the conduct book. In doing so, he showed how widely known this type of manual had become. One of his inheritors was Jane Collier, whose *An Essay on the Art of Ingeniously Tormenting* (1753) issued recommendations about how to irritate one's friends. For instance, 'If you have no children, keep as large a quantity of tame animals as you conveniently can': you should treat them with extravagant fondness, and 'Let them be of the most troublesome and mischievous sort' (squirrels and monkeys are recommended). Also: 'If your friend should come to any worldly misfortune, be sure . . . not to fail telling him (and that repeatedly), that it was entirely by his own fault.' Writing for a mainly female audience, Collier poked fun at existing paradigms for women's conduct. She suggested that women were limited by domestic convention. She urged her readers: 'Remember always to do unto everyone, what you would least wish to have done unto yourself.' In reversing the usual wisdom, she hints at some of the frustrations of conventional existence.[14]

In their different ways, Swift and Collier were deriding the contemporary notion that politeness was a kind of engineering. The sort of book they reviled was François Nivelon's *The Rudiments of Genteel Behaviour* (1737), which gave precise instructions – alongside illustrative plates – about how to stand, walk, give, receive and retreat. Nivelon appeared to think that behaviour could be presented as if it were no more than ballet. This seemed ridiculous. Yet in truth, it was precisely the limitations of such schematic guides that made them effective.

Satirists of the period were alert observers of the influence of French and Italian culture. During the eighteenth century large numbers of British men and rather smaller numbers of

British women went abroad for pleasure and as part of their education. European tourism was not confined to the British – the Germans and French were also keen recreational travellers – but British tourists were the most numerous. The Grand Tour was a ritual. It involved socializing with foreign dignitaries, examining precious artefacts and classical sites, savouring opera and stunning vistas, and collecting desirable paintings and *objets*. These activities were believed to have an ennobling effect that equipped young men for positions of power at home. The benefits were rarely explained; instead they were asserted.

It was during this period that it became common to claim that travel broadens the mind and helps one understand one's own culture. Thus Peter Beckford, an eager tourist between the 1760s and 1790s, could write that 'It is not in looking at pictures and statues only, that travelling is of use, but in examining the laws, customs and manners of other countries, and comparing them with our own.' Why? Because 'an Englishman will learn from a knowledge of other countries to set a proper value on his own.'[15] Most travellers set that 'proper value' pretty high. Whatever they claimed about their minds' expansion, the main benefits were social; the Grand Tour enabled upper-class Englishmen to be part of an international elite. It also created a vogue among men for carrying trifles such as small items of jewellery and scent bottles. Quasi-educational, it was a lesson in affectation.

In Hannah Cowley's 1780 play *The Belle's Stratagem* one character speaks of 'adventitious [i.e. non-native] manners imported by our travelled gentry', another of 'the blessed freedom of modern manners'. Cowley, a shrewd critic of bogusness, captures the changing conditions of society: Sir

George Touchwood, the possessive and ridiculous husband of a determinedly free-spirited woman, states that society is 'a mere chaos' and a 'universal masquerade'.[16] That chaos, as Sir George can barely comprehend, is partly the result of a changing social order, in which women of independent mind, if not of independent means, are more numerous.

Several prominent eighteenth-century commentators, writing for male audiences, prescribed 'the company of virtuous women' as a recipe for politeness. Swift and Shaftesbury applauded its effects; so did David Hume. As the feminist democrat Mary Wollstonecraft would point out at the end of the century, elevated ideas of female excellence had the effect of degrading women, making them resemble treasures or jewels – toys and trinkets, not free and fully rounded individuals. She wrote of the 'false system of female manners . . . which robs the whole sex of its dignity'.[17] But in the altered public and private spheres of the late eighteenth century, women, though lacking many rights and much control of property, were able to extend their influence. They constructed family life as if it were a little world, which they peopled, made comfortable and made moral, and in which they performed roles unavailable to them in public life, as diplomats and economists. Meanwhile as writers they promoted a broader sense of life's possibilities, women's education and themselves, through pamphlets, novels, songs, poems, plays, memoirs, polemics, newspapers and magazines. By the start of the next century a new idea of necessary female accomplishments was being set out, by middle-class women. Before that, though, there appeared the single most controversial book ever written about English manners.

13

Lord Chesterfield and the invention of etiquette

We can date to the late eighteenth century the beginnings of our present distinction between *manners*, a word suggesting broad principles of behaviour, and *etiquette*, which denotes the actions that articulate those principles. In the century that followed, *protocol* offered a further shade of meaning, as it became the preferred term for the etiquette of a particular sphere (most often diplomacy). The word had been used since around 1700 for records of diplomatic negotiations; it derived from a Greek term for the first leaf of a papyrus roll, on which an official stamp would have been set. But the emergence of *etiquette* is far more important.

The word was popularized by Philip Dormer Stanhope, fourth Earl of Chesterfield. In his lifetime (1694–1773) he was successful as a politician and diplomat. After his death, his reputation changed, and he was regarded as an arbiter and exemplar of good manners. This new reputation rested on letters he had written to his illegitimate son – another Philip.

Chesterfield is of consequence for two reasons. First, his letters are the culmination of the tradition of courtesy books aimed at men; after them, books of this kind are mainly written for women. Second, he chose to divorce manners from morals. He promoted self-interest rather than probity. He wanted Philip to understand how to get ahead. But his original contribution was a code of manners marked by amorality – and not the immorality of which his critics would later convict him.

The conservative moralist Hannah More was one of the main opponents of Chesterfield's school of delicate artifice. In 1788 she anonymously published her *Thoughts on the Importance of the Manners of the Great to General Society*, arguing that the upper classes had a responsibility to set a good example to those less fortunate. For More, simplicity was the true mark of sincerity, whereas patrician polish could be a mask for wickedness. The routines of gentility, such as the emptier sort of philanthropy or insisting a servant cut one's hair on a Sunday, disrupted morality. Principles were important; observing polite codes mattered much less. But the rise of etiquette books, which were more in tune with the competitive nature of the world, had already eclipsed such a view.

The first English use of *etiquette* that I have found is in the *Gentleman's Magazine* in January 1737. It relates to the behaviour of the kings of Spain before Philip V, who were 'slaves to their grandeur. They kept with the utmost rigour to a regulation called there the Etiquette; it contained all the ceremonies the Spanish monarchs were obliged to observe.'[1] The word was brought to wider attention by Chesterfield. Its first *OED* citation is in a letter he wrote in 1750: 'Without hesitation kiss his [the Pope's] slipper, or whatever else the etiquette of that Court requires.' It caught on in the final decades of the eighteenth century, applying not only to the court, but also to the more general intercourse of polite society. Among those to use it, just a little tentatively, were Edmund Burke and the novelist Laurence Sterne. In 1776 a work entitled *The Fine Gentleman's Etiquette* appeared – the first book to advertise itself in such terms. On inspection, it consists of Chesterfield's advice, turned into verse.

In adopting the word *etiquette*, Chesterfield was responding to what he considered the inadequacy of existing terminology: in place of large notions of ethics, he promoted a small ethics – *etiquette* being a diminutive that preserves a hint of the French *éthique*. In French, *etiquette* principally signified a ticket or label. A Victorian writer on manners, Eliza Cheadle, claimed that 'Centuries ago, the word "etiquette" . . . specified the ticket tied to the necks of bags or affixed to bundles to denote their contents. A bag or bundle thus ticketed passed unchallenged.'[2] The exact details of this are doubtful, but Cheadle captures a key role of etiquette: as a means of averting challenges, of protecting our bundles from close inspection.

One explanation of the word's transition to denoting a prescribed set of formalities lies in the use of tickets at the French court to show courtiers where they should sit at table or at a ceremony. Alternatively, it may have been related to the custom of annotating soldiers' billets with practical instructions. It was Chesterfield, rather than a French author, who established *etiquette* as a term for polite behaviour. A word that in French signified something small became in English a more generously encompassing term. As for kissing the Pope's slipper, the custom continued into the twentieth century, but we should note that French experts contemporary with Chesterfield regarded it as superstitious and embarrassing.

By the end of the eighteenth century, *etiquette* was a word that could be used without conceit or any very shameful sense of its foreignness. In 1791 John Walker in *A Critical Pronouncing Dictionary* defined it as 'the polite form or manner of doing anything; the ceremonial of good manners'. He rightly diagnosed the element of ceremony. In matters of etiquette a real consideration for others was secondary to an observance of whatever ceremonial acts were at the time fashionable.

The difference between the etiquette books that proliferated in the nineteenth century and the guides that preceded them was that, whereas it had formerly been assumed that socializing was inherently desirable, the new writers on etiquette emphasized privacy – the importance of not violating it and of maintaining social distance. The rise of the word *etiquette* was a marker of this change. Its popularity appears to have peaked between 1830 and 1900. It is to that period that we can trace what is now its dominant sense: the little rules about how to deal with shellfish, introductions and overnight guests.

In addressing his ideas about etiquette to his son, Chesterfield was subscribing to a mature tradition. For instance, King James VI of Scotland, later James I of England, had in the 1590s written for his son *Basilikon Doron*, an instructive guide to monarchy. In 1687 the politician George Savile, first Marquess of Halifax, had addressed some advice to his twelve-year-old daughter Elizabeth, in the form of a 'New Year's Gift'. By then, little books of this kind, redolent of a suave paternal authority, had been popular for almost a century. Lord Burghley, principal secretary and then lord treasurer to Elizabeth I, had put together a collection of 'precepts' for his son Robert: guidance about choosing a wife, how to dress, what kind of hospitality to offer, and how to treat servants. This was published in 1615, seventeen years after Burghley's death. It proved a model for many others: one of these was the controversial politician Thomas Wentworth, first Earl of Strafford, who wrote a letter of advice to his nephew Sir William Savile, the father of George Savile. Francis Osborne's *Advice to a Son* we have already encountered; another notable book in this vein was the jurist Sir Matthew Hale's didactic *Advice to his Grandchildren* (1673), which stressed the difference between acquaintances, companions and friends, as well as discoursing on matters such as the importance of quickly overcoming anger, and more unusual ones, such as the value of knowing all about the planting and ordering of a country farm.

George Savile was unusual in addressing himself to a girl; his letter would become the model for many works of instruction written by men for young women. At first his advice circulated privately in manuscript, but soon a publisher pirated the text and it was translated into French and Italian, though Savile's name did not appear on any edition until 1699, four years after his death. Some of what he says will now make us uncomfortable. Must a wife put up with marital unhappiness, overlook her husband's dalliances, and weep in order to get her way rather than using her powers of reason? And why does he urge upon Elizabeth an unquestioning adherence to organized religion, when in private he claimed that it was a fraud perpetrated by self-interested clergymen on their credulous congregations?

The tone of the advice is not always serious. Savile writes that spring brings out flies and fools and sends them thronging to Hyde Park. No soldier, he says, is more obedient to his captain's trumpet than he is to the desire to see a puppet show. Nevertheless, we can see the practical bent of Savile's counsel: he tells his daughter that 'one careless glance giveth more advantage [to predatory men] than a hundred words not enough considered', and that she must 'every seven years make some alteration . . . towards the graver side', so that she does not become like one of those 'girls of fifty, who resolve to be always young, whatever Time with his iron teeth hath determined to the contrary'. There is a well-phrased worldliness in his observations that 'Whilst you are playing full of innocence, the spiteful World will bite' and 'Your husband may love wine more than is convenient.' We may recognize a strategist's savviness in his advice that his daughter should avert the possibility of being teased by means of 'looks that forbid without rudeness, and oblige without invitation'.[3]

Savile's instructions had by 1765 gone through fifteen editions. They were widely read in the American colonies and were a staple of the colonial lady's bookshelf. Often presented to an adolescent girl by her mother or father, in the same spirit as the original was presented by Savile to Elizabeth, the 'New Year's Gift' became — as gifts so frequently are — a symbol of parents' ambitions for their children. In the colonies, English manners seemed to represent a higher wisdom, unsullied by the realities of everyday life.

The original recipient conformed to expectation. Lady Elizabeth Savile grew up to marry Philip Stanhope, third Earl of Chesterfield. Their son was Philip Dormer Stanhope, who inherited the title in 1726. The fourth Lord Chesterfield was supremely well-connected, but not blessed with physical advantages: he was squat, had poor teeth, and spoke in a manner others found shrieky. He had to work to endear himself to others. Along the way he learned lessons he was keen to pass on.

Chesterfield's first letter to his son seems to have been written in 1737, when Philip was five.[4] In 1739 he adopted a new instructive tone, and it was the letters in this mode that later became famous; he wrote the last of them a few weeks before Philip's death in 1768. The letters were not intended for publication, but after Chesterfield himself died, in 1773, a selection of them was published. The book was not cheap (its two volumes cost a guinea each), and many of those who read it took advantage of being able to obtain it from the increasingly numerous circulating libraries. Later editions helpfully organized Chesterfield's advice under headings. Among the most popular was *Principles of Politeness, and of Knowing the World*, edited by John Trusler. One of its categories was 'sundry little accomplishments' – words that sum up the whole finicky business of etiquette.

In 1775 the book was printed in America, where it was popular well into the nineteenth century. Objections to its moral ambiguity did not prevent its being adopted as a handbook for the aspirational. The hostility the letters provoked seemed a sign of their power. Samuel Pratt's novel *The Pupil of Pleasure*, an attack on Chesterfield's values that was published in Philadelphia in 1778 and Boston in 1780, was an especially vivid advertisement of the letters' worldly allure. When the criticism grew louder, subtle amendments were introduced to make the text more palatable. *The American Chesterfield* (1827) is typical in being an expurgated version with extra text to suit it better to a female audience.

The letters preached a practical and pragmatic approach to life. Chesterfield's assumed audience was his illegitimate son, but he presents his thoughts in a way that suggests he foresaw reaching a wider readership – albeit an exclusively male one. In what he calls 'good company', there is 'great variety': among these richly varied people 'morals are very different, though their manners are pretty much the same'. He says that 'moral virtues are the foundation of society in general', but it is a statement on which he quickly enlarges, explaining that the role of manners is to 'adorn and strengthen them'. Besides, Philip's concern should not be 'society in general'. Chesterfield has in mind for him not what he calls 'bare common civility', but rather 'engaging, insinuating, shining manners'.

Lofty ideals were not on the agenda. Good conduct was more about careful imitation than deeply felt authenticity. 'Good breeding,' claimed Chesterfield, is 'a mode, not a substance.' In a piece that appeared in the *World* in August 1756 he observed that English had no term equivalent to the French *moeurs*. It was a word on his mind because the French philosopher-historian Voltaire, an Anglophile whom he knew well, had just published his *Essai sur l'histoire générale, et sur les moeurs et l'esprit des nations* (translated into English in 1758 as *An Essay on Universal History, the Manners, and Spirit of Nations*). Chesterfield felt that *manners* was 'too little' a translation of *moeurs*, while *morals* was 'too much'. His own definition was 'a general exterior decency, fitness and propriety of conduct in the common intercourse of life'.[5] 'Exterior decency' is a two-word summary of his concern with well-maintained surfaces.

Haughtiness and shallowness are often evident in Chesterfield's writings, but there is also a shrewd wit, a playful perceptiveness. He seems to have inherited the ideas of Francis Osborne, though he does not at any point mention him. He also appears indebted to Machiavelli, a writer he acknowledges but does not recommend. For both Chesterfield and Machiavelli, it is imperative to accommodate oneself to one's surroundings. Inflexibility is fatal. Chesterfield expresses this view crisply when he writes that 'A man of the world must, like the chameleon, be able to take every different hue.'

For Chesterfield, there is a system of manners, akin to a machine, and it must be kept 'oiled'. This idea of a system, of manners or of insincerities, puts nurture ahead of nature. Whatever one's nature, it can be rescued or obscured. In this context it is relevant that Chesterfield refers again and again to 'good breeding'. The noun *breeding* can appear on either side of the 'nature versus nurture' debate. It can denote a person's parentage and extraction. Yet although Chesterfield refers to 'natural good breeding' and also 'easy good breeding', he regards breeding as the province of education. He can present it as 'the result of much good sense, some good nature, and a little self-denial', but suggests a keener emphasis on precedent and formal training when he speaks of 'the laws of good breeding' and 'the allowed and established models of good breeding', as well as when he states that 'in good breeding there are a thousand little delicacies, which are established only by custom.' Breeding seems to be a technique masquerading as an inherent quality. The more he uses the word, the more slippery it becomes.

Ready as ever with an *aperçu*, Mark Twain captures the essence of the matter in his *Notebooks*: 'Good breeding consists in concealing how much we think of ourselves and how little we think of the other person.'[6] For Chesterfield and his many inheritors, the term *breeding* is usefully pliable, or even intangible. It appeals to those who want to talk about behaviour with imprecise hauteur: 'His tendency to belittle others shows a lack of breeding.' The language of manners is full of such weasel words: the vague passing itself off as the specific, spongy nouns that suck the life out of reasoned debate.

From the outset, Chesterfield bombards Philip with exhortations that contain language of this kind. The letters insist on an appreciation of 'the necessary arts of the world', and he prescribes an 'easy, civil and respectful behaviour', comprising 'a thousand nameless little things, which nobody can describe, but which everybody feels'. Sometimes he hits on a form of words that overcomes the usual difficulties of description. 'You must dress; therefore attend to it . . . in order to avoid singularity,' he insists: he is like the conformist schoolkid who tells his friend not to be different because it marks both of them out as weird. *Avoid singularity.* Fear of the aberrant is a cardinal part of why people believe in manners and of the ways in which they impose them. Singularity precipitates ill opinion. It is interesting that Harriet Martineau, writing about American society in the 1830s, comments that 'The fear of opinion takes many forms. There is fear of vulgarity, fear of responsibility; and above all, fear of singularity.'[7] Fast-forward to 1999, and it's Carolyn Burnham (Annette Bening) in *American Beauty* saying to her husband Lester at a vile party, 'Don't be weird.' As Lester (Kevin Spacey) replies – 'I won't be weird. I'll be whatever you want me to be' – and kisses her with wholly bogus passion, we sense that his oddness is professionally, socially and sexually uncomfortable.

Even when Philip is nearly eighteen, Chesterfield is still asking if he has been sufficiently on his guard against 'disgusting habits, such as scratching yourself, putting your fingers in your mouth, nose and ears'. He maintains an emphasis on the need for 'attention'. 'A man without attention is not fit to live in the world,' he declares, and will be the sort of 'awkward fellow' who scalds his mouth when he drinks tea or coffee. Looking is mentioned again and again: Philip should be mindful of the perpetual observation of others – 'without staring at them' – and should always pay attention to his appearance. Attentiveness is essential to learning, and inattentiveness causes oversights and accidents, but Chesterfield is urging hyperattentiveness, which in practice can be disabling, as the process of constantly scanning one's surroundings blocks or hampers one's engagement with them. It is hardly a surprise that Philip grew up to be awkward; the novelist Fanny Burney dismissed him in her diaries as a 'mere pedantic booby'.[8]

As this suggests, Chesterfield's prescriptions were not easy to follow. He disapproved of quick fixes: spouting aphorisms and proverbs, which might have seemed a nice way to cut a dash, was condemned as gauche. 'Many people come into company full of what they intend to say in it themselves, without the least regard to others; and thus charged up to the muzzle, are resolved to let it off at any rate' – but anyone who does this is a bore. The use of the noun *bore* to denote a tiresome person seems to date from the beginning of the nineteenth century; as a verb meaning 'To weary by tedious conversation or simply by the failure to be interesting' (*OED*), *bore* sprang up around 1750. Chesterfield does not speak of bores, but he makes it clear that he deplores the type. For

Philip, the goal was to dazzle (a word Chesterfield uses). The idea of dazzle is in essence cold: it is controlling a person by overpowering him, not engaging in healthy reciprocity. Dazzling is all about a brilliant showiness, a confounding excess.

Among the arts to be mastered was sexual expertise, and Chesterfield urged the teenage Philip to make the most of his time in Paris: it was much better to enjoy 'commerce' with 'a woman of health, education and rank' than to consort with prostitutes, who were likely to be carrying infections. Women, he wrote, were 'children of a larger growth', incapable of acting or thinking 'consequentially' at any length. 'A man of sense only trifles with them, plays with them, humours and flatters them, as he does with a sprightly, forward child.'

At his most nakedly strategic, Chesterfield writes that there are certain women, expert in 'good breeding' (but of course!), who decide a man's social fortune, and urges Philip to pay 'particular court' to them, for 'their recommendation is a passport through all the realms of politeness'. He evokes a scene that feels less like the sphere of good breeding than a thicket of prickly hazards, but he is always at his most cynical where women are concerned. He says, for instance, that women are all 'either indisputably beautiful, or indisputably ugly', and 'those who are in a state of mediocrity, are best flattered upon their beauty'. By contrast, 'a decided and conscious beauty looks upon every tribute paid to her beauty, only as her due'; it is therefore much more effective to praise her thoughts, since she 'wants to shine . . . on the side of her understanding'. And yet, 'a man's moral character is a more delicate thing than a woman's reputation.'

While many have been outraged by Chesterfield's attitude

to women and his cynical idea of the motives for manners, the letters were hugely popular. Editions appeared under promising titles such as *The Art of Pleasing*, and it is a mark of the letters' fame that in 1791 there appeared a counterblast entitled *The Contrast: or an Antidote to the Pernicious Principles Disseminated in the Letters of the Late Earl of Chesterfield*. When a volume bearing the title *The New Chesterfield* was published in 1830, the editor emphasized the durability of the letters' 'valuable precepts', which amounted to 'a system of the most useful instruction'.

Samuel Johnson memorably spoke out for the opposition. His distaste for Chesterfield ran deep. He had been poorly treated by the earl, who had cast himself as the patron of Johnson's efforts to compile an authoritative dictionary of English. Two months before the work was finally published, in 1755, Johnson wrote to Chesterfield, dismissing his meagre assistance: 'Is not a Patron, My Lord, one who looks with unconcern on a Man struggling for Life in the water and when he has reached ground encumbers him with help?' It was no surprise that Johnson thought little of Chesterfield's letters. If one could remove the immorality, they 'should be put in the hands of every young gentleman'. (A bit like saying, 'If they were better, I'd like them more.') But as they stood, the letters were likely to 'teach the morals of a whore, and the manners of a dancing master'.[9]

Johnson valued manners, regarding politeness as a form of 'fictitious benevolence' useful in allowing strangers to get on. The fiction he had in mind was not insincerity; it consisted of adopting a position of benevolence on the assumption that it was warranted, rather than adopting it despite thinking it unwarranted. Believing that manners were a means of achieving equability where there was perhaps not equality, he could not stomach Chesterfield's tactical approach to the subject. One of Johnson's tenets was that you should never take provisions to other people's homes, because it implies that they are unable to entertain you adequately. Another was that asking someone a string of questions is not a recipe for civilized conversation; directed at his biographer James Boswell, this had a certain pointedness, for Boswell often inundated Johnson with queries in the hope of being able to transcribe the pungent answers. Eager to fit in, Boswell had disavowed what he thought was his fellow Scots' 'rough and roaring freedom of manners', but he retained a puppyish quality that sometimes annoyed his companions.[10]

It is apt that Johnson, whose pronouncements on manners were sturdy rather than silky, chooses to condemn Chesterfield for teaching 'the manners of a dancing master'. Even though Chesterfield thought dancing 'a very trifling, silly thing', he acknowledged that 'it is one of those established follies to which people of sense are sometimes obliged to conform', and the first of his deliberately instructive letters to Philip declares that 'It is very proper and decent to dance well.' At times he speaks of society as if of a dance, in which control and fluency are crucial, as are one's 'footing' and an air of 'douceur' (gentleness or smoothness).

In Chesterfield's reference to douceur we see another cause of Johnson's hostility. Like many of his contemporaries, Johnson associated French culture with a debilitating effeminacy. The English aping of French manners was unpatriotic. Chesterfield, who adopted French words such as sang-froid, gauche, soi-disant and *malaise*, was a representative of the wider, modish enthusiasm for Gallic *politesse*, *bons mots* and intrigue – the atmosphere of the salon. In his *Dictionary of the English Language* Johnson appears to have made a point of excluding voguish words borrowed from French: *bouquet, coterie, ennui, clique*. The equation of Frenchness with posturing and fickleness was neither new nor fleeting, but it found some particularly violent expressions during this period. Thus George Edward Ayscough, a well-travelled soldier, writing in 1778: 'I have studied the manners of the French nation, and I have found them volatile, even to a degree of childishness. To all rules there are, doubtless, exceptions; but a Frenchman is, in general, an unlettered prejudiced fop.'[11]

The tendency to decry French culture was in part an expression of anxiety about the state of British culture, and in part a reaction to the air of sexual ambiguity and moral slackness that clung to the Parisian aristocracy. It was common to suspect that French patterns of behaviour were all very well in France but were impossible to transplant. John Brown in his popular *An Estimate of the Manners and Principles of the Times* (1757) noted the 'vain and effeminate' nature of French manners and saw them as 'the very archetype from which our own are drawn'. But French 'national spirit' held firm because candidates for public office were 'assiduously trained' and imbued with 'the principle of military honour'. The French were thus 'women at the toilet, heroes in the field' and 'contemptible in private life; in public, formidable'. The English, said Brown, had aped only half of this, which threatened to be their ruin.[12]

Arthur Young in his *Travels* (1792) writes that 'In the art of living, the French have generally been esteemed by the rest of Europe, to have made the greatest proficiency, and their manners have accordingly been more imitated, and their customs more adopted than those of any nation. Of their cookery, there is but one opinion; . . . it is far beyond our own.' He cites as examples of the good manners prevalent in France the tendency of people of all classes to be 'scrupulously neat in refusing to drink out of glasses used by other people'. What is more, 'The idea of dining without a napkin seems ridiculous to a Frenchman.'[13]

True to his enthusiasm for French idiom, Chesterfield thinks that a gracious, pleasing style is a matter of '*je ne sais quoi*'. One of its ingredients is a harmonious speaking voice; he is maintaining a tradition of thinking the voice powerful and in need of control (Giovanni della Casa had urged against shrillness, Thomas Elyot had stressed the need for clean enunciation). Other factors for Chesterfield are 'pretty' appearance, appropriate dress, 'something open and cheerful in the countenance' and a lack of laughter. He expands on this last point: 'I could heartily wish that you may often be seen to smile, but never heard to laugh while you live.' He seems to have inherited this idea from Hobbes, who dismissed 'those grimaces called laughter' as 'incident most to them, that are conscious of the fewest abilities in themselves . . . [and] are forced to keep themselves in their own favour, by observing the imperfections of other men'.[14] Chesterfield is less interested than Hobbes in the idea that people with great minds should free others from scorn, rather than adding to it. But he buys into Hobbes's notion of laughter as distortion; it does unattractive things to the face, is a source of unpleasant noise, and, though he does not say as much, reveals the teeth.

In the eighteenth century, it was common even for people

of good breeding (such as Chesterfield) to have bad teeth. Modern dental care means that most Europeans have teeth that they are not ashamed to bare, except perhaps in the presence of affluent Americans, whose incisors tend to be resplendently straight and white. In the eighteenth century it was common to admire the lustre of Frenchwomen's teeth, and, although the Swiss commentator Béat-Louis de Muralt had in the 1720s identified as 'a great injury' Englishwomen's 'not taking care of their teeth', there were now much more concerted attempts to maintain dental health – for reasons of fashion as much as hygiene.[15] But while Chesterfield's censure of laughter was in part to do with preventing embarrassing dental exposure, it was more than that: we may instinctively think that laughter is happily cathartic, yet in practice we are likely to see how often laughter reeks of jeering complicity.

Chesterfield associated laughter with the mob, and he associated the mob with buffoonery, an absence of proportion, a lack of restraint and moderation. He was doubtless influenced as well by the advice his mother had received from his grandfather in the 1680s: 'It is not intended . . . that you should forswear laughing; but remember, that fools being always painted in that posture, it may fright those who are wise from doing it . . . That boisterous kind of jollity is as contrary to wit and good manners, as it is to modesty and virtue.'

From Chesterfield we may get the sense that eighteenth-century society was fantastically sophisticated. For many, it was. The rich young men of eighteenth-century London were defined by their tastes and sensibilities, and there were plenty of ways in which they could school these. They could attend the Soho academy run by Domenico Angelo, who taught gentlemanly elegance alongside the intricacies of horsemanship. They could wallow in sentimental literature, such as Henry Mackenzie's *The Man of Feeling*, the most popular novel of the 1770s and an education in the fine art of tearful compassion. More likely, though, they would associate with like-minded individuals, as per the satires of Ned Ward, within a club – literary, antiquarian, sporting, or simply of the 'roaring' sort where convivial drinking was the main concern. Clubs were important beyond London, too, with debating societies offering an alternative to boozy leisure.

There was a different side to the period: men and women being placed in the pillory, the custom of going to Bedlam to gawp at the insane, public hangings at which the condemned were pelted with offal. De Muralt wrote of English '*férocité*' – an addiction to violent sports and an indifference to death. In his view it was permitting evil, rather than committing it, that was the real English vice. Criminality affected everyone: highwaymen held up coaches, pickpockets darted through the city streets, freshwater pirates snatched goods from boats, burglars worked in gangs, graves were robbed to provide corpses for trainee surgeons, and there was widespread anxiety about the degree of violence that criminals used. This is the flagrantly vicious world of Hogarth, and it is the world vilified by John Wesley, who crusaded against barbarous ungodliness. London's swarms of prostitutes were well-known. From the 1750s to the 1790s it was possible to buy *Harris's List of Covent Garden Ladies*, an annual directory of prostitutes – a sort of Very Yellow Pages. Anarchy was answered with brutality. Until 1789 a woman who murdered her husband could be burned at the stake; until

1817 she could be whipped in public, and men could be whipped in public as late as 1868.[16]

But eighteenth-century visitors to England were struck by the uniformity of manners. They observed how little regional variation there was, a state of affairs very different to that in France or Italy. They presented the English as doers rather than thinkers, a nation of solemn men and modest women, rough children and violent schoolmasters, fast walkers and bloodthirsty hunters, melancholics and dullards, a tribe of practical, businesslike figures torn between restlessness and self-control. Yet most often the English were regarded as steady and regular, and their solid thinking and temperament were commonly traced to their very solid diet.[17]

That solidity, of temperament and body, expressed itself in frankness, an aversion to change, an almost monastic style of domestic life combined with a tendency to travel with their worldly goods bundled around them, and what William Hazlitt described as an appetite for 'hard words and hard blows'. Even pleasure-seeking seemed industrious. Some visitors found this dispiriting, and claimed that their intellects and emotions atrophied after just a brief time ashore. The French novelist Stendhal claimed that the moment one landed in England, where common sense was exalted, genius lost 25 per cent of its value. Another novelist, Robert Martin Lesuire, addressed the matter rather more tartly in *Les Sauvages de l'Europe* (1760). According to one character, the only difference 'between the English, and their brother-savages of Africa, is, that among the latter the fair sex meet with some consideration'. Friedrich Kielmansegge, a German who travelled around England in the 1760s, saw in Shakespeare's plays the essence of a nation condemned to be tragic: 'most of the characters go mad, or get blind, or die.'[18]

One form of Hazlitt's 'hard words' was xenophobia. The main targets were, naturally, the French. Visitors from France complained of meagre hospitality: an Englishman's idea of a token of friendship was a visiting card, three inches by one and a half. Anti-Catholic sentiment was rife at this time and found sensational expression in the Gordon Riots of June 1780, sparked by resentment of recent legislation that provided for greater tolerance of Catholics. Mob disorder erupted; soldiers called in to disperse the rioters shot 285 of them dead. The riots reinforced the impression abroad that Britain was undemocratic, with the threat of disorder never remote.

By the end of the century the violence was less marked, though the threat remained. In the 1780s and 1790s changes were afoot. Some were great: the French Revolution sparked political radicalism and utopianism (answered by a surge in popular conservatism), and Mary Wollstonecraft provoked a bristling debate about the role of women in society. Others were smaller yet significant: for instance, the new Sunday schools curbed delinquency and promoted a pious neatness, and lower-class amusements reportedly became less gross.

In due course commentators reflecting on this – among them Hazlitt – argued that the natural aggression of the English was simply now shielded from view, a condition of the mind that the body rarely disclosed. Carl Philip Moritz, a German who visited in 1782, noted that 'When two Englishmen quarrel, actions mean more than words. They say little but repetitions of the same thing, clinching it with a hearty "God damn you!"' Moritz was often impressed by the living standards he observed, but was struck by the casual loutishness exhibited by people of all classes. At the theatre, he was hit on the hat by one of the many rotten oranges lobbed towards the stage from the cheaper seats. 'Oranges,' he commented, 'are eaten practically everywhere in London.'[19]

Some visitors saw the gruff candour and hearty God-damning as virtues. In 1789 the Prussian writer Johann Wilhelm von Archenholz published *A Picture of England*, in which he remarked: 'It has been observed that the common people in England are more intelligent and judicious than in any other country.' He attributed this to 'the free and unrestrained manner in which they speak and write'.[20] The English had since the fourteenth century been known as *les goddems*, on account of that lack of restraint. It was a term used without affection, and it persisted into the second half of the twentieth century. Since the 1960s it has given way to a new sobriquet: *les fuckoffs*. But in the age of Chesterfield and throughout the century that followed, visitors admired England and the English – and the English responded complacently.

Meanwhile radical thinkers such as William Godwin (Mary Wollstonecraft's husband) argued against the artificial codes so popular among his contemporaries. In Godwin's eyes, mankind was perfectible: an enlarged personal morality could do the job hitherto done by politicians and the judiciary. He saw manners as playing no part in this; his language suggests he associated them with Chesterfield. He wrote that

By politeness many persons understand artificial manners, the very purpose of which is to stand between the feelings of the heart and the external behaviour. The word immediately conjures up to their mind a corrupt and vicious mode of society, and they conceive it to mean a set of rules, founded in no just reason, and ostentatiously practised by those who are familiar with them . . . to confound and keep at a distance those who, by the accident of their birth or fortune, are ignorant of them.[21]

These strong words, which will resonate with many readers now (and will appal many others), were typical of Godwin, a man way ahead of his time.

Godwin's behaviour was in most respects far removed from the insinuating methods of Chesterfield. We can see this in his correspondence especially. Godwin used letters not for disingenuous strategizing, but to tell off friends and acquaintances. He is forever issuing warnings to his correspondents, and sometimes he sternly tells them that they have earned his approval. 'You are not without some share in my esteem,' he informs the barrister Thomas Erskine in a letter that is otherwise severe: 'Take care. Learn a great moral lesson . . . Do you think you can insult the common sense of mankind . . . without at the same time insulting yourself & degrading your character?'[22] Godwin's letters, different from those of so many of his contemporaries, demonstrate the range of purposes for which letters were then used.

Letters and social change
Jane Austen and Fanny Burney

Until recently the letter, whether formal or personal, was one of the most flexible and popular instruments of communication. In the twenty-first century letter-writing is a lost art and can seem a futile activity; we associate it with a less mobile age. But the letter used to be an aid to personal freedom. Versatile and direct, it could function as a record, a petition, an incitement to rebellion, a grant of privilege or a bond of trust, an advertisement or a memorial.[1] Its tone could be, among other things, friendly, amorous, instructive, angry or apologetic.

If for William Godwin letters were opportunities to issue warnings, for Chesterfield they were performances, at once an extension of conversation and a sort of game. A business letter should be set out with 'elegant simplicity', whereas a 'familiar' letter could incorporate 'tropes, figures, antitheses, epigrams, etc.'. 'Neatness in folding up, sealing, and directing your packets, is by no means to be neglected,' he explained, for 'there is something in the exterior, even of a packet, that may please or displease'.

It is characteristic of Chesterfield to take this rather limited view of what matters in letter-writing while actually using a great range of nuance in his own letters. He embodies the spirit of an age in which letters were dramas of intimacy. We see this again and again in eighteenth-century novels, which, in a style that feels at once spontaneous and artful, use letters as a means of representing multiple points of view. The best example is Samuel Richardson's *Clarissa*, a novel that claustrophobically evokes the psychological relationships between its actors and invites the reader to be their judge.

At the same time, there were letters of an altogether less brilliant kind. Richardson in his 1741 book *Letters Written to and for Particular Friends, on the Most Important Occasions* showed that a letter could simply be a means of enlarging one's social sphere. It was a tool of persuasion. The samples he provided were written 'in a common style'; the intended audience was 'country readers' who did not know much about writing.

Richardson was the inspiration for a new generation of letter-writers, opening a fresh social vista for people who would previously have thought of letters as the preserve of the elite. Banal rather than novelistic, their efforts were part of the machinery of mercantile survival – and of Empire. Today we think of the internet as a technology that has shrunk the globe; in the eighteenth century it was the letter that made the world seem smaller. Letters facilitated connections across long distances. The postal service was improved in the 1660s, and then, between 1720 and 1760, Ralph Allen developed a national postal network. In the 1780s John Palmer introduced the mail coach.

As the infrastructure improved, so it was possible for letters to be the glue holding together individuals and groups who would previously have seemed hopelessly far apart. The historian Susan Whyman has shown that this was not just the preserve of gentlefolk, and great value was attached to mastering the etiquette of letter-writing: how to start and sign off, how much marginal space to leave, the commonplaces needed to achieve a suitable air of sincere politeness. This etiquette was set out in manuals, which aimed to instil dependence not only on certain templates, but also on stock sentiments. Up to about 1750, the model was French; thereafter a more natural, flexible style was adopted, but middle-class parents still required their children to learn penmanship, layout, spelling and forms of address, as well as an appropriate vocabulary which included standard ways of expressing apology, humility and friendship.

The second half of the eighteenth century also saw a proliferation of books about manners aimed at female readers. *The Young Lady's Companion* (1740), written by 'a person of quality', was an example of the initially limited scope of such works: sixty-eight pages long, it announced only as late as page forty-one that 'It is time now to lead you out of your house into the world.' This was 'a dangerous step', and numerous cautions followed.[2] In time works of this kind became more complex, and they illustrated the degree to which letter-writing was now a powerful vehicle for women's self-expression. In *The Ladies Complete Letter-Writer* (1763) there are traces of the old prescriptions of Richard Brathwait: a specimen letter about female education is juxtaposed with one providing a recipe for washing one's face to beautiful effect. But across its nearly 300 pages this volume suggests just how many letters and how many kinds of letter women were writing.

For novelists of the period, who focused on social detail, the letter was a usefully protean medium. It could also suffer all manner of plot-enhancing fates, being stolen, quoted, misunderstood, delayed, lost or forged. By the end of the century it had become a vehicle for some truly daring representations of women's desires. 'The post office is a wonderful establishment,' says a character in Jane Austen's novel *Emma*, the plot of which hinges on secret correspondence. Its wonder was that it revolutionized communication; for Austen, who was born in 1775, the efficient new mail coaches introduced by John Palmer were a given – but one still new enough to be appreciated. In her personal correspondence, Austen was passionate, trivial, jokey, ingenious; reading the letters can feel like listening in on someone's everyday phone conversations, and the mood is summed up when in one of them she asks her sister Cassandra, 'Which of all my important nothings shall I tell you first?' Important nothings are the stuff of intimate conversation, and in the age of letter-writing they became the material of literature.

We may think of Austen's world as narrow, and she certainly did, describing the limited scale of her work as being like painting with a fine brush on a little bit of ivory, two inches wide. But how much she can make of that small space. On one occasion she writes to Cassandra: 'Expect a most agreeable letter, for not being overburdened with subject . . . I shall have no check to my genius.'[3] The same applies to her novels. They are not full of action, but she is quietly engaged with social changes, such as those inspired by the French Revolution. Her characters' lives register the tremors of political upheaval; more straightforwardly, they are affected by faster journey times and greater opportunities for travel. In her last completed novel, *Persuasion*, she shows the tension between 'the old English style' and 'the young people in the new' with 'more modern minds and manners'. Such modern manners achieve 'a state of alteration, perhaps of improvement'. The main character, Anne Elliot, notices that society is becoming more fragmented. 'Every moment . . . brought fresh agitation,' she feels, as she gobbles up a love letter, and the words seem a summary of the social changes she is witnessing. In the manuscript of her final, unfinished novel *Sanditon*, Austen wrote the phrase 'social order', which she then deleted, replacing it with 'the common wants of society'. You sense that she was uncertain about not just the phrase, but the very idea of such order.[4]

Sensitive to the moral and wider social effects of good manners, and alert to the dangers resulting from their absence, Austen shared with her precursor Fanny Burney the technique of placing a character by referring to his or her lack of particular attributes. Theirs is literature as social vigilance. Burney appears to have originated several words that begin *un-*: *unamusing*, *unclubbable*, *unpleasure* and *unpretty*. Austen for her part seems to have coined *uncoquettish*, *unfastidious*, *unfeudal*, *unloverlike*, *unmirthful*, *unmodulated* and *unpunctuality*. The use of the negative prefix *un-* with (usually) a positive adjective can seem a telling evasion of direct diagnosis. But a word of this kind, uttered by a character, can be a means of self-congratulation. When Austen's Emma says that the scorned Miss Bates is 'so undistinguishing and unfastidious', she is not only emphasizing that a civilized person should be distinguishing (that is, perceptive) and fastidious, but also making the point that she herself aspires to be both of these things. As we speak of others' conduct, we establish an implicit set of criteria for judging our own. Emma reflects of the eligible Frank Churchill, a skilful and evasive letter-writer: 'His indifference to a confusion of rank bordered too much on inelegance of mind.' She thinks that a man's mind should be elegant, and that a clear understanding of rank and its importance – important to her, as the queen of her own little world – is a mark of such elegance.

Jane Austen's novels are full of public events: assemblies, dances, balls. Here, as so often, society comes together in order to observe itself in the act of doing so: one of the reasons you might go to an event of this kind was to watch others in attendance, savouring their little triumphs, discomforts and deficits. Austen is adept at showing 'polite' people at their most awful. There are characters for whom good manners are merely a form of self-advertisement. Then there are those who use manners simply as a means of appraising and grading others. Typically, the characters who create most trouble for others are the ones who practise an elevated politesse; their artfulness is a kind of villainy. Austen has a notion of a truly virtuous politeness, and its key elements are constancy and amiability. The latter is defined by Mr Knightley in *Emma* when he dismisses Frank Churchill as 'amiable only in French, not in English'. Critical of imported affectations, Knightley unpacks the significance of a word that others use too liberally, explaining that Frank is merely 'very agreeable' and 'can have no English delicacy towards the feelings of other people'.

The occasions and locations of polite public gathering – such as the Pump Room at Bath – had for some time been identified by moralistic commentators as the sites of sin, places suited to the very agreeable Frank Churchill rather than the properly sensitive Knightley. Austen never has any of her characters visit one of London's fashionable pleasure gardens (Vauxhall,

Marylebone, Ranelagh), but they figure in the novels of Fanny Burney, and they are the setting for tests of female virtue. Burney presents episodes that suggest the importance of being able to suspend attention when we are in modish or crowded places. Sharing communal space requires a degree of inattentiveness; although we cannot switch off all our sensitivities, we learn to show an awareness of other people's presence without making them feel that they are objects of curiosity to us. It is not easy to manage the balance between looking and not looking, between having our lights on full and having them on so low that we can't see where we are going.

In Burney's most accessible novel, *Evelina*, the eponymous heroine goes to the gardens at Vauxhall, where she has the chance to 'enjoy my first sight of various . . . deceptions'. Blundering down a dark alley, she feels threatened by a group of predatory young gentlemen, who form a circle round her and her friends, imprisoning her 'for some minutes'. The scene ends without disaster, but Burney nicely evokes Evelina's unarticulated suspicion that she may be subjected to a sexual assault. The very fact of Evelina being at Vauxhall in the first place is interpreted by the more rakish sort of men as a sexual invitation. That basic attitude survives among many men, who defend their priapic blitzkrieg with baloney along the lines of 'She was asking for it.' For Evelina, going out in public is both socially necessary and socially hazardous. In one of her letters she laments the lack of a guide to modern living: 'really, I think there ought to be a book, of the laws and customs *à-la-mode*, presented to all young people upon their first introduction into public company.'

Burney's own experience of public company and customs

à-la-mode meant that she was surprised when she encountered people whose manners felt wholly spontaneous and unaffected. In September 1787 she visited the eminent astronomer William Herschel, who lived at Slough. In her journal Burney writes of his sister Caroline, who worked alongside him and received for this £50 a year from King George III: 'She is very little, very gentle, very modest, and very ingenuous: and her manners are those of a person unhackneyed and unawed by the world, yet desirous to meet and to return its smiles.'[5]

At this time Burney was 'second keeper of the robes' to Queen Charlotte. It was a dismal role, even if an honour, and one in which she toiled for five years. Her position, into which she had been pushed by her father, gave her a distressingly close view of the king's insanity. As far as her own behaviour was concerned, normality had to be suspended. In a letter to her sister Hetty she could come across as an amused guide to the etiquette at court: 'In the first place, you must not cough. If you find a cough tickling in your throat, you must arrest it from making any sound . . . In the second place, you must not sneeze . . . In the third place, you must not, upon any account, stir either hand or foot. If, by chance, a black pin runs into your head, you must not take it out . . . If the blood should gush from your head by means of the black pin, you must let it gush.'[6] But this was before she had taken on the job, and once she was immersed in it her tone darkened. While many of her contemporaries were discussing social improvements and the reform of manners, she was stuck in a life of incessant service. Writing letters kept her in contact with a world of ideas that would otherwise have been lost to her.

15

The Englishness of English manners

Edmund Burke, an admirer of Fanny Burney's books, was instrumental in getting her released from her confinement, and his own brushes with monarchy, less intimate than hers, informed some of the most quotable words ever written about manners.

In 1790 Burke, established as a first-class orator and political thinker, published his *Reflections on the Revolution in France*. There he recalled seeing Marie Antoinette in her pomp at Versailles: 'just above the horizon, decorating and cheering the elevated sphere she just began to move in'. At one time 'ten thousand swords must have leaped from their scabbards to avenge even a look that threatened her with insult'. Now, though, 'the age of chivalry is gone', and 'that of sophisters, economists and calculators has succeeded; and the glory of Europe is extinguished for ever. Never, never more, shall we behold that generous loyalty to rank and sex, that proud submission, that dignified obedience, that subordination of the heart, which kept alive, even in servitude itself, the spirit of an exalted freedom. The unbought grace of life, the cheap defence of nations, the nurse of manly sentiment and heroic enterprise is gone!'[1]

For Burke, Marie Antoinette was the embodiment of civility. Her degradation was the mark of what he would six years later condemn as a 'coarse, rude, savage' new order. The French revolutionaries were desecrating the very principles of manner-liness: a regard for monarchy, religion and rank, and a deference to women. 'Manners,' wrote Burke, 'are of more importance than laws. Upon them, in a great measure the laws depend. The law touches us but here and there, and now and then. Manners are what vex or sooth, corrupt or purify, exalt or debase, barbarize or refine us.' They achieve this by a 'constant, steady, uniform, insensible operation, like that of the air we breathe in. They give their whole form and colour to our lives.' At their best 'they aid morals'; at their worst 'they totally destroy them'.[2]

Burke regarded a system of manners as a means of preserving political, social and commercial stability. When the traditional structures of society were overthrown, as by the French Revolution, manners also unravelled. Burke argues that what passes for egalitarianism is in fact a brutish stripping away of the architecture of civility. His thinking has played a large part in shaping conservative notions of Englishness. 'In England,' he writes, 'we preserve the whole of our feelings still native and entire . . . We have real hearts of flesh and blood beating in our bosoms. We fear God; we look up with awe to kings; with affection to parliaments; with duty to magistrates; with reverence to priests; and with respect to nobility. Why? Because when such ideas are brought before our minds, it is natural to be so affected; because all other feelings are false and spurious.' He imagines the English as a huge family with deep roots, and English society as 'a partnership not only between those who are living, but between those who are living, those who are dead, and those who are to be born'.[3] His ideas and his language, though repellent to many, have never since gone out of fashion. Perhaps more than anyone before or since, he recognized that language does not just refer to politics, but actually constitutes it.

There is a hearty emotiveness in Burke's statement that 'In England . . . we preserve the whole of our feelings still native and entire.' Some will find it absurd; others will relish its confidence. It seems grouchy to point out that Burke was not English but Irish; after all, by the time he wrote these words he had lived in England for nearly forty years, and he would not have thought Irishness and Englishness incompatible. We are likely in any case to be struck by Burke's sense of what sometimes gets called English exceptionalism. In this view, England is different from everywhere else: it has had its own political, religious and colonial agendas, its own forms of government, a special eclecticism, unusual traditions in education, a history of success. Even if you dismiss this as a self-aggrandizing myth, there is no escaping the consequences of so many people's belief in this exceptional status.

When Burke spoke of the English preserving the whole of their feelings, he was contrasting them with the French whom he saw 'filled, like stuffed birds in a museum, with chaff and rags, and paltry, blurred shreds of paper about the rights of man'. The revolutionary French were the products of a kind of shoddy taxidermy, whereas the English were brilliantly alive. English people's vitality came from their capacity 'to love the little platoon we belong to in society'; more than that, it came from a sense of place and from historical continuity.

The story of the last of these has been especially popular with proponents of English exceptionalism, and merits examination here because its facts feed into the tradition that Burke applauds: the awe of kings, the partnership between the living and the dead, the 'constant, steady, uniform, insensible operation' of manners. It begins with the arrival, in the fifth century AD, of Germanic settlers: Angles, Saxons, Jutes. This was a land grab, a voluntary economic migration in which the newcomers made straight for the fertile lowlands. The dialect these people used was *Anglisc*; they and the land they took over was known as *Angelcynn*. When Pope Gregory the Great saw some of these people in an Italian slave market in the 590s, he is said to have remarked that they were 'not Angles but angels'. The Christian mission that Gregory sent in 597 was intended to establish a single English Church – at the heart of a single English kingdom. Slowly a sense of English identity developed. This was evident in the 720s when the monk Bede wrote his *Ecclesiastical History of the English People*. Bede did not write in English and thought of himself as Northumbrian rather than English, but he presented a powerful image of these people's shared past and shared destiny, and of their status as a *single* people. The awareness of a distinctly English identity was also shaped by the experience of Viking invasion, beginning with a raid on the island of Lindisfarne in 793.

By the end of the ninth century King Alfred was able to think of himself as the ruler of all England. This view was not current beyond Wessex, but in the reigns of the two kings that followed, Edward the Elder and Athelstan, the idea of a united English people became political reality. That sense of unity was shaken by the Norman Conquest but survived it, and is captured in a memorably absurd line in *1066 and All That*: 'The Norman Conquest was a Good Thing, as from this time onwards England stopped being conquered and thus was able to become top nation.'[4] Ever since 1066, feelings of 'top nation'-hood notwithstanding, there have been attempts to recover a supposedly lost Englishness, something that might feel truly 'native and entire', a Saxon earthiness and authenticity that the Normans displaced.

It may seem odd, then, that the English have accepted monarchs of obviously un-English origin, including at least one who did not even speak the language (George I). But it is not so odd when we understand the English tradition of regarding their monarchs as subjects of the law, rather than its creators, and the tradition of monarchs also regarding themselves in this way. The philosopher Roger Scruton writes that 'Many of the peculiarities of the English can be traced to this conception of law. What is sometimes known as their "individualism" – that is, their disposition to affirm the right and responsibility of individual action in all spheres of social life – is surely to be attributed to their sense of being protected by the law from those who might otherwise coerce them.' The English common law, which has custom and tradition at its heart, is a tissue of local judgements, and, although there exists a wealth of commentary, the law itself is not explicitly set down. The articulate system of English common law is the truest expression of partnership between generations; among its gifts to us is the idea of ownership as duty, and its doctrines 'compose the face of England, which reveals in its every contour a long history of peaceful settlement'.[5]

Yet today the English past is typically seen as an encumbrance, and Englishness is a dirty secret. It is more than fifty years since the novelist Doris Lessing wrote that 'The sad truth is that the English are the most persecuted minority on earth . . . [and] like Bushmen in the Kalahari . . . they vanish into camouflage at the first sign of a stranger.'[6] Born in 1919 in what was then known as Persia, brought up in what was known as Rhodesia, and resident in London since 1949, Lessing saw English behaviour with the eyes of an extra-terrestrial — but also from close up. The vanishing act she perceived was a guilty one, a means of forestalling hostilities. It was as if Englishness, like other romantic notions, had continually to be tucked out of sight.

Whereas Celtic myth is celebrated with gusto and forms a key part of the Scottish and Irish romantic appeal to foreign visitors, the English tend to appear shamefaced about their folk traditions and ancient lore. National pride is regarded as gauche and offensive. There is no English national dress, no English national anthem ('God Save the Queen' is shared with the rest of the United Kingdom), and little formal recognition of St George's Day (which is often, it seems, inconveniently close to Easter). 'English nationalism' is an odd-sounding combination of words; instead of nationalism the English mostly practise jingoism and royalism. Rather than shaping a vision of democratic Englishness, intellectuals and political heavyweights see Englishness as something best left to the mob, and in the media the subject is presented negatively — at its most simple, through news reporting that constructs a painfully narrow idea of English culture.

In many circles the mere mention of Englishness provokes

hostile reflections on the iniquities of the British Empire, as if the two were actually the same. Overt celebration of Englishness is associated with atavism and racism, with hard-core football fans and the toxic politics of the far right. For the loudest celebrants it has become about race rather than place, on the grounds that English places are increasingly occupied by 'un-English' faces.

Englishness is often a source of fascination for people newly settled here, and may even be what attracts them in the first place, but there is a common belief that these people deplete English identity. When the popular historian Arthur Bryant delivered a set of lectures about the English national character on the radio in the early 1930s, he spoke of the 'various successions of immigrants . . . to whom this island had given a home and a country', adding that 'fortunately for England, this alien inflow has never been too rapid, and she has never suffered as other countries have from racial indigestion.'[7] 'Alien inflow' and 'racial indigestion' are not phrases that succeeding generations of commentators have taken up, but there is a large and from time to time vocal constituency that would delight in their suggestiveness, would regard them as synonymous, and would argue that Bryant's claim long ago ceased to hold true.

As immigrants have come to make up an increasingly significant part of the population of Britain, and of England especially, they have espoused new identities as, say, Black British or British Pakistani. Accordingly, the decision to define oneself as English has come to seem redolent not only of pride in one's indigenous status, but also of resistance or outright hostility towards incomers. That resistance is historically specious – the ethnic purists often turn out to be examples of what was once considered alien. Daniel Defoe scorned the English pretence to purity of pedigree in his poem 'The True-Born Englishman', which presents the English as mongrels inheriting a variety of conflicting characteristics from their many forebears. Defoe's poem was published in 1700; twenty-first-century purists are mostly on thinner ice than the ones he was satirizing. Nevertheless, a preoccupation with 'pure' Englishness is a mainstay of right-wing evangelism. Tellingly, the flying of the cross of St George, which has become commonplace in my lifetime, is widely associated with the England football team and its more combative supporters. It is also an emblem of English distinctiveness at a time when, though Scotland and Wales have established their own devolved political assemblies, England is in a state of political limbo, with no parliament truly its own.

It now seems possible that a crisis in Britishness, prompted by anxieties about the instability of that identity, may be turning people back on to the idea of being English. There is evidence of a resurgent interest in authentic Englishness, which is seen as a riposte to the homogenous banality of modern living. It is perceptible in the fresh enthusiasm today being shown for English food, folk music and nature writing, as well as for community projects and a host of other initiatives designed to preserve the soul of English experience and stave off the etiolating influence of globalization.

Yet it is normal to feel that England is vanishing or in a state of abashed torpor, and those who do so cling to their culture's relics. This is apparent in the tendency to describe as 'peculiarly English' things that are not: lunchtime boozing, cricket, tiredness, gardening, garden gnomes (which are German in origin), bad hotels, country estates, frigidity, melancholy, bell-ringing, a love of nonsense, DIY, a fascination with the sea, and being amused by foreigners. This descriptive tendency may be more peculiarly English than any of the above. It speaks of a desire for ownership – a possessiveness about traits and places and traditions, an urge to lay claim to things, especially if they are a little absurd. A desire to own, and also a desire to *own up*. For the English take a kinky delight in acknowledging their faults. By acknowledging them, they are able to control any discussion of them; the faults can be made to seem foibles and can be slipped inside curatorial inverted commas – 'Oh yes, we do have a great "love of nonsense".' At the same time, to admit possession of some embarrassing object or tendency is a stealthy way of showing that Englishness is robust.

As this suggests, definitions of Englishness are often sentimental. But a key part of any convincing definition must be geographical. There are features of English geography that contribute to making the English the way they are. Although Britain is related to Europe, its insular location enables aloofness and the illusion of self-sufficiency. Bill Bryson writes of the British having 'a totally private sense of distance', evident in the pretence that Britain is 'a lonely island in the middle of an empty green sea'.[8] The English feel this more than their Welsh and Scottish neighbours: the defining feature of English consciousness of English geography is not what the land is like, but where it is – and where it very much isn't. For most English people, Europe is somewhere close enough to fly to inexpensively – nice for a weekend of shopping, museums and meals out – but sufficiently far away to be no more than semi-relevant politically. This sense of isolation from Europe became entrenched in the reign of Henry VIII, who, in deciding to break away from the Roman Catholic Church, distanced England from the rest of Christendom.

No one in England is more than seventy miles or so from the sea. The long coast has made sea fishing an obvious way to source food; the vessels first used for this were the precursors of trade ships and of a navy that could be used to project force beyond England's shores. But for the majority the sea is alien – a destination for the occasional day trip, if that. The temperate climate makes walking and the outdoor life easy, without there being much suggestion of sultry glamour – the possibility of sitting outside a café on a summer evening or promenading gorgeously. In Shakespeare's *Henry V* a French character wonders how the English, a people who drink insipid beer ('sodden water', 'a drench', 'barley broth'), can match a Frenchman's 'quick blood, spirited with wine'; he disparages England as having a 'climate foggy, raw and dull'. When in the seventeenth century Inigo Jones tried to popularize the piazza, he failed because of the weather. In an English winter, there can be as little as eight hours of daylight, and at all times the first kiss of sunshine, though hardly unusual, is greeted with a surprised delight.

We might also remark England's general flatness, its compactness (which made it fairly easy to centralize) and its safeness from attack. What's more, all of England is habitable, and all of it has been inhabited: the ground is densely populated, with more than 400 people per square kilometre, around four times the rate of France, and ten times that of the United States. Today most English people live in cities and towns or amid the sprawl of suburbia. But, asked to conjure an image of England, they are likely to think of very different places: rural, idyllic, less populous and tinged with melancholy. William Wordsworth wrote of 'the ghostly language of the ancient earth', and we are likely to feel we have sensed this, just as we are likely to feel we recognize John Keats's vision of an English autumn, with its twittering swallows, robin red-breast whistling a soft treble, mists and mellow fruitfulness. Edward Thomas in *The Heart of England* pictured the perfumed air of an old wood, a church surrounded by white and grey headstones bowing to it, creepers melting into the brickwork of village houses, and a reedy pond where the summer heat quivered and the grasses were heavy with glowing flowers. For Stanley Baldwin, England meant 'wild anemones in the woods in April, the last load at night of hay being drawn down a lane as the twilight comes on . . . the smell of wood smoke coming up in an autumn evening'.[9]

There are real locations that exert a strong pull: be it mystical, as in the case of Stonehenge, King Arthur's Tintagel and Bede's Jarrow; at once practical and dystopian, as with the London Underground and the M25; or visceral and tribal, be it the noisy fortress of the Kop at Anfield or goth-enticing Whitby. Then there are the magic territories of fantasy, the invented Arcadias of the picture postcard and Romantic poetry, and the numinous territories of fiction, ranging from Shakespeare's Forest of Arden to Coronation Street and Albert Square. And then, most importantly, there are the archetypal, representative sites of Englishness: the village green, the local pub, the ivy-clad cottage, the blacksmith's forge and, less appealingly, the threadbare bedsit and the derelict seaside town.

There is a tension between our nostalgic affection for the warm scenes that might adorn a chocolate box or a jigsaw puzzle and the realities of modern England with its clapped-out fairgrounds, shuttered cinemas, boarding houses and detention centres, unprofitable farms, sparsely attended churches, betting shops and empty cafés, generic shopping streets and malls, Pupil Referral Units, landfill sites and industrial estates, identikit housing developments and characterless urban spaces, ubiquitous CCTV cameras and piss-drenched stairwells.

In his novel *England, England* (1998) Julian Barnes imagines the construction on the Isle of Wight of a monstrous heritage centre containing all things English. A survey carried out for the tycoon behind the project yields a list of 'Fifty Quintessences of Englishness'. I won't reproduce them all, but many are places or types of place: the White Cliffs of Dover, Wembley Stadium, Big Ben, the West End and thatched cottages.[10] Here we have a characteristically English act of displacement: instead of philosophy or ideology we nurse a waking dream, a space furnished not with articles of faith, but with metonyms. The 'green and pleasant land' poetically summoned up by William Blake – and celebrated in what is, in Hubert Parry's setting, the most English of English hymns – is a substitute for a concrete national idea. Blake's more sustained vision of Albion, a giant identified with a revitalized Britain, has significantly failed to achieve any such currency.

For many, the images used to evoke Englishness diffuse an air of complacency. But for others, they are comforting, psychologically and somatically. We may think of winding country roads, the Women's Institute and perfectly tended little gardens, or red postboxes and solid breakfasts. The last two of these, along with gloomy Sundays, were highlighted by George Orwell, whose definition of Englishness was a jumble of sensations, not a set of ideas. In his essay 'England Your England' Orwell pictured as a characteristic fragment of Englishness 'the old maids biking to Holy Communion through the mists of the autumn mornings'. That image was recycled by Prime Minister John Major in 1993, as he argued the need to reduce European political influence on Britain's national life. To a remarkable degree, ideas of Englishness are nourished by the tangible and the physical.

To see Englishness in microcosm, you need only go to a pub. There is perhaps no English (or British) institution more mythologized. One is expected to have strong views about what is desirable in a pub: intimacy, little nooks, real ales or gassy lagers or decent wine by the glass, sports-related mementoes, casually friendly staff, pickled onions in jars and equally pickled regulars, 'reassuringly' disgusting urinals or toilets scented with lavender, old panels of etched glass, hearty pies, a jukebox, a fug of slowness or an air of barely suppressed violence. (Clearly, no one person looks for all these things.) Orwell pictured his ideal pub, which was 'always quiet enough to talk in', sold aspirin and stamps, and had a snack counter offering cheese, pickles and mussels; the middle-aged women behind the bar called customers 'dear', but never 'ducky'.[11] Warmth was a crucial part of what he looked for. Most people expect the atmosphere of a pub, even in an age of gargantuan Pubcos and giant screens showing the football, to be much warmer than that of, say, a benefits office or a doctor's waiting room. At their best, and also at their worst, pubs are social hubs. Only the middling sort of pub, blandly undistinguished and inspiring no loyalty, is unimportant as a social centre. Pubs are sanctuaries, for many of their patrons more spacious and less stifling than home.

Precisely because of their sacrosanct quality – often exaggerated, it is true, and often abused – pubs are the setting not for a suspension of good manners, but for an amplified and even parodic version of them. We still expect there to be a queue. It may not look orderly, but within its apparent disorder there is at least an approximation of orderliness. We expect bar staff to know whose turn it is to be served. We may make a point of letting people order before us because we believe it is by rights their turn, and are likely to feel aggrieved if others – on either side of the bar – show less concern for these matters. Most important is the buying of rounds: a form of turn-taking that is essentially a matter of fairness, in which that fairness should nonetheless not be observed with an explicit strictness; it is a casual kind of equality, which all the same has certain rules. Kate Fox notes some of the key principles: 'the person who buys the round must also act as waiter', 'the correct time to say "It's my round" is when the majority of the glasses are about three-quarters empty', 'any sign of miserliness, calculation or reluctance to participate wholeheartedly in the ritual is severely frowned upon'.[12]

Here we see, in miniature, the principle that good manners are essentially a matter of making little sacrifices. Contrary to the old maxim, good manners do not cost nothing: they involve small amounts (usually very small, but usually noticeable) of delay, boredom and physical discomfort. Thomas Hobbes argued in *Leviathan* that in the absence of moral rules enforced by a sovereign, life was destined to be 'solitary, poor, nasty, brutish, and short'. The words are Hobbes's most quoted phrase. To avoid such a fate, and to achieve what Hobbes calls 'commodious living', we make concessions.[13]

A good pub has that quality of commodiousness, even when it is not actually a roomy physical space. And whether good or bad, the pub is a place where we find flesh and blood, evangelism of several different hues, the desire for ownership, a private sense of distance, a territorialism that can look a lot like insularity, an inclination to play fair, a close concern with precedent, and also evidence that there is perennially something 'little' about Englishness, a lack of larger ambitions and designs, a delight in the local. It is an education in Englishness and in English manners. Look around an English pub on a busy Friday night, and think of Burke: 'Manners are what vex or sooth, corrupt or purify, exalt or debase, barbarize or refine us.'

16

Island Man and his discontents

'They do things differently there'

The English know that some of the norms of their society are odd. Nevertheless, when abroad, they marvel at matters far less strange. On their travels, they prove squeamish yet also gregarious, pushy but more often docile, lacking in *savoir faire* and desperate to parade what little of it they possess, emotionally vacant yet forever on the brink of some grand epiphany. They come home with trinkets, undrinkable beverages and anecdotes of how 'They do things differently there.' What happens in England may be in many cases quite close to what happens in Armenia, Chile, Thailand or Angola, but differences in behaviour are palpable.

National character, which was once studied earnestly, is no longer a respectable subject. The standard academic line is that the attributes identified as national characteristics are illusions and distortions. If we refer to them uncritically, we are guilty of peddling stereotypes. Yet in private many of us remark on national differences, and manners are often used to illustrate national character. The eighteenth-century French political thinker Montesquieu wrote of the honesty of Spaniards, the Chinese weakness for cheating and desire for material gain, and the capriciousness of the Japanese. His countrymen suffered from what he called 'unfortunate vivacity': manners were disorderly, the cult of wit allowed virtue to be mocked, and inconsistency was the norm. By contrast the English were restless, at once the most and least patriotic of people, and consequently willing to settle elsewhere, taking surprisingly little of their native country with them.

Yet even when the English settle in far-flung places they want a few familiar comforts: Marmite, Marks and Spencer underwear, BBC radio. One can dismiss this as a cliché, but observation bears it out. And be they settlers, travellers or tourists, the English retain a capacity for being taken aback by the smallest quirks of other cultures. To see this, you need only look at the travel writing section in an English bookshop, which will be packed with whimsical stories of bemusement. The amateur English anthropologist, having toiled red-faced over several continents, reports back with an album of insights – akin to those in the advertisements that bill HSBC, sensitive to cultural differences, as 'the world's local bank'.[1]

For instance, eye contact during conversation is in some cultures highly desirable, but in others (such as among Native American Indians) is interpreted as over-familiar or hostile. In an Arab country it is an insult knowingly to show another person the soles of your feet. Shaking your head, which may seem a straightforward if not very charming way of signalling disagreement, is an affirmative gesture in some countries (Albania for one). Talkativeness is seen as a bad thing in many societies, and appears to be regarded with particular suspicion in Estonia, a country in which compliments are rare and unelaborate. In some cultures menstruating women must stay away from the sick, and among the Tlingit of Alaska they traditionally wear broad-brimmed hats to keep them from looking up at the sky and polluting it.

I know from experience that in Japan it is considered rude to blow your nose in front of another person – ruder than urinating in the street at night after a drinking session. I also know that a formal meeting there begins with the presentation of business cards; both hands should be used in offering one's card. The Japanese language has complex grammatical mechanisms for expressing politeness. Where English-speakers utter thanks, the Japanese are apt to offer apologies, although the modern *sankyuu* and the rather flat *arigato* are today replacing the traditional, polished *sumimasen*.[2]

For my sense of Chinese manners, I am reliant on second-hand information. Sir Robert Hart, who spent more than fifty years in China after going there in 1854 to work as an interpreter, characterized doing business with the Chinese as a matter of 'flowers and thistles': the 'flowers' were presents given to ease the passage of a transaction, and the 'thistles' were the extortions exacted by officials who felt that they had not been given enough flowers. Modern accounts of doing business in China make much of *guanxi*; literally meaning 'relationships', the word signifies a systematic approach to networking, the patient building and maintenance of rapport. The word comes up repeatedly in Peter Hessler's *Country Driving* (2010), a travelogue that is also a trenchant analysis of contemporary China. Hessler records many Chinese quirks. As he gets to know the countryside north of Beijing, he grows close to a local couple. He is intrigued when their son returns from elementary school with a list of 'rules of daily behaviour': there are twenty such rules, which include twenty-eight prohibitions couched in the form 'Do not . . .' Some of the instructions seem superfluous ('Don't drown'), but others are familiar: 'On public buses, give your seat to pregnant women.' Of the twenty rules, only one is specifically academic.[3]

German books on the subject of manners, such as Adolph Knigge's, place a lot of emphasis on the techniques of friendship. No surprise to anyone who has spent much time in Germany is the preoccupation with titles: in particular, the formal use of people's job titles, which might involve addressing one's head of department as *Herr Fachbereichsleiter*. Austrians are even more pernickety about this; to outsiders the insistence of qualified business administrator Tobias Huber on being addressed as *Herr Diplom-Betriebswirt Huber* may seem ridiculous, but omitting such titles can cause offence.

Perhaps we smile at this. But there is much about English ways that looks weird to outsiders: the parent-on-parent sports contests in schools, the pre-teen debating style of elected politicians, the capacity for being both patriotic and embarrassed by patriotism, the tendency to keep items one might like to brag about (awards, glitzy photos) in the loo. Trying to unravel the national character, a foreigner may observe that the English drink a lot of tea and breed ugly dogs, boil their vegetables till they turn to mush and express their grievances by calling radio talk shows. They recoil from extremes and fetishize obscure sports – cricket being a model for ethics, with its cult of the 'straight bat' and 'not batting for the other side'. They rarely mind that their windows don't close properly, fortify their homes with knick-knacks, favour archaic systems of measurement (Fahrenheit, acres, inches, pints), and regard the unextreme vagaries of English weather as an inexhaustible topic of conversation. Their underwear is bad. They enjoy booze and low-budget sitcoms, quizzes and terrible jokes. Suspicious of intellectuals and just about anything that ends in -*ism*, they take pride in a no-nonsense approach to life.

If foreigners look elsewhere for the essence of Englishness, they see it embodied in an assortment of rituals, ceremonies, traditions, uniforms, institutions and titles. Ralph Waldo Emerson wrote about this in *English Traits* (1856), a book that, though the work of a Massachusetts native, influenced English thinking about what it meant to be English. 'They keep their old customs, costumes, and pomps, their wig and mace, sceptre and crown,' Emerson noted, adding that 'The middle ages still lurk in the streets of London.'[4] London, and elsewhere: a tourist dowsing for signs of antique Englishness will be struck by the countless little festivals and community traditions, from the Shrovetide football at Ashbourne in Derbyshire and the annual cheese-rolling at Cooper's Hill in Gloucestershire to the bun-throwing on royal occasions at Abingdon in Oxfordshire and, in the Essex villages of Great Dunmow and Little Dunmow, the presentation of a flitch of bacon to couples happily married for more than a year and a day.

All this baggage is a sign of the English delight in the past, which is sometimes more truly a resistance to change, and also of the English love of snug expressions of local or social affiliation. A respect for old ceremonies co-exists with a scepticism about them: the mystery of tradition is somehow rather wonderful, but traditions don't need to be understood scientifically, can always be doctored to suit the moment, and are best explained with a benign shrug of the shoulders.

Sooner or later we must allow the word *eccentricity* into this picture of Englishness. By it we should understand an obstinate independence; or, if we reduce the word to its etymological basis, a refusal to be centrally regulated, a divergence from a rock-solid centre. The English eccentric is his own rock-solid centre: an island man who is himself an island. It is this quality, in some views, that differentiates the English from their less defiantly individual continental counterparts. As Christopher Hitchens remarked: 'The English have long been convinced that they are admired and envied by the rest of the world for their eccentricities alone. Many . . . are now more durable as touristic notions than as realities.'[5] Anglophilia means loving not the English, but the more archaic fragments of the English past. In the US, arguably the most Anglophile country of all, the British monarchy is generally treated as if the stuff of fairy tale, and first-time American visitors to the much mythologized attractions of London, Windsor, Bath and Oxford are often dismayed to find that the natives aren't elegant and noble-spirited or even necessarily house-trained.

The touristic notions to which Hitchens referred are a staple of books about Englishness. Here are some statements taken from *The English Inside Out*, written in the early 1960s by Pearl Binder, a colourful presence on radio and TV. 'Understatement is the trademark of the English.' 'Cleverness is distrusted in England.' 'The English people . . . don't like being pushed.' 'English people like efficiency only so long as it can be played like a game.' 'England badly needs more festivals, more occasions to dress up for.' ' "Home." This curious English word has no equivalent in any other language.' 'England, as all the world knows, is really a man's country, no matter how gallant and able our women.' 'Even an artificial dog in England can spark off an orgy of protective tenderness.'[6]

Better known than Binder's book is the earlier *How to Be an Alien* (1946), the work of George Mikes, who was born in Hungary in 1912 and settled in Britain in the 1940s. 'The English have no soul,' declared Mikes; 'they have the understatement instead.' 'In England it is bad manners to be clever.' Et cetera – except that Mikes, being a foreigner and inclined to see the comical side of Englishness, is more perceptive. Thus 'in England they hardly ever lie, but they would not dream of telling you the truth' and 'An Englishman, even if he is alone, forms an orderly queue of one.'[7] Mikes identified queuing as the national passion of a mostly dispassionate people. To this day, the queue seems the perfect example of the tacit understandings that inform English ideas of decency and democracy. As Mikes recognized, the English were adept, where no formal queue existed, at improvising one. The individuals in the queue may be thoroughly miserable about being stuck there, but their resentments are likely to simmer, looking very much like patience, rather than erupting into confrontation.

Before Mikes, a Dutchman called G. J. Renier scored a hit with *The English: Are They Human?*, which appeared in 1931. Renier's was one of a slew of 1930s guides to English character written by foreigners; others were the work of the Belgian poet Emile Cammaerts, the German visitor Karl Silex, and Félix de Grand'Combe (really Félix Boillot), a French army officer. More extreme was another German, the geographer Ewald Banse, who wrote that the English were very much the same as Lower Saxon peasants, fiery behind their cold exteriors and graspingly materialistic.[8]

G. J. Renier's book, which chimed with the period's shrill mix of Anglophobia and Anglophilia, was perceptive and clinical. He wrote of very much the same things that Binder and Mikes later discussed, noting that 'Throughout the day, the Englishman performs acts and pronounces words, not because they have a significance in themselves, but because they happen to be the acts and the words which, for one reason or another, it is deemed right to perform and to pronounce.' And later: 'The English used to practise all the little gestures and courtesies of continentals[,] which their nineteenth-century descendants gave up because they tend to diminish the distance between the individual and the outside world.' His summary view of the English, hardly a surprise to us, was that they were 'unintellectual, restricted, stubborn, steady, pragmatic, silent and reliable'.[9] In light of the popularity of Renier's book and those like it, another apposite generalization, itself edging towards cliché, would be that the English enjoy hearing themselves genially run down: it provides an opportunity for defiance or apology.

The desire to make forecasts about Englishness, or itemize its vices and virtues, is persistent, even if unfashionable. It fits in with the very English love of the more poignant sort of whimsy, as well as with the English appetite for collecting. This is a culture in which the true experts are often hobbyists. Pleasures are small. Many of them have a touch of the morbid. Today's eagerness to load up on luxury is a habit (an addiction or affliction) learned from America. Unrestrained consumption is at odds with the traditional English stoicism and cult of modesty. George Orwell wrote in 1941 that 'We are a nation of flower-lovers, but also a nation of stamp-collectors, pigeon-fanciers, amateur carpenters, coupon-snippers, darts-players, crossword-puzzle fans.' Such besottedness reflects what he called the essential 'privateness' of English life. 'All the culture that is most truly native centres round things which even when they are communal are not official.'[10]

The 'privateness' that Orwell diagnoses means that shared space is shared only in quite a limited sense. Imagine you are in a museum, for instance. Do you touch the exhibits? Where do you eat your sandwiches? Do you strike up conversation with other visitors? Rules of place, which tend to be learned unconsciously, are claimed as ingredients of public order – strategies for avoiding chaos and all the costs associated with it – but they also preserve privacy within public space. A humdrum example is the seating in restaurants: although refectory-style tables may be found in some (which recreate the busy atmosphere of a canteen), we generally expect when we eat in public to be afforded a good deal of privacy. I am likely to feel uncomfortable if the tables are very close together, and adjacent diners will be offended if I touch any of the items on their table.

Victorian travellers to America were appalled to discover that they were expected to take their meals in a room shared with people they had never met. Appalled, too, when requests for privacy were met with derision or bafflement. We may now laugh at this kind of thing, but we all have notions of what might count as unwelcome encroachment on our personal space. In a café, do you vault into the conversation that's happening at the next table? How do you react when someone sits down opposite you on a train and proceeds to devour an elaborate picnic? Do you object if someone touches you to get your attention while you are waiting for service at a bar? *Debrett's Etiquette and Modern Manners* states that an essential part of civilized living is 'every person's right to privacy, even in public'; consequently, 'distracting behaviour of any kind – speaking loudly, shouting in the street, excessive gesticulation, whistling, singing, playing radios, or arguing – breaches good manners'.[11]

We carry around with us what I think of as an invisible hula-hoop, a portable boundary marker or buffer that others cannot see but are (we hope) able to sense. It seems to prevent our autonomy being taken away from us and to keep us from being exposed to an excess of stimuli. The hula-hoop, or bubble if you prefer, expands and contracts according to our mood and environment: it is bigger when I am using a cash-point than when I am in the mosh pit at a rock concert. Even at its most contracted, it is bigger than I am. All of us expect a modicum of privacy on public transport or a crowded beach. We expect it when we are shopping, too. Do you look point-edly at the contents of someone else's shopping cart? Do you point out to another shopper that he has selected a bruised bunch of bananas? Do you say, 'You don't want to buy all that processed shit you've got there'? It is normal to be inter-ested in what other shoppers are buying, and normal also to make a point of averting your gaze from them.

More than a hundred years ago, the critic George Slythe Street called for 'absolute silence' in the hottest rooms at Turkish baths 'so that languorous poetry may lightly fan our brains'; he proposed that a special code be drawn up for those who frequented them, and any broken rule 'should be tattooed on the offender's back'.[12] The specific terms may seem bizarre, and the appetite for languorous poetry may sound fey, yet the spirit is one we understand: people who pierce the skin of our privacy are regarded not just with distaste, but with violence.

The desire for privacy is not distinctively human. It appears that all species possess mechanisms with which they define the space that individuals occupy: what's too close, and what's too far. If you pack rats or rabbits into an unusually tight space, they become sadistic and even murderous (or suicidal). Animal sensitivity to territory, trespass and distance plays an obvious part in breeding, raising young, maintaining health and fostering a stimulating kind of sociability. Social life involves episodes of companionship and moments of reserve, the rewards of interaction and those of restraint. We fear isolation, but we also fear antisocial curiosity – which seems harder to prevent. In a classic study of notions of freedom, Alan Westin argues that it is the mark of a totalitarian society that it favours surveillance more than privacy, whereas in a liberal democracy the balance will be tilted towards 'strong citadels of individual and group privacy'.[13]

Wanting to keep somewhat apart from others hardly makes bonhomie impossible. But we are suspicious of people whose bonhomie feels sticky: we recognize it as a substitute for real involvement, and automatically wonder if it is a means of compensating for some deficit. The word *bonhomie* was imported from French in the nineteenth century, and it has always been tinged with an air of the ridiculous or the forced, a hint of English aversion to French affectation – and also of upper-class French aversion to less patrician values, Jacques Bonhomme being before the Revolution a nickname for the lesser sort.[14] The related adjective *bonhomous* has never gained much acceptance, as is reflected in the alternative and tellingly nervy ways in which it has been spelled: *bonhommous* and even *bonhommious*. The closest English synonym for *bonhomie* is somewhere between 'good nature' and 'good fellowship'; the French word was adopted to fill a gap, but the gap wasn't quite as big as was imagined – wasn't, and isn't.

The urge to secure a private space even while appearing to participate in public life is apparent also in the affection for clubs. Some of these are grand, others modest, but all are furnished with protocols and rituals of access, their ambience at once a re-creation and an evasion of the domestic. They need not offer anything very special by way of facilities or refreshment. The food in so-called gentlemen's clubs is either awful or reassuringly old-fashioned, and less lofty clubs often resemble bad hotels, complete with unsmiling staff, antique plumbing and improbably incommodious furniture. Many of these clubs continue to admit only male members. The clubmen cherish the particular comradeship that this fosters, which calls to mind the single-sex boarding schools they once attended (or wish they had attended). Such exclusiveness is typically represented by clubs not as a choice they are actively pursuing, but as a function of nebulous historical forces.

However, privacy is now widely treated neither as an ideal nor even as a social norm. A lot of what would once have been kept private is loudly proclaimed. You have only to pick up a newspaper or magazine to read famous people reciting intimate details of their sexual fantasies, family life and finances. This is not to say that the desire for privacy has evaporated. Rather, our expectations have blurred, as the division between what people want to make public and what they wish to keep private has become unclear.

In the 1890s the German architect Hermann Muthesius, writing about English houses, expressed surprise that the English screened their homes using hedges, which 'very often serve the practical purpose of a protective fence'.[15] In his own country this was forbidden. The formal English hedge seemed, and still seems, a pleasantly verdant means of enclosure, yet also a battleground, for one person's idea of necessary privacy is another's of obstruction, a selfish and unsightly encroachment on amenity. What's more, the moment a hedge has been established as a safety barrier, there is curiosity about what lies on the other side. Hedges, as planted and maintained by English householders, are at once defensive and provocative, a request for privacy but also an assertion that their proprietors have something they wish to keep from view.

This capacity for being both genteel and defiant perplexes outsiders. Yet, puzzling though it may be, it is less fascinatingly strange than the English attitude to abroad. There is a tendency among those deep in love with foreignness to squirm when they are in its midst, to treat their adventures either as a bit of a joke or as an activity with a particular pretext, and to boast clinically about where they have been, as if sticking pins in a map on the kitchen wall. There is a goading, counterintuitive interest in the claim made in 1918 by the poet T. S. Eliot, an American by then based in England, that since the exploits of his fellow poets Lord Byron and Walter Savage Landor almost a hundred years before, 'no Englishman appears to have profited much from living abroad'.[16] With that in mind we now turn to an English woman whose travels, in America, enabled her to profit – financially, even if in no other respect.

17

Fanny Trollope and the domestic manners of Americans

'A single word indicative of doubt, that anything . . . in that country is not the very best in the world, produces an effect which must be seen and felt to be understood. If the citizens of the United States were indeed the devoted patriots they call themselves, they would surely not thus encrust themselves in the hard, dry, stubborn persuasion, that they are the first and best of the human race, that nothing is to be learnt, but what they are able to teach, and nothing is worth having, which they do not possess.'

These damning words come from *The Domestic Manners of the Americans*, a two-volume work published in 1832 by Frances Trollope, commonly known as Fanny. An industrious and sociable bluestocking who embraced liberal political causes, Trollope was also a sharp satirist, whose vitriol earned her the nickname Old Madam Vinegar and etched her name on the consciousness of Americans. In *Domestic Manners* she observed a society that, unlike Britain with its careful gradation of privilege, seemed all bustle and impatience and affray.

Fanny Trollope is important because, writing for an audience who had with few exceptions not been to America or contemplated going there, she established a sense of what that country and its inhabitants were like. *Domestic Manners* introduced a generation of Britons to the quirks of American idiom, and created idiom of its own, for the verb *to trollopize*, roughly meaning 'to abuse the American nation', acquired some currency. Although there is more to the book than a cavalcade of slurs, the abuse is plentiful, and it is worth noticing, because, while a huge amount has since changed, Trollope's hostility is of a kind we will straightaway recognize. It is the sort of hostility that is often still directed at Americans – but also now at the Chinese and at Indians. In each case the reproof and disdain stem from fear of a civilization that is flourishing.

Trollope matters to the story of English manners because she articulated – before it was common to do so – a fear of American influence. That fear remains. English abhorrence of Americanisms, in both language and behaviour, expresses a shaky sort of confidence in the purity of English diction and deportment. Trollope was in little doubt that English manners were the best. Yet there was doubt about whether they could prevail, and, as she complains about her experience of American manners, it is clear that she is thinking, 'If it's happening here, could it happen elsewhere?' Could Americans' depravities take root in Britain? Could an aristocracy based on money replace the established British aristocracy? Would Britain eventually fall victim to a clumsy cult of equality, of a sort that in America made it possible for a slaughterhouse to be put up next to a smart family home? In America, she claimed, 'the moral sense is on every point blunter than with us'. Harking back to the age of chivalry, and invoking Edmund Burke's imagery of tradition ('the unbought grace of life'), she reflected that 'this knightly sensitiveness of honourable feeling is the best antidote to the petty soul-degrading transactions of everyday life', and 'the total want of it, is one reason why this free-born race care so very little for the vulgar virtue called probity.'

Trollope sailed for America in November 1827. She travelled with her son Henry and her two daughters Cecilia and Emily. Her destination was Nashoba, a Tennessee community run by Frances Wright, a feminist reformer who had left her native Scotland to pursue utopian projects. Nashoba was intended to prepare slaves for emancipation – and for new lives in Liberia and Haiti. On arrival, it became clear that the commune was ravaged by malaria, and Trollope, regretting this 'maddening misadventure', moved to Cincinnati, which was at that time the fastest-growing city in America. There she came up with several schemes to support herself and her brood, including a bazaar for fancy goods (locally known as 'Trollope's Folly') and a couple of shows at the city's Western Museum. She was there for two years, then travelled for a year, and returned to England in 1831.

The fruit of the three and a half years she had spent abroad was 600 pages of scribblings, which she turned into *Domestic Manners*. The book caused outrage in America and mirth everywhere else. Its success was immense ('I awoke one morning and found myself famous,' she wrote to her son Tom), and she would capitalize on it delightedly, producing books in a similar vein about the Belgians and the Austrians.

It was Trollope's view of the Americans and their country that made a lasting impression. She pictured her arrival in the country not as a glorious or even curious moment of discovery, but as a descent via the Mississippi Delta into murk and mud. Arriving at Cincinnati, she found a town 'about the size of Salisbury' but without any of its charms; pigs and their stink were everywhere. Yet the company aboard a Mississippi steamboat was worse even than that of hogs. This, to be sure, was a country very different from her own: 'Everything English is stigmatized as out of fashion – English material, English fashions, English accent, English manner, are all terms of reproach,' and if a woman was described as looking English this was meant as 'the cruellest satire'.

Trollope depicted a land of religious factions and sexual mania, the two sometimes closely connected. She complained of the boring uniformity of American homes, the noise and oniony stench of crowds, the scrawny women and hollow-chested men, the 'general feeling of irksomeness . . . which hangs upon the memory while recalling the hours passed in American society'. Money was spent and discussed too freely. Diet was abundant and indelicate; food was seized at table with 'voracious rapidity', and teeth were cleaned with pocket knives. Women did not walk nicely. At the theatre, men sprawled grotesquely, and on one occasion she saw a man in the pit vomiting profusely, 'which appeared not in the least to annoy or surprise his neighbours'.

Commenting on Americans' enthusiasm for watermelons, she wrote that 'their manner of devouring them is extremely unpleasant', the juices pouring from each slice as it is 'applied to the mouth . . . while, ever and anon, a mouthful of the hard black seeds are shot out in all directions'. Besides such specifics there were febrile generalizations: Americans were guilty of 'overweening complacency and self-esteem, both national and individual', and 'in taste and learning they are woefully deficient'; confronted by the vastness of their country and its natural resources, they were busily 'hacking and hewing their way through it'; and the 'universal pursuit of money' produced a 'low tone of morality'. Philistinism was rife. Literature was unloved, but newspapers were adored. Magazines were full of trash, and people's imaginations seemed to 'kindle with alarming facility'.

Informality was a licence for savagery – a constant threat. Trollope noted a 'familiarity of address' that was 'universal throughout all ranks'; as an example of 'violent intimacy' she cited her children being called 'honey' by one of the neighbours. Granted, there was something to be said for the idea that 'any man's son may become the equal of any other man's son'. But if this was 'a spur to exertion' it was also 'a spur to . . . coarse familiarity, untempered by any shadow of respect', and while Americans boasted of the equality prevailing among them, evidence of slavery and of suffering was abundant. 'You will see them with one hand hoisting the cap of liberty,' she wrote, 'and with the other flogging their slaves.'

Trollope's son Anthony, the novelist known for his chronicles of life in the fictional and distinctly matriarchal county of Barsetshire, would accuse her of flagrant exaggeration. He had been left behind in England while she travelled, resented his abandonment (he was twelve when she travelled to Nashoba), and argued that 'No one could have been worse adapted by nature for the task of learning whether a nation was in a way to thrive.' But Mark Twain, better qualified to judge the veracity of Frances Trollope's account, wrote that it was true to life – a 'sort of photography'.[1]

One of Trollope's themes is 'the incessant, remorseless' spitting of Americans. She writes of the 'vile and universal' habit of chewing tobacco. She claims that American men have lips that are 'almost uniformly thin and compressed', and suspects that this is connected to 'the act of expressing the juices of this loathsome herb'. Rather than dealing with the matter once, she refers again and again to spitting, 'that plague-spot . . . which rendered male colloquy so difficult to endure'. She was not alone in observing the habit, or in finding it rebarbative. Charles Dickens in his *American Notes* (1842) wrote that 'In all the public places of America, this filthy custom is recognized' and in some places it is 'mixed up with every meal and morning call, and with all the transactions of social life'. In 1858 Philip Kelland, a distinguished English mathematician, published his impressions of America as *Transatlantic Sketches*. He complained that 'even the ladies in some districts speak with a lazy nasal twang' and that 'business men, seizing an opportunity to quit their desks for a midday meal, do not think it necessary to sit out three courses and a dessert'. Above all, he claimed, 'Spitting is the monster vice of the country; next to slavery it is the great obstacle in the way of perfect civilization.'[2]

We know that the distaste for spitting was nothing new. But in the nineteenth century the objection to it became medical as well as aesthetic. It was associated with the spread of disease; after Robert Koch identified the tubercle bacillus in 1882, spitting was linked with the spread of tuberculosis. By the start of the twentieth century, 150,000 Americans were dying each year of TB. Crusaders for public health, in Britain and France and America, promoted an anti-tuberculosis message with religious vehemence. American cities passed no-spitting ordinances. Trollope would have been impressed. As it was, though, she found spitting incessant and unchecked.

Cultivated Americans regarded Trollope's book with horror. One of its consequences was an increase in the literature of American manners: volumes that set a practical, clear and often pious agenda. Literature of this kind had previously been either imported or derivative. Among the early colonists, the elite read Castiglione and Guazzo; later generations took their lessons from Peacham and Brathwait, Allestree and Savile, and especially Chesterfield. Of the books written by Americans, Eleazar Moody's *The School of Good Manners* (1715) was popular but based on earlier works (including Erasmus's *De Civilitate*). As a teenager in the 1740s, George Washington wrote a list of the principles of good manners (110 in all), reproducing maxims that had appeared in an English version of a sixteenth-century French book. Thomas Jefferson fretted about this tendency to copy European behaviour; he set out his own ideas about a specifically American etiquette in a memorandum dated November 1803, but his main concern in it was to do away with the pageantry of political office.

The efforts of Benjamin Franklin were wider in scope and more original. In his autobiography he recalled how in 1726, aged twenty, he devised a programme by means of which he could cultivate, in sequence, thirteen virtues. The virtues Franklin listed were temperance, silence, order, resolution, frugality, industry, sincerity, justice, moderation, cleanliness, tranquillity, chastity and humility. Of these, chastity was understood in a way we might consider unusual, for Franklin wrote that sex was to be reserved 'for health or offspring' and should not be used to 'the injury of your own or another's peace or reputation'.[3] Franklin's programme exalts virtues rather than manners, but is of interest here partly because he believes that personal growth is all about developing habits, and partly because he sees virtues as having practical uses – as instruments of worldly success, not just guarantees of heavenly reward. Franklin later elaborated his ideas of civility and good manners, always keeping in view this principle of utility and stressing the valuable effects of amiable compliance.

It was only in the 1820s, though, that a truly American literature of manners began to develop. As this literature grew, it created the illusion that America was a classless society. The reality was that inequalities were rife; manners were a means of obscuring this uncomfortable fact. One historian of American manners comments that 'the plain, republican citizens of the United States have shown a remarkable appetite for cere-monious titles . . . cling[ing] to them as tenaciously as molecules of water to ethyl alcohol,' though this is matched by 'an ability to take the measure of pompous and self-important men'.[4]

In the 1830s Alexis de Tocqueville pictured the relationship between democracy and manners. In his masterpiece *Democracy in America* he wrote of the tendency for aristocratic societies to run according to rules that 'adorn and hide what is natural'. By contrast, in a democracy manners are 'like a thin and poorly woven veil, through which each person's true feelings and indi-vidual ideas can easily be seen'. In the America de Tocqueville described, there was less politeness than in Europe, but there were also fewer disputes about rank and status. Society was compara-tively unrefined, certainly, but it was authentic and straightforward. Henry David Thoreau, preaching the value of simplicity in the 1850s, wrote in his journal about the kind of men whose fine manners are 'a lie all over, a skin-coat or finish of falsehood'.[5]

American writings on manners flowered in the years after the Civil War of 1861–5. In this period, one of industrial progress and urbanization, the American gentleman ceased to hide behind a parapet of whiskers, and a concern with clean skin and fresh underclothes was usual among writers who aimed to teach respectability without surrendering realism. The historian Andrew St George observes that the mid-Victorian English etiquette book took everything for granted, finding its models among an established aristocratic class, whereas the American version argued from first principles.[6] As he shows, the vital quality was 'ease': this in the sense 'freedom from embarrassment' rather than casual convenience. The new American guides to manners spoke optimistically of community, tranquillity and social cohesion, of openness and purpose.

These books had a strongly patriotic feel. Sarah Josepha Hale, a prolific poet and editor, published in 1868 a work with the title *Manners; or, Happy Homes and Good Society All the Year Round*. It contained chapters on 'the importance of needlework' and 'pets and their uses'; in the latter she suggests that 'The small wood-tortoise will be found to be one of the best, safest, and most convenient pets for little boys.' Another sample statement: 'Married women are usually more agreeable to men of thought than young ladies, because the married are accustomed to the society of a husband, and the effort to be a companion to his mind has ingrafted the habit of attention and ready reply.' Hale's writings may make us grimace or smirk, but she is astonishingly certain of her country's excellence. 'America has all needed means of making her history unparalleled in the reality of happy homes and good society,' she says, and then: 'there are, in the texture of American life, certain threads that, like telegraphic wires, reach across all obstacles, and awaken the sympathies of the world.'[7]

By the end of the century, it was common for American writers to declare that the manners of their country were superior to those of their former colonial masters. This could happen even in a volume with the title *'Good Form' in England, by an American Resident in the United Kingdom*, which was published in New York in 1888 and intended to help Americans understand 'how things are' in England. It contained the stinging assessment that 'Reversing in the waltz . . . is not "good form". Why it should not be can only be accounted for by the fact that English men and women (whom candour compels me to say, after many years' observation, are the worst dancers in the world) *can't* reverse themselves, and therefore, in the spirit of "sour grapes", excuse their awkwardness by stigmatizing what they only wish they could do as "bad form".' There was more in this vein, as well as a note of mystification in statements such as 'in England, *money* has nothing whatever to do with social status', and of outrage in the revelation that 'there is a stupendous number of utterly occupationless men', many of them 'dependent upon an allowance . . . [to keep them] in genteel idleness'. American visitors to England also complained of mechanical behaviour and its results: narrowness of mind, narrowness of conversation. A 1901 volume outlining *Etiquette for All Occasions* claimed that the riches of English hospitality were abundant, but could be made available only 'after one has passed one's examination and been accepted'.[8]

The most striking feature of the new American literature of manners was the degree to which it was created by women. They wanted to improve themselves. They also wanted to improve their menfolk; as the domestic expert Marion Harland observed, the American man of the late nineteenth century did not take polish readily. The general tone was at once dismissive of European flummery and vigorously competitive. Much more than in Europe, the story of manners in America is one not of practices trickling down, but of people – women – reaching up.

18

'You're the most important person!'

the trouble with children

'Before I left England,' wrote Fanny Trollope, 'I remember listening, with much admiration, to an eloquent friend, who deprecated our system of public education, as . . . paying little or no attention to the peculiar powers of the individual. This objection is extremely plausible, but doubts of its intrinsic value must, I think, occur to everyone who has marked the result of a different system throughout the United States.'

The raising of children, and not merely their education, was a subject that weighed heavy on Trollope's mind. She saw in America an alarmingly unsystematic approach to all aspects of this, and concluded that 'No people appear more anxious to excite admiration and receive applause than the Americans, yet none take so little trouble, or make so few sacrifices to obtain it.' Trollope would have been astonished to discover that in the twentieth century America would be the fountainhead of ideas about child-rearing.

We are used to the idea that children are taught manners by their parents. The teaching involves more *don't*s than *do*s. Exasperation is often audible. Few parents have the time to explain in detail the reasons why particular conventions exist;

children grow used to hearing that certain behaviours are dangerous or rude. Conservatives argue that more time and effort should be spent on this instruction. For one such conservative, the American law professor Stephen Carter, 'Teaching civility, by word and example, is an obligation of the family.'[1]

We are also used to observing that in practice children are much of the time not taught manners by their parents, who leave others to do the job. Typically this is because the parents don't have the energy, inclination or patience to do it themselves. Parents are apt to argue that manners should be taught at school; teachers complain that manners are not taught at home. What is clear to both parties is that habits formed in childhood tend to last. It is as children that we learn, if we do so at all, to play fair, clean up our mess, and put things back where we found them.[2] I can remember being taught these lessons: what I learned at school reinforced what I learned at home, or perhaps it was the other way round. The process undoubtedly involved the explicit endorsement of principles that had already been presented implicitly. I learned by precept, and by observation and imitation.

The concept of good parenting is a modern invention. In medieval society there was a limited awareness of the particular nature of childhood. Sustained interest in the nature and roles of children was rare before the seventeenth century, and until the later stages of that century English children were mostly treated in a controlling, punitive manner that at times became ferocious. While historians have exaggerated parents' lack of tenderness, it is clear that children were considered neither innocent nor autonomous. Adults and children shared few activities. Children were peripheral and were regarded as property rather than the centre of the household.

John Locke, who in the 1690s argued that children should not be treated as little adults, is sometimes said to have 'invented' childhood. This is not quite right, but he did establish the belief that childhood is a key phase in the formation of character. Locke was influential in his conception of children as citizens in the making. He suggested that coercion and physical punishment, which aimed to instil conformity, were counterproductive. Children should be 'tenderly used' and 'not be hindered from being children, or from playing'. Fresh air and comfortable clothes were important. So was learning through trial and error. Education was essential to the development of free, rational, functional beings. 'Manners, as they call it . . . are rather to be learnt by example than rules.'

Locke saw the child as a blank slate. 'God has stamped certain characters upon men's minds,' he claimed, and these cannot be completely altered, but they 'may perhaps be a little mended', and it is as children, when they resemble 'white paper, or wax', that they are best able 'to be moulded and fashioned'. It was for this reason that Locke rather startlingly argued that children should be 'wholly, if possible' kept from talking with the lower sort of domestic servants. They risked picking up 'tricks and vices', and 'the contagion of these ill precedents . . . horribly infects children.'[3] Jonathan Swift would later remark on this in *Polite Conversation*, ironically observing that 'a footman can swear, but he cannot swear like a lord. He can swear as often, but can he swear with equal delicacy, propriety, and judgement?' For Locke, servants should be 'hindered from making court' to children, which they might do 'by giving them strong drink, wine, fruit, playthings, and other such matters, which may make them in love with their conversation'; the young should be 'kept as much as may be in the company of their parents'.[4]

The eighteenth-century philosopher Jean-Jacques Rousseau shared Locke's conviction that honing children's minds was among the chief duties of society. Children should play not on their own, but 'all together and in public, so that there will always be a common goal toward which they all aspire'.[5] Today we accept that playing is crucial to children's development. Its purpose is not merely to allow children to blow off steam, but to practise activities that will continue throughout their lives, not least the regulation of aggression and arousal. As they play, children try on different roles, solve problems, understand stimuli, learn about sharing and intimacy, deal with conflict, and discover the limits of their power. If we fail to give them an opportunity to express themselves through play, instead channelling all their surplus energies into academic study, we produce young people who are socially inarticulate and inept.

Rousseau differed from Locke in claiming that children were born not 'blank', but in a state of purity and nobility. Thus from the moment of their birth they were susceptible to corruption. According to Rousseau, children should be allowed to develop without the pressure of expectation and without fear of authority. His idea of them as society's precious raw materials – which did not prevent his abandoning his own children in a public orphanage – has contributed to an enduring anxiety, not only about the processes of parenting but also about the public spectacle of parenting, the drama of responsibility for the child.

Modern parents are hoverers, lacking in confidence, busy, fearful of seeming oppressive, keen to be humane and be seen to be humane, jittery about even the tiniest sign of what might be deformity in their offspring, and cursed with total answerability for them – without total authority. Modern children are for their part regarded as vulnerable, and also as a threat. According to which earnest new study you happen to be reading, they are artists, blessings, flowers, oppressors, cost centres or potential victims of abuse. The child is both innocent and savage, a cherub always teetering on the brink of repellent wildness. One wide-ranging book on the subject notes that 'while parents find valuable advice and comfort in childrearing manuals, they are also being told that their own impulses are likely to be wrong.' 'Growing psychological expertise [has] brought many adults to question their own childhoods and the ways they were raised,' and it has become routine to blame one's parents for one's problems.[6]

Today's children treat their parents with an informality that would have been unimaginable a century ago. The proverb that 'Children should be seen and not heard' is more than 600 years old. It used to be applied exclusively to girls, and was once a commonplace, but anyone now uttering these words is likely to be regarded as a crank. More often children are regarded as little wonders, their excesses excused as healthy self-expression. Once, when a four-year-old boy narrowly failed to jab me in the eye with a cocktail stick he had somehow acquired, I was told by a bystander who claimed to be a childcare expert that this was my fault as I should not have been sitting 'within range of him'. In many cases children's violence is tolerated, even indulged, by parents who pride themselves on liberalism and flexibility. Public piety about children is not the same as taking care of them; often it serves as a substitute for doing so.

Reading *Bossypants*, a memoir by the comedian Tina Fey, I am struck by her recollection that 'When I was a kid there was a TV interstitial during Saturday morning cartoons with a song that went like this: "The most important person in the whole wide world is you, and you hardly even know you. / You're the most important person!" Is this not the absolute worst thing you could instill in a child? They're the *most important person? In the world?* That's what they already think. You need to teach them the opposite.'[7] Some children are told that they are the most unimportant of people and are abused into believing that they matter less than everyone else. But mostly, it's true, children are encouraged to believe in their superlative importance, and while this is meant to empower them, its result is often a cosseted, bratty egomania.

Modern attitudes to children are part of a cult of family life. This is represented as something wholesome, but its manifestations are in practice hard-nosed – or sharp-elbowed, to use an adjective of more recent vintage. A broad sense of social responsibility has been squashed by the cult of family, which is a licence for selfishness and unfettered consumption. Our public life is poorer because our investment in the private values of the family is so deep. Deep, that is, and narrow.

Reviewing a number of recent books about parenting, Elizabeth Kolbert suggests that today's children are some of the most indulged young people in the history of the world. She is writing about Americans, and clearly not about America's poor, but everything she says applies in Britain. Relative to their forebears, children in the twenty-first century have huge amounts of stuff – which spills into all areas of their homes – and an unprecedented degree of authority. In a reversal of tradition (and nature, too, one might argue), parents seek their children's approval. They also encumber their offspring with help that keeps them from taking responsibility for themselves.[8]

French Children Don't Throw Food (2012), by the American journalist Pamela Druckerman, highlights how different this is from the French approach. French parents, she explains, 'aren't panicked about their children's well-being', 'don't treat pregnancy like an independent research project', 'don't worry that they're going to damage their kids by frustrating them', and 'aren't obsessed with far-flung eventualities'.[9] As a result, French babies sleep through the night, and French children play quietly and eat the food that is put in front of them. Although Druckerman admits that these are generalizations, she is again and again impressed by how relaxed French parents are and how compliant yet also autonomous their offspring. Some of her critics have uncharitably observed that these benign French children grow up to be French adults – *et après ça, le déluge*. But *French Children Don't Throw Food* drives home the point that a lot of the parenting practices cultivated today in Britain and America don't work very well, failing to instil compassion, empathy or even just the habit of basic courtesy.

19

What were Victorian values?

Victorian Britain was youthful: throughout the period, more than a third of the population was under fifteen. We are used to images of the poor Victorian child stuck up a chimney or toiling in a factory. Either that, or pressed into a suit and starched collar. But there was more to Victorian childhood than silence and servitude. Victorian children benefited from the campaigns of activists who sought to improve their lot. A good guide to this is the tailor and social reformer Francis Place, whose diaries are crammed with details of everyday life and commentary on London's changing character. In 1829 he notes that, compared with forty years before, 'people are better dressed, better fed, cleanlier, better educated, in each class respectively, much more frugal, and much happier.'[1] He cites the cheapness of cotton as a key factor.

Cotton garments were easy to wash, and it was obvious when they needed washing, whereas the leather stays and dyed linen petticoats worn by previous generations had been preserved unwashed until they rotted and fell to bits. Physical cleanliness was linked to better standards not just of presentation, but also of behaviour. Filthy children, observed Place, were likely to be unhealthy, miserable and morally squalid. Children who wore cotton could be preserved from pollution of all kinds, and good manners were another form of armour, protecting them from injury. In the year that Place commented on improvements in London life, there appeared a little volume with the title *A Manual of Manners; or, Hints for the Proper Deportment of School Boys*. It decried the 'false and tinsel politeness of Lord Chesterfield' and proposed instead something more resilient, a 'true and sterling politeness'. With its numbered points, clipped military style and emphasis on cleanliness, this manual felt like a new kind of *vade mecum* for the well-scrubbed schoolchild.[2]

There was still much in Francis Place's England that needed to change. Friedrich Engels could write in the 1840s of the urban poor 'forced to sacrifice the best qualities of their human nature, to bring to pass all the marvels of civilization', of the streets' repulsive turmoil, the 'barbarous indifference' of people in the larger towns, the 'whirlpool of moral ruin' in the slums, and also the 'cramped and desolate' condition of the rural poor, living 'with no comforts whatsoever'. Engels was nauseated by the rough dirtiness of the streets, their poor ventilation and the foul water. In public sanitation, there had been few changes since the medieval period. Place and his contemporaries would have recognized much in Jonathan Swift's description of the open drains of the early eighteenth century: 'Sweepings from butchers' stalls, dung, guts, and blood, / Drowned puppies, stinking sprats, all drenched in mud, / Dead cats, and turnip-tops come tumbling down the flood.'[3] Swift had been exaggerating, but not wildly, and in the first half of the nineteenth century facilities were still inadequate. When Queen Victoria took the throne in 1837, Buckingham Palace did not have a bathroom.

In a quirky history of the bath and loo, Lawrence Wright notes that in the eighteenth and nineteenth centuries a bath was normally regarded as a medical therapy, with the person taking the bath being treated as a patient. Only around 1860 was the bath established as a place for private cleaning routines. Other improvements followed. Wright declares that '1870 was the *annus mirabilis* of the water-closet.'[4] At last the apparatus was effective, and sewage systems helped make effluent more remote. The first sewage system in Europe was built in Hamburg in the 1840s, and London's was created in the aftermath of 'the great stink' of 1858 when the smell of the Thames was so foul that MPs considered moving parliament out of town. Indoor bathrooms remained rare until the end of the nineteenth century, and the modern lavatory was not common until the 1940s. But the Victorian period saw politicians, public servants, philanthropists, scientists, doctors and civil engineers combine to raise standards of health, welfare and preventative medicine.

Efforts of this kind are now seen as having a particular Victorian character, combining practicality and benevolence. From time to time we hear that we should revive Victorian values, and it is a moral ideal that is being invoked – an amalgam of deference, piety, self-reliance, reasonableness and traditionalism, expressed through thrift, sobriety, patriotism, hard work and an attachment to family life, all underpinned by religion. Although today's neo-Victorians are conservatives, many of those who espoused what we now think of as Victorian values were progressives.

While Victorians would on the whole have seen their good qualities as perennial, and while the true narrative of Victorianism is in any case much more complex, this distillation of

Victorian Englishness has had enduring appeal. Famously, it was embraced by Margaret Thatcher as she campaigned for re-election in 1983, though in her own account she said she had spoken of 'Victorian virtues'.[5]

The Victorians' emphasis on fortifying morality was a product – as it usually is – of social uncertainty. Theirs was a period of extraordinary affluence, political strength and industrial progress for Britain. The last third of the eighteenth century had laid the basis for this: innovative machines and then machines made by machines, higher incomes, cheaper commodities, a longer working day, new horizons and appetites. As technology made agriculture more efficient, labour was released and moved into manufacturing. Improved transport also sped up social change: canals and roads were built to serve industry, but it was not just coal, textiles and metal goods that moved around this network.

As geographical mobility increased, social mobility did the same. While received ideas about social status did not collapse, notions of class became more fluid. For those intent on upward mobility, the refinement of their manners appeared a pivotal concern. Insights into the cosmetic codes of etiquette were widely available. A series published in 1845 in the *London Journal* bore the symptomatic title 'Etiquette for the Millions'. Even when presented as highly exclusive, books on conduct catered for a mass audience. This was especially apparent from the 1830s, when the middle classes gained greater access to power as a result of political reform. Manuals of correct behaviour pictured a lifestyle that was rich and aristocratic, but they were read by people – mostly women – who could emulate only elements of this.

The emphasis was on the external rather than the internal.

John Stuart Mill wrote in his 1869 essay 'The Subjection of Women' that 'The English, more than any other people, not only act but feel according to rule.'[6] Feeling according to rule meant not *feeling* at all. The formulae of proper conduct suppressed character and emotion, and they were set out in language bereft of either. Books of etiquette were often published anonymously; authorship might be attributed to 'a member of the aristocracy', but there was little trace in their prescriptions of an individual style, and their tone was impersonal. The printed volumes tended to be pocket-size; they had to be portable and easily digestible.[7] Morality was treated almost as if a medical matter. The priority was avoidance of the distasteful, rather than positive virtue; shared comfort, not shared goodness; inhibiting the spread of the coarser human tendencies, more than promoting the growth of the higher ones.

The rise of etiquette was also an education in detachment. Physical intimacy between friends, once considered normal, was seen as not only undesirable but unnatural. In the Renaissance, detachment was discussed in mainly negative terms; by the Victorian period, it was advocated.[8] Around 1800 the noun *tact* started to have connotations of keen social perception and a delicate understanding of how to avoid giving offence; *tactful* and *tactless* established themselves half a century later. The word had previously signified touch or the sense of touch. But the nineteenth-century idea of tact was of *not* touching: it came to mean a kind of prescience, knowing what not to touch or when not to, knowing not to voice potentially disruptive questions or sentiments.

So, to be polite was to be detached. To be detached was to be polite. These are tenacious principles, and if we think about the everyday language of politeness we can see many distancing effects inherited from the Victorians. The damning use in social contexts of *over-familiar* and *over-familiarity* is a Victorian development. So is *detachment* as a synonym for *aloofness*. And so is *sorry* as a short form of 'I am sorry': the verb disappears, and all that's left is an adjective conveniently cut off from the person feeling sorrowful. We can also trace to this period the emergence in British English of the phrase *stiff upper lip*. However, this posture of unyielding stoicism did not become a proverbial English attribute until the early twentieth century.

An item in the *Blackburn Standard and Weekly Express* (of Saturday, 2 September 1893) reproduces a no doubt apocryphal story about a young woman who boards the smoking carriage on a train, with her Skye terrier in tow; objecting to the smoking of one of her fellow passengers, she snatches his cigar from his mouth and tosses it out of the window – about which he says nothing, though a minute later he seizes her Skye terrier and flings it from the window. The young woman says nothing, the two travellers descend at the next station without exchanging a word, and a French passenger who has witnessed these events is left reflecting bemusedly on '*les Anglais taciturnes*'.

Smoking was, as it always had been, a contested pleasure. 'The habit is more perfectly artificial than almost any other in which man indulges,' declared a pamphlet published in 1842, and it is 'disagreeable to those who do not practise it'. An 1838 volume entitled *A Present for an Apprentice*, which was at least partly the work of the publisher Thomas Tegg, gave guidance about when it was unacceptable to smoke. The short answer was that 'Tobacco . . . is offensive in a high degree,' and the smoking of cigars a 'wanton and fruitless expense'; if one had to smoke, it should certainly not be done in the street, which was the sign of the 'pseudo-fashionables'.[9] Smoking was a form of conspicuous consumption (a term not actually coined till 1899 by Thorstein Veblen). This was still the case in 1893, when the piece above appeared in the *Blackburn Standard and Weekly Express*. Smoking was a predominantly male practice, and what a man chose to smoke – a pipe, cigars or, by the 1870s, cigarettes – was an indication of his class and style.

Above all, though, the story of the smoker and the Skye terrier leaves us with an image of wordlessness. 'Silence is golden' seems a peculiarly English saying, yet it was in fact a Swiss proverb which English readers imbibed from Thomas Carlyle's *Sartor Resartus*, a curious blend of satire, biography and philosophy published in serial form in 1833–4. In this headily innovative work, the main character represented speech as 'too often . . . stifling and suspending thought', and suggested that holding one's tongue for a day would help order one's thoughts: 'what wreck and rubbish have those mute workmen within thee swept away, when intrusive noises were shut out!' Whereas speech was 'of time', silence was 'of eternity'.[10]

There is a Victorian thriftiness in any talk today of someone 'wasting' words. I am struck, for instance, by the *Dragons' Den* panellist Deborah Meaden saying in an interview with the *Guardian* that 'I don't believe in wasting time, in wasting words. I don't speak for the sake of speaking.'[11] Yet what one person perceives as wasted words will be another's idea of healthy interaction: conversation, and indeed all social life, involves redundancy. The word *redundancy* carries a certain stigma, but I am using it here to refer to things that appear superfluous rather than things that have no function. When we communicate, the apparently redundant elements of what we say (or write) prevent ambiguity. They also help the effectiveness of messages – consider, for instance, the repetitive nature of a lot of advertising – and assure social ease by keeping channels of communication open and by avoiding a directness that might seem aggressive or just too tightly packed with information.

The Victorian aversion to wasted words was part of a new science of conversation. Writing at the end of the century, Beatrice Knollys in her *The Gentle Art of Good Talking* (1899) asserted that 'A good conversationist [*sic*], unlike the poet, is made, not born', and 'To be a social success . . . a bright, sparkling champagne style of conversation is . . . to be cultivated.' She referred to the 'golden tongue of silence', evidently superior to the 'silver tongue of speech', and to other types she identified, such as the 'electro-plated tongue of deceit', the 'satin tongue of courtly hypocrisy' and the 'india-rubber tongue of tact'. She was able to review an age in which conversation was treated as if a discipline with exact principles. To be the Demosthenes of the drawing room was to be the master of a rigid, morally scrupulous exercise. In a volume entitled *Conversation: Why Don't We Do More Good by It?* (1886), George Seaton Bowes identified four types of conversation: informational, cheerful, helpful and spiritual. Examining other books on conversation, he reflected that 'They are most of them of a negative character. They tell us what our talk should not be, and dwell upon the evil of trifling, backbiting, slander, pedantry, exaggeration.' The proper purpose of conversation was to provide 'food for the mind'.[12]

English taciturnity was matched by a dislike of noise. This was supposed to be racial in origin. Paul Langford glosses the view then common: 'The Gothic peoples of the sunless north were given to introverted brooding forced on them by their domestic isolation in an adverse climate.' Sensitivity to noise was a way of demonstrating superiority. James Sully, a psychologist, wrote in 1878 that 'The sufferings which afflict the sensitive ear in our noisy cities are largely due to the general dullness of people with respect to disagreeable sounds.'[13] Among those exceptionally elevated above such dullness were Thomas Carlyle, who took refuge from crowing roosters and the shouts of street hawkers in a soundproof study, and the mathematician Charles Babbage, whose public outbursts over the noise made by organ-grinders caused his neighbours to terrorize him, breaking his windows and leaving dead cats on his doorstep.[14]

Campaigners against noise associated it with crime, sickness and a distaste for the life of the mind. Their efforts embodied the middle-class Victorian zeal for collective action, and that zeal was often focused not just on curbing lawlessness, but on defining it. This was a period seized by a mania for legislation. For instance, the laws of association football were codified in 1863, converting a raucous, reckless pastime into a regulated activity and a means of shaping character. Football had long been associated with gratuitous aggression. In his immense history of the sport, *The Ball Is Round*, David Goldblatt traces this, reproducing early on a proclamation issued by Edward II in 1314 about 'certain tumults arising from great footballs in the fields'. The Victorians recognized that football could be something else: a means of teaching young people about co-operation. Sportsmanship was not exactly an invention of this period – it was as old as the ancient Olympics – but it thrived as compulsory games flourished in the new boarding schools, which espoused an ethos of vigorous amateurism. Sport was intended to keep violent instincts at bay, and football, once its codes were clear, could be 'an instrument of Darwinian selection' and a lesson in the healthiness of competition.[15]

The Victorian appetite for legislation was evident in both the public and private spheres, and it extended to all departments of existence. There was nothing Victorian polite society liked more than having its ordinary beliefs packaged as nonpareils of wisdom. One man who excelled at this was Martin Tupper, a poet with a facility for grand-sounding proverbial philosophy. His books, now forgotten, were immensely popular; a tour of America and Canada in 1851 enlarged his reputation, and his platitudes, though they gave rise to the disapproving adjectives *Tupperish* and *Tupperian*, were treated by his many admirers as if they were the words of an oracle. 'To join advantage to amusement, to gather profit with pleasure,' he wrote in one of his poems, 'Is the wise man's necessary aim, when he lieth in the shade of recreation.'[16] Tupper tapped into the Victorians' enthusiasm for having their qualities itemized, labelled and sold back to them.

The myth of idyllic domesticity, a product of the 1830s and 1840s, was an example of this. In the home it was possible to regulate life precisely. The disparity between the public and the private was emphasized, and the privacy of family life was treated as the true location of respectability. This idea was developed through a vast literature that made women the leading actors in the theatre of domestic life. Especially popular were the writings of Sarah Stickney Ellis, who in a succession of books defined the sphere of influence of women in middle-class families. One such work was *The Wives of England* (1843), in which she set out the duties of wives along with details of their 'domestic influence' and 'social obligations'. She spoke of 'the way to make others happy, and consequently to be happy ourselves', and of the necessity 'for all women to have learned to manage themselves, before undertaking the management of a household'. The essential principles of a well-run home were 'order, justice, and benevolence'; its mistress 'should appear calm . . . whether she feels so or not' and should maintain this 'by the mastery of judgement over impulse'.[17]

Domestic virtue and domestic management were the unseen pillars of Empire. Rafts of magazines aimed at a female audience combined instruction in thrift with (mild) entertainment. Housekeeping was an area in which women, so often treated as passive or as if children, could exert real influence. On the first page of *The Book of Household Management* (1861), a splendidly decisive volume, Isabella Beeton declared that 'As with the commander of an army . . . so it is with the mistress of a house.'[18] But the robust tone of works in this vein could not conceal their basic emphasis on female sacrifice.

Before Stickney Ellis, many of the publications aimed at young women were concerned with recreation. A representative example is *The Young Lady's Book* of 1829. This offers guidance on moral deportment (uppermost are 'piety, integrity, fortitude, charity, obedience, consideration, sincerity, prudence, activity, and cheerfulness' – a sort of Ten Commandments) and the appreciation of flowers ('A bunch of wild flowers is a gallery of landscapes'), as well as presentation ('Jewellery should never be used to cover any imperfections of form in the neck') and archery (in shooting, the arrow should be 'brought not towards the eye, but the ear'). Stickney Ellis and the many others like her wrote of the lives of young women in terms that had little to do with personal amusement. In *The Wives of England* it is suggested that 'young women should cultivate habits of attention to the public as well as the private affairs of the country in which they live, so far as to obtain a general knowledge of its laws and institutions.' The correct use of such knowledge would allow them 'to carry out the views of an enlightened legislature through . . . minor channels'.[19]

One of the period's key developments was a new emphasis on timekeeping. This was crucial on the railways and in factories. But it was also important at home, especially where meals were concerned. As more and more people had clocks in their homes and watches on their person (the watch, a luxury item until well into the nineteenth century, became a badge of solvency), exactness about time became the norm. However, openly checking one's watch was considered impolite. A lady was expected to check the time behind a fan and to have the dial plate of her timepiece concealed within a case. Among the consequences of closer timekeeping was a greater arbitrariness about what were the right and wrong times for certain kinds of activity. Prescriptions about timing replaced an intuitive understanding of it. Lewis Carroll's White Rabbit, constantly fussing about the time, is a true Victorian.

Sarah Stickney Ellis warned her readers that they should make a habit of 'minute calculations upon the value and progress of time', as 'Every year, and month, and day, have their separate amount of responsibility.'[20] It was necessary to be as careful about spending one's time as one was about spending one's money. Yet amid all this concern with precise timing, women of the upper classes were understood to have a great deal of leisure. Increasingly, they were able to socialize away from home. There were more places for the nineteenth-century woman to go, and she could go there more freely. In the second half of the century, the use of chaperones declined. The sheltered miss was still common, but the streets of large towns were full of unaccompanied women.

The development of lunch as a social occasion was part of a broadening of what we might call 'the public day'. This became noticeable in the 1860s. By the end of the century, lunch was established as a necessary part of a lady's schedule – the beginning of the day's sociability. Men were likely to lunch elsewhere, at clubs or taverns or restaurants. Although eating away from home has long been necessary, the restaurant has existed in Europe for not much more than 250 years, and in Britain it did not catch on till the second half of the nineteenth century.

Only at evening engagements were men and women equally represented. Deference was a mechanism for preserving dignity in such situations. Historian Michael Curtin itemizes the three main types of deference paid to Victorian ladies: the right to be first or occupy the best places, the right to have their physical needs attended to, and the right to be introduced only to those who had been carefully selected for the privilege. In each case this looked very much like the deference traditionally due to superiors, and 'the deference paid to ladies superseded that given to superiors: in almost all cases a superior gentleman deferred to an inferior lady. He carried her packages, passed through doorways second, yielded her right of recognition after an introduction, etc.'[21]

Even so, some of the mechanisms of deference, such as the bow and the curtsy, were in decline. Still required on formal occasions, they had otherwise given way to less theatrical greetings, and where curtsies were performed they were more economical – part curtsy, part bow. *A Present for an Apprentice* discoursed at some length about handshakes: 'never receive the hand even of a stranger with coldness or suspicion' and, in approaching another, 'throw your kindling and gladdened eye right into his, and give him your hand at once without any preliminary flourish.'[22] By the end of the century, books of etiquette had moved on and were giving details of when it was acceptable to 'cut' acquaintances (i.e. pretending not to recognize them).

Alert to their readers' liking for using first impressions to inform social judgements, Victorian etiquette writers tended to expatiate on linguistic faux pas. Purity of expression could quickly be measured, and was understood as a sign of moral purity and patriotic good character. But the 'proper' use of English was conceived in defensive terms rather than positive ones. In this vein Oliver Bell Bunce published in 1883 a manual entitled *Don't: A Manual of Mistakes and Improprieties More or Less Prevalent in Conduct and Speech*. Bunce's linguistic guidance consisted of injunctions such as 'Don't speak ungrammatically.' More interesting than his remarks about improper language are his proscriptions about what one can do in public: 'Don't carry cane or umbrella in a crowd horizontally', 'Don't smoke in the street, unless in unfrequented avenues', 'Don't eat fruit or anything else in the public streets', 'Don't be over-civil' ('haste to wait on others is over-civility'), 'Don't at any public entertainment make a move to leave the auditorium before the performance is over.'[23] The trouble, as we all recognize, is that an instruction beginning with the word *Don't* immediately has an effect that is the opposite of the one desired. Don't think of a grey kitten.

Saying 'Don't' is an abrupt kind of censoriousness. The term we now inevitably associate with this kind of attitude is *snob*. Snobbishness is seen by foreigners as a peculiarly English ailment – and one that masquerades as a talent. The history of the word *snob* is worth unpacking. Originally a slang term for a cobbler or his apprentice, it had by the middle of the nineteenth century become a term for someone who was trying to advance socially (a businessman seeking to pass himself off as a gentleman). Yet by the end of the century, its sense had shifted and it denoted someone who on the basis only of background regarded himself as better than those of lower social rank. This was a striking inversion. Theodore Zeldin has observed that 'The purpose of snobbery is to limit conversation.'[24] Snobbery is a form of vulgarity practised by people intent on identifying and repelling vulgarity; it is the beacon of an unearned sense of their own excellence. It comes in many varieties (intellectual, aesthetic, sexual, sartorial) but is always an attempt to consolidate a superiority that may not actually exist. The snob shows us the difference between civility, which makes a virtue of tolerance, and etiquette, which is uncompromising and looks a lot like intolerance.

As far as linguistic snobbery was concerned, Oliver Bell Bunce was subscribing to a mature tradition. A good deal of snobbery involves not using words and expressions that have been soiled by heavy use. The most notable book on this theme is Hester Piozzi's *British Synonymy* (1794), billed as 'an attempt at regulating the choice of words in familiar conversation'. Mrs Piozzi, once a close friend of Samuel Johnson, observed that parents and teachers 'wear out their lives in keeping the confines of conversation free from all touch of vicinity with ordinary people, who are known to be such . . . the moment they open their mouths'. Using vulgar words here seems very much like having bad breath.[25]

But it is not enough to avoid ordinary words and their nasty smell. Using twee alternatives is in fact a graver offence, a mistake made while trying to avoid a mistake. The most celebrated discussion of this is comparatively recent: Nancy Mitford's collection *Noblesse Oblige* (1956) includes a simplified version of an article by Alan Ross about 'class indicators' in English. This draws a distinction between 'U' and 'non-U' terms: the legitimate, correct, upper-class words, and the illegitimate, incorrect, lower-class ones, which tend to be pretentious evasions of the everyday. Thus *jam* is U, *preserve* non-U; *rich* is U, *wealthy* is non-U; *napkin* is U, *serviette* is non-U; *lavatory paper* is U, *toilet paper* is non-U; and so on. This is the kind of distinction most people today affect to find laughable and maybe even odious. But we certainly make judgements about the little details of people's vocabulary that speak of their background and aspirations (the receptive and the elective), although we are likely to insist that we do not.

Though not a uniquely Victorian pursuit, regulating language was a Victorian obsession. There was a pernickety concern with the 'best' usage; those who deviated from it could expect to be punished, and their offences were discussed as if moral rather than linguistic. Arguments about pure and proper English were pursued by bossy amateurs with a pretence of scientific precision, but the fixation with shibboleths and tests reflected a limited understanding of both language and science.[26]

Today there are New Victorians who profess admiration for the rigid values of their forebears, though they hardly honour them. Their paternalism is clumsily literal-minded. As Gertrude Himmelfarb writes in a fierce critique of this 'travesty of Victorianism', the New Victorians create legislation that their supposed antecedents would have found embarrassingly overt. 'Today's moralists,' writes Himmelfarb, have a 'far-away, fanatical glint in their eye'. Their concern is not 'the kinds of crime that agitate most citizens – violent, irrational, repeated, and repeatedly unpunished'. Instead they push for 'new legislation to punish speech or conduct normally deemed uncivil', and seek to criminalize words and behaviour that were formerly regarded as simply vulgar or distasteful.[27]

Perhaps what is truly Victorian in the modern world is the tendency to treat as sacrosanct things that are arbitrary: colonial borders, for instance, or the exact size and format of a visiting card. People uphold and defend contingent values precisely because they are contingent – an expression of *their* truth. 'We do things this way because this is the way we do them,' a starchy train manager tells me, when I ask why in a so-called quiet carriage I can't silently listen to my iPod to drown out the noise of the adjacent travellers playing Connect Four. When he catches me in the act for a second time and I question the sense of the rule, he threatens to involve the British Transport Police. We have the following exchange: 'There are good reasons why you can't listen to your MP3 player in a quiet carriage.' 'What are they?' 'I couldn't tell you.' 'Is that because they don't exist?' 'No, it's because it doesn't matter what they are. What matters is *that* they are.'

20

Curb your enthusiasm

new ways for new times

Although my use of an iPod in a quiet carriage precipitated a volley of Victorianism from a train manager, the situation was in most respects a colourfully modern one. It made me feel like the often-offending, often-offended Larry David in *Curb Your Enthusiasm*. This is apt, for there is perhaps no better primer in the prolixity of modern manners than that HBO comedy series. In every episode Larry comes up against the miserable truth that there is a difference between being right and doing what's considered polite. In principle Larry favours good manners, but in practice they seem archaic or nonsensical.

In the first episode of the opening season, Larry argues with his irritating friend Richard. Larry has had a run-in with Richard's new girlfriend at the cinema: he wanted her to move her legs so that he could get past her to his seat, and she was ungracious about it. Richard defends his girlfriend, and attempts to convey her good qualities by saying she likes to read the Jewish writer and activist Elie Wiesel. Larry responds, 'You know what she should be reading? Emily Fucking Post.'

The reference will be lost on a large part of the show's

international audience. But in America, Emily Post is the doyenne of Doing It Right. Although she died in 1960, her legacy continues. Her writings and the work of the Emily Post Institute highlight an important fact about Americans' attitude to social niceties: they are much less embarrassed (than the English, than pretty much anyone) about asking what is correct and aspiring to self-improvement. Post's principles permeated the American middle class, and live on in the many places American middle-class values now reach. While the English may not read Emily Post, and may not even have heard of her, they have seen the fruits of her work.

Post stumbled into writing about manners. A socialite and the author of half a dozen novels, she was contracted in 1921, aged nearly fifty, to write an encyclopedia of etiquette. This was a time when, thanks to a flood of advertisements introduced with statements such as 'Everybody tittered when I took an olive with my fork', a lot of people tittered at the mention of a guide to etiquette. A lot of people – but not everybody. Alongside advertisements for soap, deodorants and mouthwash, magazines frequently contained articles bemoaning the decay of American manners. Post prospered by responding to this perception. Her syndicated advice column would eventually appear in more than 150 newspapers, and during the Second World War her *Etiquette* was reportedly the most requested book among GIs. Her attitudes, as a *New Yorker* profile remarked in 1930, were idealistic. She believed that a gentleman 'affected by alcohol' should not appear in the presence of ladies. In the words of the profile's author, Helen Huntington Smith, 'The problem of a lady affected by alcohol she neglects to take up.'[1]

There were rivals, chief among them Lillian Eichler, whose *The Book of Etiquette* (1921) was for a time an even bigger bestseller. But, as the critic Edmund Wilson observed, Eichler's manner was comfortable and made social life sound jolly, whereas Emily Post had real imaginative powers and a much stronger snob appeal. F. Scott Fitzgerald told Wilson that reading Post's *Etiquette* had inspired him to think of writing a play in which the characters were preoccupied with doing the right thing.[2] Post scored with the public precisely because she was alive to the unjolly, uncomfortable competitiveness of the world.

From the outset Post provided a wealth of detail about what to do at dances, christenings and funerals, how to write letters, how to dress and how to greet people. Yet she also recognized that society was forever changing. She made this plain in the first edition of *Etiquette*, published in 1922, and her attention to change is evident if we compare successive editions of her work. The first edition was presented on the title page as a guide to etiquette *in society, in business, in politics and at home*; the tenth, published in 1960, was simply *The Blue Book of Social Usage*, reflecting the work's established status. Some of the changes are as we would expect, the society of *The Great Gatsby* having turned into the world of *Mad Men*; the 1960 edition addresses travel on aeroplanes, whereas the 1922 edition naturally has nothing to say about this. Another shift, less immediately obvious: the fear of disagreeable occurrences, to the fore in 1922, has by 1960 been displaced by a fear of criticism.

Post's coverage of restaurants is a sign of changing habits. In 1922 she is concerned with whether one can wear a headdress in a restaurant, and explains that an engaged couple may have lunch or tea in such an establishment, but should not take their evening meal there. In 1960 she is more concerned with tipping, a subject that in 1922 came up in the context only of hotels, steamboats and other people's domestic servants. 'It is impossible to give definite schedules for tipping,' she writes in 1960. She does her best, but mainly seems startled that 'The ten per cent rule of yesterday is today at least fifteen and sometimes even twenty!'[3] As 'rules' go, that's vague. Yet here she offers a useful perspective on one of the more vexed forms of gratitude.

As a word for a small present of money given to a servant or a dutiful schoolboy, *tip* emerged in the eighteenth century – not, as myth has it, an acronym for 'to insure promptness' – and gained real currency in the nineteenth. (The word *gratuity* was used with this sense by the middle of the sixteenth century; it sometimes had connotations of bribery.) The tip is embarrassing because it is a brief acknowledgement of unequal status, of the fact that different lives have momentarily touched. Walter Donaldson's *Synopsis Oeconomica* (1620) stressed that servants should be paid on time, but advised against handing out gratuities. In 1760 the Select Society, an Edinburgh debating club that included David Hume, considered the question of whether one should tip servants and firmly concluded that one should not. Hannah More was among many writers of the period to condemn giving tips (often known as *vails*) in the home; Voltaire, having dined once with Lord Chesterfield, turned down a second invitation because the servants expected such great vails. The Victorian actor Sir Henry Irving was noted for the generous tips he gave; he laughed off the complaints of his frequent collaborator Ellen Terry, who felt such generosity was vulgar. The modern service charge, automatically added to one's restaurant bill, is a sanitized version of the tip, supposedly designed to insure against the meanness or forgetfulness of customers, guarantee staff a decent wage, and satisfy the taxman.

'You will not get good service unless you tip generously but not lavishly,' states Emily Post. 'Tipping is undoubtedly an undesirable and undignified system, but it happens to be in force.'[4] One of the ironies of guides to manners is that they often bolster practices they would prefer to condemn. Saying that something happens to be in force implies a degree of nuisance or absurdity, but it does not have the effect of quelling that 'something'.

Post's central credo was that codes must be observed as strictly as possible, even if their logic is questionable. The key to success was conformity. Her first rule of behaviour was 'Try to do and say only that which will be agreeable to others.' If you were to abide by this religiously, you would never say anything of consequence. However, Post offers many pieces of counsel that, scrupulously followed, would avert life's awkwardnesses. That they are no longer observed does not make them worthless. For instance, 'Don't plaster your face with powder until it no longer has any semblance of skin . . . Remember that a mask can never take the place of a face'; 'Intimate letters of condolence are like love letters in that they are too sacred and too personal to follow a set form'; and, when playing cards, 'The good loser makes it an invariable rule never to play for stakes that it will be inconvenient to lose.'[5] We may find the pronouncements a touch prim, but there is wisdom here, a sense of life lived and examined.

Many have taken up Post's mantle. One of her inheritors, Amy Vanderbilt, hosted a TV show called *It's in Good Taste* in the 1950s, and her writings were carried in numerous newspapers during the the 1950s, 1960s and 1970s. In 1968 she noted how widely it was asserted that American manners were uniformly bad, and argued against this, suggesting that 'The very mobility of American society brings into sharp focus the bad manners of the minority, thus making bad manners seem to be the norm.' Nevertheless, she identified certain reasons for the deterioration of manners: 'the decline of the mother's influence', a 'revolution in homemaking' that meant that 'houses are not necessarily homes', and a public language 'so free . . . that even grandmothers have become shockproof'. Her essential maxim was simple: 'Good manners . . . are the traffic rules of society.'[6] Her readers were perpetually anxious to give the right signals. In her final years she received 25,000 letters a month, and these enabled her to keep abreast of new bugbears and anxieties, ranging from when to take off one's sunglasses to how to behave in a sauna.

Another writer in the mould of Emily Post was Letitia Baldrige, who offered volumes of guidance aimed at executives, brides and mothers. A typical pronouncement from her *New Manners for New Times* (2003) is 'When children see parents accept situations that are morally wrong, it inspires them to grow up to become liars, cheats, and thieves – or perhaps extortionists, inside traders, and stock manipulators.'[7]

But the leader of the pack is Judith Martin. Since 1978 this American journalist has written a popular and widely syndicated advice column under the name Miss Manners. The title of her magnum opus suggests her temper: *Miss Manners' Guide to Excruciatingly Correct Behavior.* Like Emily Post before her, she invents characters, and her greatest invention is herself – poised, humorous, at times starchy, but the opposite of naïve. 'What is the proper way to eat potato chips?' a correspondent asks. Miss Manners mocks: 'With a knife and fork. A fruit knife and an oyster fork, to be specific.' She quips that arguments between husband and wife should be conducted in a foreign language: 'You'd be surprised what an inducement that is to the education of children.' Reflecting on matters of domestic taste she declares, 'No house can be truly elegant unless it contains at least half a dozen atrocities of varying sizes and uses. This must not include the residents.'[8]

Miss Manners has described her abhorrence of the 'Jean-Jacques Rousseau School of Etiquette': in a speech to Harvard students in 1984 she argued that Rousseau's ideas about children, filtered through the thought of Thomas Jefferson, have licensed sloppy parenting and an attitude summed up in the phrase 'I'm just as good as anyone else'.[9] Her preferred view is that 'the world needs . . . more false cheer'. The only acceptable answer to the question 'How are you?' is 'Very well, thank you. How are you?' Any other response is a symptom of the failure to discipline one's natural selfishness.

Curiously, one of the three epigraphs to Bret Easton Ellis's notoriously grisly novel *American Psycho* is a quotation from Miss Manners:

One of the major mistakes people make is that they think manners are only the expression of happy ideas. There's a whole range of behaviour that can be expressed in a mannerly way. That's what civilization is all about – doing it in a mannerly and not an antagonistic way. One of the places we went wrong was the naturalistic Rousseauian movement of the 1960s in which people said, 'Why can't you just say what's on your mind?' In civilization there have to be some restraints. If we followed every impulse, we'd be killing one another.[10]

The purport of this quotation is ambiguous. Is Ellis abjuring the attitudes of the 1960s? Or is he in fact hinting that mannerly behaviour and psychosis are compatible? Is he endorsing Miss Manners's view that codes of behaviour are essential to – and effective in – the repression of our violent urges, or is he playing ironically with this idea? This epigraph is sandwiched between a long quotation from Dostoevsky's *Notes from Underground*, about the inevitability of society engendering deformed characters, and a short one from a Talking Heads song: 'And as things fell apart / Nobody paid much attention.' Ellis's novel depicts moral apocalypse as the result of misdirected attention: by focusing on signs rather than meanings, modern capitalist society has sent into exile the very idea of meaning.

The essay in *Fortune* magazine from which Ellis took his Miss Manners quotation posed a number of workaday questions: Should you invite colleagues to your wedding? If someone lays claim to your handiwork in a meeting, should you speak up? Is it ever okay to bring your kids to the office? Miss Manners is clear-cut in her answers: 'I'm firmly against it', 'Yes', 'Basically, no.'[11] Most people, confronted with such questions, will hedge and fudge. Those who don't will generally be regarded as too abrupt and direct. Miss Manners has a rigid idea of common sense; her judicial process admits few grey areas. How should you respond when offered drugs, one of her readers wonders. The answer is that one should say either 'Yes, please' or 'No, thank you'.

Modern guides to manners have, naturally, to address questions that would not have troubled our great-grandparents. A selection of prescriptions from *Debrett's A–Z of Modern Manners* (2008) shows this: 'Trust your fake tan to the professionals'; 'Don't be an online bore: blogs that enumerate the minutiae of your day . . . won't make you popular'; at office parties 'Steer clear of mistletoe and dirty dancing'; when embarking on internet dating 'Use the best photograph you have'; and in the realm of social networking, 'Remember, it's not a competition to see how many friends you can get.'[12]

Debrett's A–Z is a British publication, whereas all the writers I have previously mentioned in this chapter are American. It is significant that in Britain guidance on etiquette is purveyed by a company that has existed since 1769, while in America there is a more personal touch – or at least an illusion of the personal. Americans seem to prefer a touch of homeliness, where the English like their etiquette served *de haut en bas*. Who is the leading English expert on manners, the equivalent of Judith Martin? It is hard to think of an individual whose authority is taken seriously. Indeed, people who present themselves as authorities on manners are automatically not taken seriously; they are treated as self-important throwbacks. It is as though the act of talking about manners makes manners disappear beneath a froth of drivel.

The closest we come to an English version of Miss Manners

may be Drusilla Beyfus. Her *Modern Manners* (1992) is substantial and wide-ranging but as a result has the appearance of a cookbook. It is sensible and worldly, yet sometimes causes unintentional amusement, as when it proceeds directly from thoughts about the etiquette of using condoms to discussing how to offer a proposal of marriage. A 1950s volume that is partly the work of Beyfus has the title *Lady Behave: A Guide to Modern Manners*, which says a lot about its intended audience and that audience's attitudes. An updated edition from 1969 is much concerned with 'the new woman', 'the new staff', 'the new manners' ('a slimmer's best compromise is to make her dieting as unobtrusive as possible') and 'new relationships' (which is mainly about dealing with doctors and nurses).[13]

The American market for straightforward guides to etiquette dwarfs the British one. Even though large numbers of the British and especially the English are sticklers for etiquette, they pretend that such matters are either unworthy of discussion or in no need of it. Much more popular are guides that give them cynical or supercilious treatment. These reflect, wittily and sometimes not so wittily, on when it is a good idea to lie, how to navigate the hell of a second family, and the art of deflecting people who threaten to be tedious. It is a defining feature of English manners that they can be treated, simultaneously, as vitally important yet also comical. But then one could apply the very same terms to Englishness itself.

21

Creative hubs and 'extreme phenomena'
negotiating the modern city

In an anonymously published dialogue dating from 1579, a gentleman called Valentine lists the reasons for preferring town life to country life. Among these are the better opportunities for education, public service and making money. His inter-locutor, Vincent, is at first unconvinced. He believes that urban folk have little love for one another; instead they hide behind 'ceremonies of civility'. But Valentine makes his case forcefully, and ends up persuading Vincent that city life is healthier and quieter than life in the country.[1]

Even in 1579 that was a brazen claim, and our own view of city life is likely to be more equivocal. The architecture scholar Elizabeth Collins Cromley, an expert on the resort hotel and the history of bedrooms, chose for her academic study of New York's early apartment buildings a singularly apt title: *Alone Together*. The apparent gregariousness of modern living is an illusion. In reality, towns and cities are scenes of impersonality and transience. True, they afford opportunities for collaboration – and may allow us, in the recent and popular view of the Harvard economist Edward Glaeser, to be happier, richer and greener. Freed from a preoccupation with obtaining food and shelter, people moving to cities from the country have long been able to engage in business and creative projects. But amid the social churn, anxiety festers. Urban citizens have tended to be more fearful about plague, fire, floods, foul smells and vermin, as well as more beset with rumours.

In cities, our physical proximity makes manners useful as a means of co-operating to achieve the best use of limited space, yet they are also a means of maintaining social distinctions that are constantly under pressure. Jonathan Raban evokes the psychological climate of city living in his book *Soft City*, published in 1974. 'In a community of strangers, we need a quick, easy-to-use set of stereotypes, cartoon outlines, with which to classify the people we encounter.' Accordingly, 'People who live in cities become expert at making . . . rapid, subconscious decisions,' and 'mechanical aids to such character-reading are at a premium in cities.' It is certainly a feature of modern city-dwellers that they are quick to pigeonhole those around them. 'The riot of amateur astrology,' observes Raban, 'is one of the more annoying expressions of this city hunger for quick ways of classifying people.' At the same time, though, character seems fluid in the city. One's presentation and personality appear to be constructs: 'Identity is presented as plastic, a matter of possessions and appearances.'[2]

Urban living exposes people to a relentless stream of stimuli. In the modern city this can be overwhelming, and the best defence against being overwhelmed is to develop cool indifference. That indifference can be a sterile inexpressiveness, or it can be something more callous, calling to mind George Orwell's alarming remark about England: 'In no country inhabited by white men is it easier to shove people off the pavement.'[3]

Anonymity makes rudeness easy. In cities, we avert our eyes from the sufferings of others because, if we allowed ourselves to become involved in their affairs, we would never get anything done. Or so we imagine – and so we have been conditioned to imagine.

'The deepest problems of modern life,' wrote the German sociologist Georg Simmel in 1903, 'flow from the attempt of the individual to maintain the independence and individuality of his existence against the sovereign powers of society.' Simmel argued that city life, fragile and dangerous, may stimulate the nerves to the point where they cease to be able to produce a reaction. He concluded that amid the impersonal culture of cities, individuals feel the need to save what he called a 'personal element'; the result is a cultivation of 'extremities and peculiarities'.[4]

A century on from Simmel, the public sphere feels anything but intimate, and we associate cities with a lack of social cohesion, with randomness and perhaps also unnaturalness (a state of decay rather than fertility). In a small, tightly woven community it is hard to do wrong with impunity, but a city's sheer size weakens social constraints, and the impersonal nature of its regulations seems almost to invite disregard.[5] In the modern city different cultures are meeting all the time, and so are different assumptions about conduct. These encounters resemble collisions more often than felicitous convergences. Communication with strangers seems impossible because it interferes with the apparently automated flow of human traffic. To make this personal for a moment: When did you last travel on the London Underground? And when did you last talk there to someone you'd not previously met? How do you react to a stranger addressing you on the Underground? (If you've never travelled on the London Underground, imagine using your local bus service at its busiest – and add in an extra batch of disgruntled commuters.) Cities feel like archives of grievance and grime, which we traverse mechanically.

Today most Europeans live in urban environments. Among the great narrative strands in twentieth-century history was the transformation of urban living. At the start of the century, three-quarters of England's population was urban – a high proportion compared to, say, France – and the crucial change was not that people moved to towns and cities, but that the towns and cities altered. They burst the boundaries that had previously contained them, becoming intricate clusters. According to the historian Emily Cockayne, the period from 1919 to 1944 was one of suburban development and semi-detached living; between 1945 and 1969 the spirit of semi-detachment became less harmonious; from 1970, detached living and home ownership increased; and today our informal encounters are ever more infrequent, with less and less significance attached to one's reputation on the street where one lives, and long-distance relationships, conducted electronically, often seeming more important than physically immediate ones.[6] It is not just the texture of home life that has altered; changes in the way we travel and the environment in which we work have transformed attitudes to space and the people with whom we share it.

Statistics afford a more precise sense of some of the key changes in Britain during the twentieth century. The number of permanent dwellings trebled, and the rate of owner-occupation of property increased from around 10 per cent to around 70. The number of children in the average family halved. The population of England and Wales increased by roughly 20 million (about 60 per cent). Life expectancy for newborn children increased by thirty years, and the rate of infant mortality declined from 15 per cent to 0.5. In 1904 there were 1.4 telephones per 100 people in London; in 2005 the figure nationally was 56.4 landlines per 100 people, while the number of mobile phones exceeded the number of people. At the start of the century there were 8,000 cars in Britain; by its end, the figure was above 20 million. To take a longer view: the crowd today attending a sold-out football match at Wembley Stadium contains more people than lived in the whole of London 500 years ago.

The data relating to phone ownership are arresting. Immediacy of access to people has had numerous beneficial effects, professionally and socially. But it erodes formality and privacy. While working on this chapter, I found myself on a bus sitting next to a fortyish man who began a phone conversation as follows: 'Hi, it's Dave, right? I just want to tell you to *fuck off*.' Nothing so very unusual in that, but imagine how the same communication would have had to be handled a hundred years ago. Standing on someone's doorstep and haranguing him, or penning a poisonous letter, is much more demanding than simply calling him up and insulting him. Evelyn Waugh, writing in 1962, referred to the telephone as a 'pernicious device', observing that 'People leave all arrangements vague in the knowledge that they can always ring up at the last moment and change them.'[7] This makes me wonder what Waugh would have thought of the mobile phone.

The telephone can also be held responsible for the popularization of the greeting *hello*. Thomas Edison suggested this as an alternative to the word favoured by the device's inventor,

Alexander Graham Bell, which was *ahoy*. *Hello* established itself, and in 1880, at America's first National Convention of Telephone Companies, there was a debut for the ingratiating 'Hello, I'm Henry' style of conference badge.[8] The rise of *hello* seems a small thing, but originally the word was a variant of *hallo*, which expressed a degree of surprise. A note of surprise remains in *hello*; it is a greeting more ambiguous than an assured 'Good morning' or 'Good evening'. The telephone changed not just our ability to communicate, but also the way we talk; when we don't have face-to-face contact with the person to whom we are speaking, we have to find verbal rather than visual methods of conveying attitudes, confirming attention and giving feedback.

Increased car ownership, beginning in the 1920s, played an even larger role in creating new departments of manners. There are rules of the road: the Highway Code has since 1931 been the official version of these. Then there are common courtesies: I acknowledge someone who lets me out at a junction, avoid tailgating other motorists, park so as not to block a driveway or the entrance to a garage. Behind both the rules and the courtesies is an awareness, which we necessarily blot out, that the car is a weapon. Kate Fox comments that English drivers are justly renowned for their orderliness and courtesy. Notwithstanding the way drivers shout insults and honk their horns, or even occasionally indulge in violent road rage, the norm is restraint, 'an extension of our queuing behaviour', redolent of inhibition and insularity.[9]

The car has transformed society, by enabling us to travel alone or only with people of our choosing. Traditionally, private travel has been the preserve of the rich; everyone else has had to share. The rise of the automobile created a new flexibility, and it also changed the landscape: suburbs grew, the function of streets narrowed, and motorists were better able to socialize beyond their immediate neighbourhoods. Increased use of cars led to public transport being thought of as a location of incivility. Meanwhile, in reality as in the advertisements, the car was a vehicle of fantasy and escape, allowing its owner to luxuriate in solipsism. In the late 1930s the American carmaker Nash Motors advertised one of its models with the apposite slogan 'It'll lead you astray – and you'll like it!'

As cars became more affordable and ownership grew, people drove themselves rather than being driven. By taking responsibility for something that would traditionally have been done for them, the new motorists made certain roles obsolete. This was also happening through the proliferation of domestic appliances such as vacuum cleaners. The double-edged nature of the term 'labour-saving' was implicit in the slogan 'Let electricity be your servant.'

Here we touch on a major change that took place in Britain in the twentieth century: the decline of domestic service. In 1901 the Ladies' Sanitary Association, a voluntary group that had sprung up in the 1850s, published a booklet entitled *Rules for the Manners of Servants in Good Families*:'Move quietly about the house', 'Never sing or whistle at your work', 'Always answer when you receive an order or a reproof . . . to show you have heard', 'Do not smile at droll stories told in your presence.'[10] By the 1940s such publications were redundant. There was a sharp fall in the number of men and women – especially women – employed in other people's houses. When P. G. Wodehouse's Jeeves first appeared in 1915, the immaculate valet was a familiar contemporary figure; by the time of the last Jeeves novel, in 1974, Wodehouse's creation had become a benign archaism. In America, too, domestic service declined; Emily Post first thought to pen a chapter 'On the Servantless House' in 1928.

The decline of domestic service is part of the larger story of the changing world of work: more jobs in the service sector and fewer in industry and agriculture, women's increasing participation in the labour force, global competition, outsourcing, rising unemployment, and employers seeking more flexible arrangements with those who work for them. This accelerated in the final decades of the twentieth century as technology destabilized old notions of employment and blue-collar jobs vanished. While political rhetoric about job creation has not abated, temporary and freelance work have come to seem ordinary. As with the rise of car culture, the changes in infrastructure have affected not only practicalities, but also attitudes. Modern workers' feelings about their jobs are likely to be insecure, uncommitted or mercenary. In the late twentieth century, perhaps for the first time ever, it did not seem absurd to claim that on average the rich worked harder than the poor. This is not to deny that some of the richest people are gallingly indolent. But members of today's affluent executive class are shackled to their jobs, and one consequence of this is that they are embarrassingly remote from members of all other classes.

At the same time, the physical experience of being at work has changed, in all sectors, thanks in large measure to new technology. This is true for those employed on the land, in factories and in offices. For Britain's legions of office workers, conduct in the workplace is shaped by the design of the workplace and the systems that are used there, as well as by the law, the particular culture created by an employer, and of course the nature of the work being carried out.

In the final decades of the last century, there were significant changes in the architecture of offices: a move from the cellular to the open-plan. This in fact had less to do with architects than with the insights of management consultants: the watchwords were flexibility, democracy, teamwork and reduced overheads. The German consulting firm Quickborner revolutionized office landscaping in the 1950s; in America, Hewlett-Packard pioneered open-plan office space, apparently leading to a surge in demand for ear plugs.[11] Additionally, the commercial development of air conditioning in the 1950s made it possible for offices to have 'deep space'. Those who have spent much time in this kind of space will attest that, while it seems convenient to planners, it suffers from a depressing lack of sensory richness and dampens cognitive activity. Only in one sense is it deep.

These changes have meant that in the realm of business, where class distinctions were previously tenacious, hierarchy has been flattened. But the push for egalitarianism hasn't really eradicated images of status, and, for all the rhetoric about creativity and collaboration, mutual respect and team players, flexibility and informality, the modern workplace is a sphere still stiff with etiquette. It is one kind of etiquette replacing another, rather than the eradication of any such code: now we are obliged to believe in a professional world where the transaction is more important than the relationship, though we talk about relationships more and more, to make up for our flitty, momentary work life, the defining feature of which is impatience.

22

Location, location, location

The phrase I have chosen for the first half of this chapter's title could easily have come up before now. Grating though it may be, it is more than just the smug mantra of estate agents. Our understanding of all behaviour is tied to location. Our very sense of self is positional: when I think of myself, it is not as a dislocated entity, but as a being in a place. The ways we express our psychological and emotional states are similar to the ways we express physical ones. The language we use of our everyday activities and feelings is suffused with *in* and *out*, *up* and *down*, *here* and *there*, *towards* and *away*. Principal among these words is *in*. We have a consistent sense of being located, *in* space and *in* time. We also think in terms of boundaries: we have strong feelings, not necessarily explicable, about when *here* becomes *there* and *in* becomes *out*.

When we think about manners, we think about places: the places that bring on particular kinds of behaviour, the places where we are likely to face challenges. We are conscious of the rules of place. At the same time, the unconscious is sensitive to circumstances. Two episodes from my own life may serve to illuminate this a little.

First, I am sitting in a café in a small town in the West

Midlands, eating a late breakfast. A burly man in his forties flumps down at my table. 'Mind if I sit here?' It isn't really a question. He personalizes his side of the table, lining up sauce bottles and slapping his newspaper into submission. He looks at the book I am reading – short stories – and eyes me in a manner I find threatening. 'You're not from round here, are you?' I acknowledge that I am from London. He snorts ('Not a London type of place, this'), apologizes for having a cold ('It's not even a proper cold'), and asks what my politics are. The conversation unfurls: football, TV, the music buzzing from the café's radio. We somehow miss out the weather. He offers to buy me a cup of tea – 'Oh, coffee, is it? Very *cosmopolitan*' – and we keep talking. After twenty minutes he gives me his email address, explaining that he will be coming to London soon and it would be useful to get the details of one or two decent pubs. 'I like a personal recommendation,' he says. 'Nothing posh, mind, just pubby pubs.' He insists on paying for another drink for me ('I spoiled your lunch, didn't I?'), and then leaves, saluting most of the other customers by nicknames as he exits and belching theatrically in the doorway. 'Couldn't help myself,' he says with undisguised glee. When I look again at the email address he has written down – a playful handle – I realize I didn't ask his name and wasn't told it: this is one of those things foreigners remark on, the English tendency to withhold their names as if guarding a secret (or making a mystery out of something prosaic, for until we know that Bob is Bob we may imagine he is Duwayne or Galahad). A moment later he pops back to 'grab a sandwich for later'. 'We're not good at goodbyes,' he muses. He could be speaking for himself or a whole nation.

A few days later I go to the bar of a hotel in London's Mayfair. It is a five-star establishment and not the sort of place I usually visit. Although I am not dressed all that differently from other patrons, and although my companion certainly doesn't look out of place, we are treated shabbily. We seem to be invisible to the bar staff. They are not invisible to me; I register the studiousness with which they ignore me. In the end we do manage to order drinks, but, once we have sat at a table, we are unable to order a second round. Staff look past us, and fawn over other customers. The table next to ours is cleared, slowly, by three waiters: this is intentional inefficiency, a passive-aggressive move. We decide to find a more congenial location, but it takes more than ten minutes to interest someone in bringing the bill. This includes a 'discretionary service charge'. I ask for it to be removed, as the service has been non-existent. I am told that it cannot be removed. Perhaps I should make a fuss, but instead I meekly pay. I use cash, which is examined sceptically. As we leave, the manager ushers me towards the exit with a ludicrously insincere flourish. At no point does anyone tell me I have done anything wrong, let alone tell me *what* I have done wrong.

Our reactions to places are strongly linked to our experience of people we encounter there. Thus we dislike a restaurant because of bad service or the proximity of obnoxious diners. We find a health spa calming not only because of the facilities it offers, but also because of the unruffled demeanour of its staff and the placidity of other patrons. The reverse can apply: a spa fails to restore us because it is full of abrasive people, and a restaurant's appeal stems partly from its clientele. A space's tone can have a positive influence on those who use it, but it can also be violated.

Particular locations call for particular kinds of behaviour. This may seem an obvious point, but, precisely because it feels obvious, we do not tend to scrutinize it. We understand the tonal purposes of spaces: location influences what we think of as acceptable behaviour. And, in ways that we are barely able to recognize, the imagery with which we are surrounded orients our behaviour.

Even within an apparently unified culture, and at a specific time, manners vary. We know this well. One person's idea of necessary decorum is another's of archaic fussiness. The shepherd Corin in Shakespeare's *As You Like It* tells Touchstone, a witty townie, that 'Those that are good manners at the court are as ridiculous in the country as the behaviour of the country is most mockable at the court.' Quite so. What's more, as individuals we apply different standards of manners in different situations. This is akin to code-switching (or style-shifting, as it is also known) in language: I speak and behave one way in a job interview or at a funeral, and in another when at the races or in a roadside diner. This isn't a sinister feat of dissimulation; it is a largely predictable and strategic move, driven by our sense of what is appropriate in a particular situation as well as by our need to define our relationship to that situation.

I am likely, unconsciously or semi-consciously, to alter the way I express myself according to whether I'm speaking at a wake or trying to defuse an argument in a bar, and in much the same way my sense of what's offensive will change according to whether I'm visiting a shrine or sitting in a jacuzzi, shopping at a supermarket or browsing in an antiquarian bookshop. Many instances of rudeness stem from a failure to suit words and actions to occasion and setting. But the capacity to judge suitability is not innate. Rather, it relies on a grasp of convention. In the Chamber of the House of Commons one must not refer to another Member by name, but it is all right for the Chancellor of the Exchequer to drink alcohol while delivering his Budget – Gladstone used to take sherry with a beaten egg. This is hardly a state of affairs one could intuit.

Our experience of rudeness has a lot to do with our sense that the conventions of place are being breached. Contrary to what we might imagine, the locations of incivility are not places where we feel out of our depth (a 'dodgy' area) so much as places we frequent: the supermarket, the road when we are driving, residential streets near where we live, pubs and bars, cafés and restaurants, public transport, car parks, the gym, and maybe the cinema, a park or a concert venue. We experience rudeness more when 'getting somewhere' than when 'being somewhere'. In their study of the role of the rude stranger in everyday life, sociologists Philip Smith, Timothy Phillips and Ryan King conclude that we meet with rudeness mainly among 'ordinary' people and in ordinary places. In fact, the peak moment for experiencing it is around lunchtime. The explanation is straightforward: the denser our interactions, the more potential there is for rudeness (or at least for spying it). Rudeness most often occurs when the victim and the perpetrator are in motion.[1]

The home is usually thought of as a refuge from such abuses. The idea of home as a place of sanctuary is summed up in the well-worn line that 'An Englishman's home is his castle.' This is more than just an image of the inviolable threshold, of the delight we take in pulling up the drawbridge and lowering the portcullis; it touches upon questions of law, politics and psychology. Privacy is paramount. This is why English people like their homes to be hard to find, and make expertly unhelpful use of signs and barely visible house numbers to ensure this. It is also why front gardens exist for display, whereas the garden at the rear of a property, much less visible and usually much less carefully tended, is for enjoyment.

The desire to live in a house is strong. Apartments may be practical and adequate, but the wish for something more is almost universal. The trailer, even though it usually affords less space than the meanest sort of apartment, is presented as a house on wheels. In places where we are surrounded by vast numbers of other people – as at a music festival, for instance – there is the urge, even as we exult in shared experience, to summon up the atmosphere of domesticity. In fact, one of the pleasures of festival-going and camping seems to be that it is an excuse to spend the night in a little room you erect and then nest in, surrounded by your clutter. Your tent is another kind of castle.

The places we live announce to others who and what we are. Yet if a house can be a projection of character, it can also shape one's behaviour in unintended ways, creating identity rather than expressing it. In a shared property, a lot depends on whether you have a room of your own with a door that locks. If you live in a palace with 1,000 rooms, you will behave differently from how you would in a bedsit where sleeping and eating happen in the same space. 'Differently' does not mean 'better'. The houses of the social elite have long influenced ideas of politeness; they have typically been hard to get to, or at least hard to get into, and have thus embodied the relationship between grandeur and exclusivity – a patrician aloofness.

The story of domestic space and its development is, in broad terms, one of specialization: different rooms for different purposes. Even at the top of society, it was once usual to do everything in a single space, as is still the case for some people in Britain and many in less economically developed countries. As Bill Bryson writes in *At Home*, his genial history of private life: 'No room has fallen further in history than the hall. Now a place to wipe feet and hang hats, once it was the most important room in the house. Indeed, for a long time it *was* the house.'[2]

A large medieval house was a collection of rooms surrounding a central unit: hall, kitchen, chapel. By the sixteenth century, the most important room was the great chamber, sometimes known as the dining chamber. By the seventeenth, many houses had corridors, and voluntary isolation was possible; even if few people enjoyed much privacy, there was at least a sense that not all areas of the home were communal. By the eighteenth century, the hall had generally been reduced to a vestibule, servants were consigned to the backstairs (a word that came in around 1650), and a series of communal rooms running into one another were used for social occasions. Polite entertainment required compartmentalization: separate rooms for gathering, dancing and taking meals. These had to be some distance from the front door, to reduce the chances of anyone tumbling muddily into a sophisticated gathering.[3] As domestic space became more specialized, so manners seemed to have more particular departments. In Victorian England, guides to manners were concerned with the behaviour appropriate to each room and the circumstances in which one moved from one room to the next.

The fundamental truth here is that you cannot talk about manners without an awareness of environment. Our experience of environment primes our decisions. A particularly curious demonstration of this was an experiment conducted in 2010 at Cornell University, in which psychologist David Pizarro and PhD student Erik Helzer found that students quizzed about their political attitudes voiced more conservative views if interviewed while standing near a hand sanitizer dispenser.[4] This is a small-scale example of something that happens on a much larger scale: we respond to cues that are environmental (and perhaps also olfactory in the case of the hand sanitizer), and as we do so we are largely unaware of what these cues are. Our bodies do not merely register the effects of the choices we make; often they inform our judgements.

23

A fluid world

Although middle-class domestic space became more specialized in the nineteenth century, the living conditions of the
poor, especially the urban poor, remained cramped, high rents
notwithstanding. There was space in the suburbs, but not in
the neighbourhoods where workers needed to live in order
to be near their places of employment. The poor could not
retreat to a soundproof study, as Carlyle did; their lives were
noisy and always available for inspection – by their neighbours,
and also by philanthropists who came to examine them. Tools,
crockery and clothes were jumbled together. Children might
sleep three or four to a bed. Family matters were unavoidably
public.

Although there are still people in Britain who live in such
conditions, in the last hundred years the amount of domestic
space enjoyed by the poor has increased a great deal. Patterns
of land ownership have changed, too. Today 70 per cent of
the population has a stake in Britain's land; less than 150 years
ago, the figure was 4.5 per cent. In the 1870s a population of
28 million occupied 3.84 million dwellings, 703,000 of them
privately owned. Between 1873 and 2010, the population a

little more than doubled, but the number of dwellings went up sevenfold, and the number of privately owned dwellings increased to nearly 20 million.[1] With ownership has come a sense that privacy is an entitlement – a means of selectively controlling access to one's space, a guarantee of some degree of autonomy and one of the planks of a more equal society.

In 1882 William Hurrell Mallock, a novelist who was also an economist, published a book called *Social Equality: A Short Study in a Missing Science.* We may now grimace at that title. The twentieth century can be characterized as the Age of Equality, and as one in which the approach to improving equality was scientific. This is not to say that the distribution of wealth and opportunity is now equal, but, as one history puts it: 'The twentieth century saw the transformation of our world from one where most people's lives were short and spent living at close to subsistence level to one where the majority enjoy unprecedented material well-being and greater longevity.'[2]

Greater social equality has been achieved not in a linear fashion, but in fits and starts. Attitudes to courtship have represented this: there was an obvious relaxation of formalities between 1900 and 1930 (especially during the prosperous, dance-mad, materialistic, playful Roaring Twenties), followed by a period of comparatively modest change between 1930 and the early 1960s, at which point informality sharply increased. Over this timespan parental influence on courtship declined, and sex was more frankly discussed, amid loud complaints from traditionalists about the rise of permissiveness. In the 1960s and 1970s there was a surge of enthusiasm for expressiveness, experimentation and radical activism. Mingled with this were negative feelings about the inauthentic and hierarchical authoritarianism of traditional manners. Deference was mistrusted. The pressure for change was 'bottom up' rather than 'top down'. In freeing up the emotions and valuing many kinds of behaviour that had previously been considered dangerous, the period's movers and shakers were expressing what is sometimes dignified as *nostalgie de la boue*, a longing for the primitive and the degrading, a desire to get down and get dirty. Openness, a reduced concern with self-regulation, a desire to discover ironies at every turn: this was the John McEnroe approach, and a harbinger of the kind of mass entertainment in which everything is allowed to hang out (the world of *The Oprah Winfrey Show*) or slither out (the world of *The Jeremy Kyle Show*). In pop psychology, which would go super-pop on *Oprah* and *Jeremy Kyle*, restraint was associated with pitiful repression.

We can see evidence of these developments in changing styles of dance. At the start of the twentieth century dancing often meant waltzing; new styles to emerge before the 1920s included the foxtrot and the tango; with the 1920s we associate the Charleston; with the 1930s, jitterbugging to swing music; with the 1940s and 1950s, the jive; with the early 1960s, the Twist; and with the 1970s, disco. What's happened since requires a whole book of its own. But what we see here is a move away from structured dance with a partner towards greater individualism and spontaneity – and towards much less strict control of dance's sexual elements, from connotations of sex towards an exhibition of it.

A more integrated and open society naturally involved a more emancipated and unbuttoned approach to social life. A small example: we use people's given names where once we would have addressed them more formally – in the workplace, for instance, or in the classroom. Harold Nicolson writes in *Good Behaviour* (1955) that 'had I been addressed by my Christian name at . . . school, I should have blushed scarlet, feeling that my privacy had been outraged and that some secret manliness had been purloined from me.' He suggests that the wider use of given names became fashionable in the reign of Edward VII (1901–10). Yet the old practice hung on.

In the context of calling it 'old', I should explain that hereditary surnames were first used in the eleventh century but were not common even in urban families until 300 years later. Before surnames were in wide use, the limited range of personal names meant that people had to be identified using bynames – a reference to their antecedents, occupation or where they lived. In many cases surnames crystallized bynames. Today, given names are incredibly varied; often they compensate for the drabness of a surname (Keyboard Smith, Queequeg Jones). Yet many surnames have deep, romantic associations, and it is not so very hard to imagine an age in which addressing people mainly by their surnames seemed not only judiciously formal but also more tuneful.

A book on contemporary manners from 1933 reports that 'In no way is the offhand attitude of these days as apparent as in the extravagant use of Christian names.'[3] A year later, the mountaineer Eric Shipton, after a month or so sharing a small tent with his fellow Himalayan explorer Bill Tilman, asked if they could stop calling each other by their surnames. Tilman replied, 'Are you suggesting that I should call you Eric? I'm afraid I couldn't do that. I should feel such a bloody fool.'[4]

In 1939 Laura, Lady Troubridge, whose guides to etiquette

were popular before the Second World War, wrote that 'Friendships are made far quicker now that the barrier of undue formality has been lifted, and Christian names follow swiftly on mutual liking in a way which would make old-fashioned people aghast.' Yet thirteen years previously, her attitude had been different: she had warned that 'everyone, and women especially, should be extremely careful in making friends and acquaintances in hotels', on the grounds that 'strangers still remain strangers, even though you sleep under the same roof with them.'[5] It is striking, too, that Lady Troubridge's thoughts were in 1926 being packaged as *The Book of Etiquette* – subtitled *The Complete Standard Work of Reference on Social Usage* – whereas by 1939 they were presented as *Etiquette and Entertaining* – with a jaunty explanation on the cover that the book would serve 'to help you on your social way'.

In the twentieth century etiquette ceased to be regarded as a form of law and instead came to be thought of as an art. At the same time the Victorian pattern persisted: the readers of etiquette books were, to an ever greater extent, women. The development of low-cost paperback publishing, which began in 1935 when Allen Lane launched the Penguin imprint, made books of this kind accessible to all but the poorest. Advertising in magazines promoted the idea that guides to etiquette were an aid not only to social ease, but also to self-sufficiency.

In *Austerity Britain*, a vivid picture of the post-war years, the historian David Kynaston lists some of the things that Britain did not have in 1945. There were 'No supermarkets, no motorways, no teabags, no sliced bread, no frozen food, no flavoured crisps, no lager, no microwaves', and yet there were 'Shops on every corner, pubs on every corner, cinemas in every high street, red telephone boxes'. Abortion and gay relationships were illegal. Capital punishment was still in force. This was a world of 'dresses and hats, cloth caps and mufflers', in which every Monday was wash day and the hearth was the centre of people's homes.[6] The rigidity of such a society may seem the stuff of a mercifully bygone age, but it is common to look back on that time as one of decency and stoicism, typified by the 'make do and mend' philosophy of a people bound together by feelings of shared purpose.

We speak of lost communities, the precious solidarities once valued but now scorned. This is a romantic view of the past. The extensive findings of the Mass Observation Project, begun in 1937, dispel the image of a golden age of neighbourliness and community spirit. Instead they reinforce the impression of what the anthropologist Geoffrey Gorer called 'distant cordiality'.[7] Gorer was writing in 1955, a time we might incline to think of as steeped in a warmth now gone. Yet in his analysis of the findings of a questionnaire filled out by readers of the Sunday newspaper the *People*, he noted that while two-thirds knew their neighbours well enough to speak to them, fewer than 5 per cent felt able to drop in on them without an invitation. A larger percentage complained that their neighbours were nosy, noisy, snobbish or stupid.

The question of how we behave towards our neighbours is interesting, because we misrepresent our feelings on the matter. It is normal to idealize neighbourly behaviour as an overt chumminess, but in reality being a good neighbour, especially in a closely packed environment, is more likely to be latent – it often involves averting our gaze. Neighbourliness is really the art of managed indifference, a selective inattention. Ask people to talk about good neighbours they have had, rather than about the idea of a good neighbour, and you will glimpse a negative sort of solidarity: 'She never complained about my music', 'He kept his nose out', 'I barely heard a peep out of them.'

Some of the questions in Gorer's survey are framed intriguingly. Respondents are asked to identify the main reasons behind an apparent recent increase in crime 'especially among young people'. The options available are 'People got into bad ways in the Forces', 'Children whose fathers were in the Forces didn't have proper discipline', 'Children who were evacuated weren't properly looked after', 'Modern parents aren't strict enough', 'Modern schools aren't strict enough', 'Young people follow the bad example of crime films and crime stories in books and on the radio' and 'People are neglecting religion'.[8] Gorer's findings chime with the spirit of a good deal of 1950s journalism. For instance, in 1953 the *Daily Express* ran a series of pieces depicting 'The New Poor', middle-class strivers struggling to keep up appearances while paying high taxes. Their conformity was proverbial, yet found frequent expression in an almost paranoid aversion to anything 'common'. That word has been used to mean 'ordinary' and even 'inferior' for more than 600 years, but towards the end of the nineteenth century it came to be a term for unrefined, lower-class people, and it caught on amid the social competitiveness of the post-war years.

Gorer's findings, together with the Mass Observation Project, unsettle familiar assumptions. Is intimacy always a good thing? It has become customary to suggest that it is. But rather than being democratic, intimacy can be troublesome. Today we are obliged to be relaxed. Casualness is mistaken for fairness. The idea that each of us should do what makes us feel comfortable does not result in other people's comfort and hardly seems to improve our own. I'll call this the paradox of laxity: to para-phrase Norbert Elias, we are constrained to be unconstrained. There is a self-consciousness about this relaxedness: when someone professes to be 'chilling', the mood is not in fact sedate.

The flipside of instant intimacy is instant hostility. We are quick to adopt a hollow or at any rate cool intimacy, as for instance when kissing someone we barely know on the cheek, but quick also to tear into others or pepper them with candid advice and personal remarks. An example from my own experi-ence: in a restaurant in Egypt, another British tourist – to whom I had never spoken, though we knew each other by sight – stopped me as I was helping myself to pudding, saying, 'Don't eat that: a minute on the lips, a lifetime on the hips.' When I smarted, she insisted that she was 'only trying to be helpful'. This taunting semi-helpfulness concluded with the observation that 'It would be awful if one day you just keeled over.' It is but a step from this to rank abuse, the overt hostility we feel able to show people because we don't know them and expect not to see them again. Walking through a railway station, at Christmas, I chance on a shopper berating a worker from a nearby building site; I have no idea what he has said or done to her, but she is spraying him with invective, confi-dent that she can at any moment retreat through a ticket barrier – 'Who the fuck do you think you are? You don't fucking *know* me, you deaf cunt.'

I don't believe that this kind of behaviour is completely new, but it feels as if it is on the rise. I say this a little tentatively because it may simply be that I have become more sensitive to it. Writing a book about manners has made me notice conduct I might previously have overlooked. Still, the view prevails that manners have declined (or are in decline).

Canvassing opinions about why this may have happened, I heard about multiculturalism, sexual freedom, the perils of individualism, the impact of technology, the Sunday Trading Act of 1994, the decimalization of currency in 1971, the end of the ban on *Lady Chatterley's Lover* (in 1960), the encroachment of liberal values on school teaching, the encroachment of capitalism on just about everything, the cult of efficiency, the shrinking of the public sector, the bloated public sector, tight clothing, very loose clothing, men no longer wearing ties, the pampered ennui of James Bond, the concept of 'unisex', in-ear headphones, hip-hop, the 1960s, the 1970s, the 1980s, the European Union, TV, the gutter press, hard drugs, the growing acceptance of soft drugs, atheism, lazy agnosticism, religious extremism, the poor quality of modern diet, the wide use of agrochemicals and food additives, mass-produced housing and the rupturing of long-established neighbourhoods, the decline of the 'family business' and the fraying of family life. I also heard about institutional sloth and political niaiserie. Samuel, a sixty-two-year-old jeweller, spoke for many in declaring that 'Good manners have disappeared because there's no discipline. Nobody trusts the fucking government, nobody trusts the fucking police. The Church is mostly run by . . . you know' – he makes a pungent claim – 'so you can't trust them, can you? Who do kids look up to? I'll tell you who – fucking celebrities. Where's the good of that? Women's lib has got something to do with it, too.'

Samuel touches on an important subject here. The move towards greater gender equality began before the twentieth century, and the suffragettes achieved significant progress, especially after becoming more militant in the years just before the First World War. In the 1960s a fresh wave of activism, partly inspired by the writer Betty Friedan, addressed issues in law as well as in culture. Friedan wrote powerfully about the need for women to turn away from investing in domesticity, which made a woman 'an anonymous biological robot' who 'looks for security in things' and 'lives a vicarious life through mass daydreams and through her husband and children'. Long after Friedan's disavowal of female servitude, iniquities remain, but there have been palpable improvements in women's political, educational and legal opportunities. As Theodore Zeldin has written: 'There are two types of women in the world today of whom there were very few in the past: the educated and the divorced.'[9]

The rhetoric that has accompanied the improvement of women's rights has complicated many men's understanding of how they should behave towards women – or rather, towards individual women they encounter. The questions that result are often small but fraught with serious implications. Is a man on a bus or train who gives up his seat for a woman an example of sensitivity or a patronizing patriarchy? If he does not give up his seat, is he failing to be chivalrous or renouncing what he sees as an outmoded practice?

As a child growing up in the 1970s and 1980s, I was encouraged to believe that I ought to hold doors open for others, especially if they were encumbered. But I can remember, when I was no more than nine, holding the door of a bakery for a heavily laden woman and being berated as 'a bloody sexist'. About twenty years later I was surprised, as I helped an elderly woman with her heavy shopping bags, to be abused by a woman cycling past: 'Don't think you're something you're not, you sexist prick.'

Fundamentally, sexism is the belief that one sex is superior to the other. Yet it is a many-headed monster. Clearly my behaviour in the two cases just mentioned was not hostile missionary sexism, but it would be construed by some as benign sexism – an act of differentiation, though not of discrimination, seen as paternalistic and condescending, though many people of both sexes might regard it as charming, honourable or simply human.

We are a long way here from the large history of sexual injustice and the mainly peaceful revolution that, over the past 200 years, has transformed the lives and expectations of women. We are a long way, too, from the salient fact that in the western world the key ideas of feminism have circulated as books (*The Second Sex*, *The Female Eunuch*, *The Feminine Mystique*, *Sisterhood is Powerful*, *The Beauty Myth*), in magazines and on television.

It is worth taking note of the positive effects of television – as a chronicle of our times, an educational stimulus and a means of augmenting existing pleasures – because so much of the comment about television is negative, dwelling on its alleged distortion of reality, its role as an insidious instrument of consumerism or its capacity for turning us from careful watchers into careless glancers.

Criticism of television often targets what is on (the violence of drama, the fatuous nature of game shows), but the very existence of television has changed patterns of sociability. If you spend your evenings slumped in front of the box, rather than going out for your entertainment, you are very likely avoiding other kinds of activity that would demand greater participation. Watching TV can be a social event, but typically it is isolating. Once upon a time you would have given the hours you now spend watching TV to voluntary groups or hobbies that were likely to involve others. 'I don't watch TV,' you may say, 'or only PBS.' Perhaps you are not even addicted to HBO box sets. But you know exactly what I am talking about.

Watching TV reduces our engagement with people. In his lament *Anyone for England?* (1997) Clive Aslet writes of 'privatization . . . taking place in the home', of 'individuals and groups . . . splintering off from the collective mass of principles and activities that form a community . . . Now habits, manners, morals, codes of conduct, ways of life . . . have similarly been privatized. In deciding which to adopt, the individual has never been more on his own.'[10] Although you may find the language hyperbolic, Aslet has a point: TV is a domestic medium and asks little of its consumers, while the now ubiquitous remote control, though it enables grazing, seems to leave its users in a state of being both entranced and inattentive.

As the rhythms of communal life have grown fainter, so they have become something to nurse or cherish. Yet could the phenomenon identified as collapse really just be a reflection of the multifariousness of our interests? Is the much mythologized communal sociability a way of putting off the need to take charge of one's own well-being? Is there a case for saying that the mechanisms of communal living, which create webs of dependence and reciprocity, exist (or existed) only so as to dampen the threat of our crude animal drives? That in a highly technologized society, which is also a heavily medicated one, this threat can be – and is – dampened in other ways?

Steven Pinker shows the present state of manners in a different light. He has written about how, if we review the history of violence, we will be struck by the peacefulness of the modern world, even though it is conventional to speak of the twentieth century as a period of exceptional destruction. 'The decline of violence,' he argues, 'may be the most significant and least appreciated development in the history of our species.' When he narrows his focus to look at the very recent past, he identifies in the 1990s what he dubs the Great Crime Decline, 'part of a change in sensibilities that can fairly be called a recivilizing process'. In his view, society has become so peaceful that we can relax the mannerly inhibitions that were once necessary to curb violence. Lots of people look edgy and bohemian, rebellious and dysfunctional, but really they are just experimenting with styles and roles; on investigation, they turn out to lead pretty conventional lives. What pessimists see as evidence of a deep social malaise can instead be interpreted as evidence of society's comfortableness: 'the fact that women show a lot of skin or that men curse in public is not a sign of cultural decay . . . [but] a sign that they live in a society that is so civilized that they don't have to fear being harassed or assaulted in response.'[11]

To return to a theme from my opening chapter, never quite out of sight since: decline is something we are always noticing. Long historical perspectives are not usually available to us; we see what is in front of our noses, rather than slow processes of the kind described by Pinker or Norbert Elias. The comparisons we make are confident but historically dubious. We regard ourselves as good at identifying excess and deficit: someone drinking or eating too much, not getting out enough, working too hard or too little, spending too little time with family or too little effort on personal grooming, being too loud or failing to make enough noise to be heard. Evidently we fancy that we know what the right amount of these things is. Yet the right amount is something we establish by reacting to our experience of what feels like the wrong amount; it is rarely appreciated when present. Something similar occurs when we talk about decline: we praise a state of affairs for which we would never have expected to feel such affection. Declinism is the dark side of nostalgia, homesickness for a place we never really loved.

Even in today's fluid society there are still enclaves of old-fashioned ceremony, which satisfy the desire for a connection to a more pristine world. Weddings and funerals are two examples; another is interacting with royalty. Ideas today of the significance of marriage are very different from those that prevailed in the 1950s or the 1850s. But the wedding itself is a rite of passage and a public declaration with public repercussions. The English think of privacy as essential to matrimonial ease, but before that privacy is possible there must be a glare of public scrutiny. From the moment of proposal onward, the process is steeped in tradition: the reading of the banns, to check for legal impediments to the marriage; the rectangular invitations with their formulaic wording; the presence at the ceremony of a best man, ushers and bridesmaids, all with their defined roles; the bride wearing white, and her father giving her away; the signing of the register; the reception with its toasts and speeches, the first dance, the cutting of the cake; and then the honeymoon, a practice known to the French as a *lune de miel* but also as a *voyage à la façon anglaise*. True, it isn't always like that, but even a fairly inventive secular wedding or civil partnership will incorporate elements of this blueprint. Whereas Victorian guides suggested that the pageantry should be limited, the modern wedding is a gluttonous and expensive affair. Nevertheless, it remains a very formal way of affirming private feelings. Sacred or not, it is a ritual of transformation that resonates with solemn imagery of pledges and covenants.

The funeral is the most solemn example of a durable ceremony. In other cultures there may be sacrifice, ritual washing of the deceased, rending of garments or of symbolic ribbons, and later exhumation and reburial. Some communities in Britain maintain these practices. But the English funeral is a confined occasion, a family gathering marked by sobriety rather than festivity. Extravagant displays of grief and lamentation are taboo; the norm is quiet tribute. The funeral sermon includes some testimony, however meagre in its information, about the character of the person who has died. For all its poignancy, this eulogy is an appeal to the communal and the acknowledged; it is not the place for revelation or confession, drama or evaluation. The most modern funeral rites seem conservative when compared with other parts of the lives of those in attendance. But technology is changing the parameters of mourning and commemoration.

In the final decades of the nineteenth century, a popular

guide to conduct was *Manners and Rules of Good Society*. Presented as the work of 'a member of the aristocracy', it contained a wealth of instructions such as 'A gentleman should not take his stick or umbrella with him into the drawing-room, but leave it in the hall' and 'Ladies and gentlemen, whether related or not, should never walk arm-in-arm, unless the lady is an elderly one, or an invalid, and requires the support.' Especially striking to us now are the stipulations about acceptable periods of mourning for the deceased: for an uncle or aunt the correct period is said to be between six weeks and three months, and for a second cousin it is three weeks, though 'Mourning for a second cousin is not obligatory.'[12]

The rituals of bereavement, once so precise (with conventions about social seclusion and the wearing of hat-bands), are now relaxed. An article in the *New York Times* in April 2006 quoted messages left on a young woman's Myspace page after her death in a car accident: one of these was 'Hey Lee! It's been a LONG time. I know that you will be able to read this from Heaven, where I'm sure you are in charge of the parties.' Social networking has made grief a much less private matter. Peter Hitchens, writing in the *Daily Mail* in December 2011 about the death of his brother Christopher, reflected that 'Much of civilization rests on the proper response to death, simple unalloyed kindness, the desire to show sympathy for irrecoverable loss, the understanding that a unique and irreplaceable something has been lost to us.'[13] The 'proper response' now has, even for a traditionalist such as Peter Hitchens, a latitude few Victorians could have imagined.

24

Technology and the revenge effect

As we have seen, manners typically used to filter from the top down – not least from the old and experienced to the young and callow. But modern communications technology has changed that. Online, and throughout electronic culture, the young dictate the mood, and the rest of society learns from them or gets left out. In *Talk to the Hand* Lynne Truss writes: 'Just as the rise of the internet sealed the doom of grammar, so modern communications technology contributes to the end of manners.'[1] Not everyone will nod assent. But while I don't believe that grammar is doomed or that manners are finished, I know what Truss means.

Technological evangelists claim that the internet is forging a better world, converting us from couch potatoes addicted to passive consumption into creators and sharers who collaborate on projects. Some of these are worthwhile, others admittedly less so; of the former, the most staggering have been the Twitter revolutions, achieved in countries such as Iran and Egypt, which made use of the microblogging service to co-ordinate protests and relay news.

Instead of squandering our lives inhaling opiate entertainment

– such as vacuous TV shows – we now split our time between making things, disseminating them and consuming them. Such, at least, is the new received wisdom. An alternative view, articulated best by the contrarian computer scientist Jaron Lanier, is that technology, while it can and should be used to enrich our interactions, tends to deplete our relationships, encouraging shallowness and a hollow obsession with diffusing information – a culture in which human understanding, even as we believe we are enlarging it, becomes dwarfish. The writer Sherry Turkle used to celebrate the capacity of technology to liberate us, but has recently cast doubt on this. 'Technology proposes itself as the architect of our intimacies,' she observes, but these days our networked existence 'allows us to hide from each other, even as we are tethered to each other'.[2] Oppressed by busy-ness, we use technology in the hope of clawing back some time for our discretionary use, but instead it makes us feel more overwhelmed. The playwright Richard Foreman, in the online magazine *Edge*, has spoken of the emergence of 'a new self that needs to contain less and less of an inner repertory of dense cultural inheritance as we all become "pancake people", spread wide and thin as we connect with that vast network of information accessed by the mere touch of a button'.[3]

Pancake people cover a lot of territory, as readers and writers. But they tend to share themselves before there is anything much to share. In my experience, one is most likely to be a pancake person when using social networks. While there is something rather beautiful about a complex network of sentient nodes, social networks can also provide ugly examples of the ways in which contagion works. Amid the swarm of information, there is increasing uncertainty about concepts such as ownership, copyright, privacy and free speech.

The vulnerability of our personal information online creates opportunities for people we know and people we don't know to jeopardize our privacy and security. One of the things many of us love about the internet is that it makes it possible to broadcast ideas and images that might otherwise get no notice. But it also allows others to broadcast our ideas and images, for their own benefit or merely to our detriment.

A practice that is apparently trivial yet actually intrusive is the photographing or filming of our everyday activities (and their less humdrum moments: the time you danced in just your underwear or cracked a regrettable joke about your best friend). The camera, from the moment of its development, posed a threat to privacy. Now many of us have a camera on our person all the time, on our increasingly sophisticated phones. We can be filmed at any moment, and the footage can be shared with ease. Having had a stand-off on a train with a man who was trying to use his phone to film under – and up – my girlfriend's skirt, I am alert to the potential for this to turn sour. I don't think those pictures were merely for furtive private consultation, not that it would have been all right if they had been. Yet my reaction to this man's behaviour surprised him, and he argued that because we were in public we were at his mercy: 'If you want to be private, stay at home.'

Using the internet prompts a host of other concerns, mostly small but not paltry. Is it prudent to announce your new relationship on Facebook? What about a bereavement? Is it okay for your avatar on a networking site to be a logo rather than a picture of you? Can you reject a 'friend request' from your own parent or child? Do you have to follow your friends on Twitter? Can you tell someone he's exposing too much of himself in his updates (be it his boringness or his appetite for random sex)? How perfunctory can you be in your response to an email? When do you use 'Reply to All' rather than 'Reply', and, more importantly, when shouldn't you? Are emoticons tacky or charming? Is looking at pornography on the internet somehow 'more okay' than looking at it on film or the printed page? (Clue: No.) Where do you draw the line between researching the personal history of new acquaintances and snooping on them? Can you use your phone to check your email under the table during dinner? Are goods you buy online more likely to be faulty or counterfeit, and what can you do if they are? Exactly how secure are your credit card details? What information is your web browser sequestering for future use? How, if at all, can you massage your online reputation? What are the dangers of digital technology's everlasting memory?

Where social networks are concerned, several principles of etiquette have emerged: promote others more than you promote yourself; if you are trying to sell something, disclose the fact that you are doing so; don't voice your resentment of other people's reluctance to back your cause; if you are recycling something you were directed to by another person (let's say a lovely YouTube clip), acknowledge who alerted you to it; be aware that in correcting other people's 'netiquette' (or their grammar), you are at high risk of committing offences every bit as bad as those you are choosing to condemn; don't be a troll, dishing out rancour from behind a mask; and don't use sockpuppets to praise yourself.

There are issues here that go far beyond the realm of etiquette. Across social media there are users keen to avoid generic interactions and instead engage with others personally, sensitive to the need for concision and visual appeal, mindful of others' vulnerability, and respectful of the sources of ideas and information. Their practices are the ingredients of a new civility. But this is not far past its infancy, and it has grown out of users' unhappy experiences, a familiarity with those parts of life online that seem scrappy, immodest, churlish, sadistic, corrupt or degraded.

The internet creates myriad new ways to be rude. It is a carnival. We try on alternative personalities. Anonymity makes it possible to insult people without their knowing who's insulting them; often a troll abuses someone he does not know. A different sort of impoliteness is spam. I am thinking not just about the oddly phrased blandishments (promises of sexual enhancement or invitations to have your bank account emptied), but also about the communications you receive from acquaintances and associates who think you might want to sponsor them to run to the end of the road or might care to know that they're really looking forward to post-work drinks on Friday (LOL, ROFL, BRB).

Spam is noise in your inbox. And in the modern world noise, which we might define as 'unwanted sound', is everywhere. One person's unwanted sound is another person's source of pleasure, sounds often being associated with the cherished items that produce them (a mobile phone, a stereo system, a TV, a car, a dog, a child). As the novelist Andrew Martin observed in his 2012 BBC radio essay 'The Sound and the Fury', it is much easier to make a noise than to get someone else to stop doing so, and 'we cannot close our ears'.

Modern communications technologies have turned up the noise in our lives. The mobile phone exemplifies this best. The novelist Jonathan Franzen, a brilliant if grumpy cultural commentator, suggests that the device came of age on 11 September 2001. Before that the world was 'not yet fully conquered by yak' – and he's not talking about the Himalayan bovines. Now yak is everywhere. The one positive consequence of this is that while the notion of 'civilized public spaces, as rare resources worth defending, may be all but dead . . . there's still consolation to be found in the momentary ad hoc micro-communities of fellow sufferers which bad behavior creates'.[4] You know how that moment looks and feels: the shared gawps of distress as Trendster McFuckpig blurts once again into his tiny electronic conch. Yet the moment soon passes, and the digital toys beep and whirr, and their owners belch and snipe. Rather than freeing us, these technologies risk making us bored commuters, dissociated from everything except our febrile and inconsistent self-love.

But here's a different way of looking at this. Advertising barrages us with unwanted information: we have been spammed since the day we were born, and most of us have grown up in a world where rudeness and interruption glare from a multitude of surfaces (billboards, walls, screens) and pollute the airwaves. To the extent that we now make choices about how we circulate messages, from ourselves and others, we are able to set filters, and in doing so we challenge the centralized dissemination of ideas and images. We are thus in a position – perhaps – to teach the corporations that govern us some manners.

In this snapshot of the battle between the individual and

the corporation, we see one of the leading motifs of our age. Corporate values, which have such a pervasive influence on our society, do a lot to frame our choices and channel our desires. I am thinking not of the values that are officially espoused as visions or missions (the guff about delivering exceptional customer experiences), but of the prevailing attitudes and convictions of corporate life. Among these is an idea of what people are like and how they behave: we at all times resemble shoppers, making choices as if comparing brands of energy drink, and are intent on maximizing our pleasure, which is narrowly defined. Masses of data are crunched in order to map our habits and preferences as consumers. But as the data multiply – retained, regurgitated, augmented – so it appears as if nothing else matters: whatever cannot be quantified and entered into a spreadsheet is insignificant. The world is arranged in such a way that we no longer have to experience it.[5]

25

'Are we there yet?'

manners now

Worrying about the end of manners is not a uniquely English affliction. In America there is a special class of commentator who makes a living out of declinism, and there is a sub-class within it that consists of writers who like to explain that the *real* decline is happening in places where most of us aren't looking.

In a much quoted essay published in 1996 in the *Nation*, the cultural critic Benjamin DeMott examined claims by the 'leader classes' that American society was suffering from 'rampant intemperateness on the one hand . . . and distaste for associated living on the other'. Most citizens, it was being alleged, had 'forgotten how to listen and respect and defer'. DeMott sniffed at this, and argued that, as they clamoured for more civility, privileged Americans were expressing their impatience with the idea that social divisions might have something to do with a lack of justice and fairness. In his view, people's disengagement from civility was the result of a perceived 'need for an attitude – some kind of protection against sly, sincerity-marketing politicos and boss-class crooks'. What others diagnosed as the 'new incivility' was according to DeMott a form of protest, a 'justified rejection of leader-class claims to respect'.[1]

DeMott's prose may have left something to be desired, but he usefully summed up a significant difference: one person's idea of a riot is another's idea of protest, and what to some seem the mechanisms of a happy society seem to others the instruments of oppression. To jump from 1996 to the more recent past: after unrest flared in London in August 2011, a study by the *Guardian* newspaper and the London School of Economics found that many of those who had rioted felt aggrieved about what they perceived as discourteous treatment by the police.[2] According to this view, rioting was not a form of incivility but an expression of discontent with the hollow norms of civility.

In October 2011 the Young Foundation, a self-proclaimed centre for social innovation, published a report about contemporary civility. Entitled *Charm Offensive*, the report disclosed that interviewees, though often unfamiliar with the word *civility*, understood what it denoted; they regarded it as central to shaping their lives, and in many cases felt that there was nothing that contributed more to quality of life.[3] Although few would go so far as to support David Cameron's assertion (before becoming Prime Minister) that 'Rudeness is just as bad as racism', it was common to think that rudeness damaged the sense of community whereas civility improved it.

Though hardly a revelation, this was an eye-catchingly conservative, traditional view. It was based on research done in three places: the borough of Newham in London; Cambourne, a new town in Cambridgeshire; and the Wiltshire communities of Salisbury, Trowbridge and Devizes. So, not 'Cultivating Civility in 21st Century Britain', but 'Cultivating Civility in 21st Century England'. The report did not gloss over the frequency with which incivility is encountered. Yet it noted that, rather than there being a crisis of civility, there was in fact an impressive persistence of faith in it.

The report's title is a phrase we associate with politicians and psychopaths. Charm is used as an instrument of enchantment; its attractions are skin-deep. Though often applauded, it is essentially a substitute for competence. The things that charm us and the things that irritate us are not as divergent as we tend to imagine. To put it another way, the capacity to be charming and the capacity to irritate occupy the same space in people. Both give them power over others and specifically over others' moods. We are all familiar with the idea that what one person finds charming can seem exasperating to someone else. More than this, though, charm and irritation work in the same way, by teasing the sweet fibres of our narcissism.

Whatever its title may suggest, the focus of the Young Foundation's report is not charm, but civility. Seeing these two words side by side, though, highlights both how readily they are confused and how fundamentally different they are. Charm is a power to fascinate and delight, which comes easily to some and is impossible for others; civility has none of charm's talismanic attractiveness, but it is altogether more robust and is something everyone can achieve. In the sober words of the sociologist Edward Shils: 'Civility is a belief which affirms the possibility of the common good . . . [and] recommends that consensus about the maintenance of the order of society should exist alongside the conflicts of interests and ideals.'[4] I am reminded here, I know incongruously, of the story of the porcupines that huddle together in order to avoid freezing, but stand far enough apart to ensure that none of them is impaled on another's quill.

Among the key statements of *Charm Offensive* is the idea that civility, although partly 'a matter of individual disposition', needs to be cultivated. Developing civility involves mastering 'a learned grammar of sociability', and it is underpinned by an expectation of reciprocity. Thus a taxi driver in Newham: 'Civility? We give out and we get back.'[5] Erving Goffman has written about 'supportive interchanges', the little rituals through which we acknowledge that we are connected to others, even if only by our shared humanity: we signal our awareness of the connection, and its receipt and appreciation are signalled back – all of this briefly, with no great ceremony.

But observation suggests that many people, far from confident of getting anything back, have stopped giving out little portions of civility – each of which requires a small amount of unselfishness. It has become customary for sociologists and the journalists who popularize their findings to define the decline of manners and the rise of selfish individualism in a snappy soundbite, with talk of 'bowling alone' or the 'lonely crowd'. There are complaints about diminished trust, an atomized society, dwindling social attachments, and the passing of what the political scientist Robert Putnam – he of 'bowling alone' – has called the 'long civic generation' and its values. That generation, born between 1910 and 1940 (Putnam was born in 1941), exceeded their predecessors and their successors in their engagement with citizenship: 'voting more, joining more, trusting more'.[6] Thus George, a retired manual worker, born in 1934: 'I look at the kids now and they don't do nothing *together*. They've all got their noses in their phones –

d'you know what I mean? Most of my friends, growing up, was lads I knew from the Boys' Club, playing football. My mother – she'd have known most of their mothers. There'd have been some respect. But now, even the ones you see out with all their friends, they're lonely-looking, trying to look like they're not all lost. And the old? They treat us like we're dinosaurs. They've no respect, not even for their own lives.'

We hear a lot today about respect: for laws and rules, for tradition, for exemplary individuals, for ourselves. We hear about it most when it is absent. Here is the sociologist Richard Sennett: 'Respect is an expressive performance. That is, treating others with respect doesn't just happen, even with the best will in the world; to convey respect means finding the words and gestures which make it felt and convincing.'[7] Sennett dismisses the idea that respect is a matter of combining goodwill with deft improvisation; that's just the social equivalent of modern jazz. The alternative he describes begins with respect for oneself: a mixture of self-sufficiency, charity and self-improvement. Though widely endorsed, not least by Tony Blair's British government with its 2006 Respect Action Plan, this seems a quiet and tentative project. In reality, respect is today formulated in terms of rights, and it is understood as a legal concept rather than as a human quality. Legislation is a blunt instrument; it reduces principles and powerful values to dry technicalities.

Respectfulness is a theme addressed by Stephen Carter, who writes about the sense of positive duties that is the kernel of civility. His notion of these positive duties comes from Christian faith. He notes that there is a school of thought that insists that religion and civility are incompatible; members of this school claim that believers do not want to enter the marketplace of ideas, preferring instead to try to shut it down. Carter takes issue with the very notion of such a marketplace. In his view, the language of the marketplace is something to be resisted.

The arguments advanced by Carter are widely endorsed, even if the specific terms vary. In *Coming Apart* (2012), a portrait of the divided nature of contemporary American society, Charles Murray makes a link between religious faith and a training in 'important civic skills'. 'People who are religious,' he says, 'account for a large proportion of the secular forms of social capital.' These include youth groups, political clubs, professional societies and school fraternities or sororities. As society has become less religious, so the argument goes, the general sense of social affiliation has diminished. Murray perceives decline in family and community, faith and vocation. He suggests that the deterioration he sees in contemporary America resembles the disintegration of other great civilizations. Right now, among the most privileged Americans, there is 'a rejection of the obligations of citizenship'. With this comes a 'vulgarization of manners, the arts, and language'. Murray identifies an unsettling 'adoption by the middle class and upper-middle class of behaviours that used to be distinctly lower class', a 'proletarianization of the dominant minority' that reflects 'the collapse of confidence in codes of honourable behaviour'.[8]

Although this kind of writing is more common in America than in Britain, you need hardly be Fanny Trollope to suspect that what happens in America is a portent for what will happen in Britain – if it is not already happening. Britain used to think of America as its runaway child; now the relationship seems to have reversed, though with 'runaway' replaced by something less racy. Many readers will find Charles Murray's vision alarmist, and will disagree with a lot of his contentions and provocations (including his proposal that a universal guaranteed income should replace the programmes that make up the welfare state). Still, *Coming Apart* and the numerous books of its kind are not just diagnoses but also symptoms of a society in which civility is under threat.

Mining anecdote, I sense that most people believe manners are getting worse. There are familiar stories of drunkenness at office parties, off-colour speeches at weddings, the decline of thank-you notes, drivers using their car horns gratuitously, dog-owners doing nothing to clear up their mutts' profusely deposited shit, the use of a mere 'sorry' to excuse sickening behaviour, sodcasting on public transport (i.e. playing loud, tinny music on a mobile device), shop assistants chatting to their friends rather than serving customers, theatregoers checking the time on their brightly illuminated phones, and others' readiness to discuss their earnings or sex lives. I hear strident complaints about what seem pretty small things: it is the gravest faux pas to wear brown shoes 'in town' or after six o'clock in the evening, only children and the infirm should use napkins, and folks who hang wind chimes in their gardens should be guillotined. I gather that crisps shouldn't be eaten on public transport, as well as that you should never offer to pour your host a drink. The inappropriate question is another bugbear. Not the kind of question that encroaches on taboo, but the hazardous query: 'How's business?', 'Have we met?', 'Have you been on a diet?', 'What are you wearing *that* for?'

Many voice concerns about gracelessness in electronic communication, too: writing an email entirely in upper case is shouty, using the wrong font for a document can be grotesque, and one must never use Comic Sans for anything that isn't casual – or, according to one school of thought, for anything at all.

In some of these areas, the lack of received wisdom seems an invitation to improvise new etiquette or at least fantasize about it. One female friend, single at the time and bored of the flirtatious attentions of married men, insisted that all people who are married should be obliged to wear wedding rings. Less surprising was another friend's complaint about the intrusive use of mobile phones: 'I basically think that unless someone is a doctor on call his phone should be banished during all social interactions.' One rejoinder she had been tempted to try out – inspired, she thought, by Tom Hodgkinson, editor of the magazine the *Idler* – involved carrying a volume of poetry at all times and, whenever friends get their phones out, holding up a hand in the manner of a traffic policeman, intently examining a poem for a moment and then saying, 'Sorry, carry on – where were we?'

A recurrent theme when I discuss English manners with other people is the depravity of the young: looseness, slackness, self-indulgence, a callous malignity and coarse truculence, a desire for adult rights and pleasures without adult responsibilities. Though occasionally celebrated for their sexual precocity, tech-savvy and resourcefulness, young people are convicted of cultural deafness and a hazy internationalism, and of being apathetic and aggressive, barbarous and hypersensitive. Can they be all these things? Generalizations – sometimes teed up with a reference to 'the youth of today', and sometimes prefaced with a briefly noted exception – judder along incoherently. The hiatus between childhood and adulthood, once marked with the words *adolescent* and *teenager*, is represented as a deep abyss with indistinct boundaries. One friend traced the pattern thus: 'Manners seem to be learned in childhood, forgotten in youthful exuberance, and returned to in middle age, with plenty of tutting at those who don't know the rules.' There is a large gap between the learning period and the return.

There are several points here that need teasing out. First of all, the young are likely to behave in a depraved way because they have yet to experience the consequences of such behaviour, or because they know what the consequences are and don't consider them significant, or because the consequences are much smaller for them, or because there is a masochistic thrill to be had from inviting the consequences. The 'forgetting' of manners referred to by my friend is in part a wilful abandonment of manners, an expression of independence. It is also a test of the structures that manners appear to hold in place.

Complaining about young people is part of maturity – of passing beyond the age of experiment, in which boundaries seem to exist in order to be tested, into an age of acquiescence and comfort, in which the boundaries seem reassuring and the business of testing them seems jejune. In the past fifty years, youthful groups that have been demonized have included punks, hippies, hoodies, Teddy boys, skinheads, mods, goths, emos, ravers, bikers, casuals, greasers, grungers, gamers, hipsters and skaters. Arguably, it is as if none of these subcultures has truly existed until it has been excoriated. Their members' appearance is 'spectacular'; they conscientiously try to look different from their parents and authority figures, acting out a ritual of resistance to social norms without actually resolving their fundamental discontents. The main objective, often tacit, is to create a social space for themselves. Marking that space is an important part of the transition from childhood to adulthood, and being troubled by the recalcitrance of youth is a sign that one has found one's space and now wants to defend it. As Florence Bell observed with understated irony in *The Minor Moralist* (1903): 'Young people do not, as a rule, write articles on the manners of older ones.'[9]

From time to time the young are the target of phobic political policies. The Anti-social Behaviour Orders, introduced by Tony Blair's Labour government in 1998 and now scrapped, are a recent example. ASBOs criminalized what might previously have been classified as nuisance or rudeness. While they were not designed to police the behaviour of a specific age group, attention focused on their being applied to young people, and the media seized on stories like that of a ten-year-old in Middlesbrough 'banned from throwing things', an eleven-year-old in Manchester prevented from riding his bicycle on footpaths, and a four-foot-five-inch twelve-year-old from near Bolton whose offences including stealing beer from a liquor store.[10] An instrument for dealing with problems as disparate as spitting, loitering, joyriding and drug-dealing, the ASBO tapped into the 'broken windows' theory advanced by James Q. Wilson and George L. Kelling in the 1980s: that fixing smallish problems is a means of averting graver ones. It appealed to a large and anxious section of society which felt that civic order was crumbling, not because they had been victims of violence or other extreme forms of crime, but because of their daily experience of small abuses. The high percentage of breached ASBOs suggested their ineffectiveness. But the principle behind the ASBO has a lengthy history. As long ago as 1599 Alexander Goozey, a Salisbury man, was prosecuted for behaving 'barbarously' and 'uncivilly', his gravest offence having been to yank his wife's hat off during a church service.[11] ASBOs were civil orders, not criminal ones. As such, they could be handed out in response to hearsay. Their name may have sounded modern, but their temper was medieval.

In 2012 the novelist Martin Amis published *Lionel Asbo*, described by one critic as 'a full-on indictment of a debased culture'.[12] Early on in this satire, which has the subtitle *State of England*, we learn that the protagonist, a generic yob who works as a debt collector, changed his name when he reached eighteen. The decision to switch from Lionel Pepperdine to Lionel Asbo may not quite ring true, but the desire to brandish one's name as a badge of dishonour suggests the mood of the ASBO age. Among the many quirks of modern manners is an appetite for parading one's lack of them.

We hear a lot about modern manners – their complexity, their absence, the difficulty of documenting them. It is a field densely populated with experts, again mostly American: some are hucksters, others perceptive and helpful. Richie Frieman, a one-time professional wrestler now billed as Modern Manners Guy, offers 'quick and dirty tips for a more polite life' on his website (http://manners.quickanddirtytips.com/). Modern he certainly is, confronting issues such as 'What is proper karaoke etiquette?' and 'How to politely handle a negative tweet'. Elsewhere, Steven Petrow at http://www.gaymanners.com focuses on questions of gay and lesbian manners, such as 'If I'm not sure my new neighbours are a gay couple, may I ask?'

At http://www.slate.com Emily Yoffe deals with problems of every hue: 'I've been offered a scholarship for Hispanic students, but it turns out I may not even be Hispanic. Does it matter?', 'My husband's brain injury ended our romance. Should I take a lover?', 'My boss walked in on me touching myself, and now he won't stop flirting. What do I do?' A British slant on the subject is provided by *Debrett's A–Z of Modern Manners*, which sets out rules such as 'if you are leaving a voicemail message don't ramble' and 'wear . . . deodorant when working out . . . [and] wipe equipment down when you have finished with it'. Some of the advice is whimsical: if you pass wind, 'blame the dog, even if there isn't one'.[13]

In the late 1990s John Morgan regularly answered questions from concerned readers of *The Times* about 'modern manners', some of them in truth not so unaccustomed. For instance: 'Should widows continue wearing their wedding rings? . . . Would it be suitable to wear the ring on my right hand?', 'How should one address a letter to a person of unknown gender who is known only by surname and initials?', 'What is good form when reclining one's seat on a commercial flight?' The answers Morgan provided were as follows: 'No . . . as this could be interpreted as your being committed to Christ in a relationship analogous to marriage', 'The only safe solution is to use the styleless, sexless, but increasingly prevalent form, i.e. "Dear N. V. Bloggs"', 'There is no reason to ask permission as seat-reclining is an accepted convention shared by all air passengers.'[14] The confidence of the prescriptions is striking, but perhaps misplaced.

A less recent volume, by Anne de Courcy, suggests that 'Much of modern manners is moulded by issues first made

fashionable in the Sixties – racism, the right to free contraception, a vague and benevolent Socialism.' I fancy the 1960s
'made fashionable' racial sensitivity rather than racism, but de
Courcy speaks aptly when she notes the prevalence today of
attempts to reconcile affluence with 'an anguished liberal
conscience'.[15]

People have been talking about 'modern manners' since the
eighteenth century. A reviewer of a book on the subject
complains that 'Modern Manners are, in general, so trifling
and insipid, with so little either instructive or entertaining in
them' – this in 1782.[16] Depending on whom you talk to,
modern manners are either something that desperately need
codifying (we must have a new system of manners to take
account of the peculiar textures of the world in which we
now live) or the final insult, a flimsy travesty of older and
more rigid codes of behaviour.

Today's world poses challenges not countenanced by traditional etiquette books, with their resolute guidance on how
to respond to a wedding invitation or set a table. At what age
should my daughter be required to cover the upper half of her
body at a public swimming pool? How should my sister react
when people see her mixed-race son and, observing their very
different looks, assume she is his nanny? In a restaurant, can
you order something that's not on the menu – an egg-white
omelette, for instance – or request alterations to a dish? Is it
acceptable to rebuke another person's child? Can I ask you to
remove your high heels when you come into my apartment,
which has wooden floors that are easily scratched? If you do
remove your high heels, is it polite to offer you my slippers
(much loved, comfortable)? Can I insist, when you ask to smoke

in my apartment, that you go outside to do so? On a crowded train, is it okay to read a newspaper over another person's shoulder, and what about reading someone else's Kindle?[17]

One answer that covers most of these questions is 'Do what you like'. The I-do-what-I-like crowd is always keen to add to its numbers. Its message is one of solipsism rather than tolerance, and it is especially disdainful of English reserve. That fabled reserve could be summed up thus: just because you have a feeling doesn't mean you need to express it. But now we are taught that expressing feelings is authentic, and we are taught to believe that there is a true self that we can recover from the clutches of our false self – the latter the creation of a society that has supposedly blunted our sensitivities or smothered them. According to this view, the true self is one without inhibitions; anything that creates inhibitions, as manners do, is false. Nevertheless, many of us are deeply afraid of causing offence. Characters in the novels of Jane Austen and Fanny Burney were afraid of this, too, but look how much there now is to cause offence *about*. Observe, too, the shamanistic susceptibility of the people who get offended, frequently on behalf of others who have not yet learned to be so touchy.

I dispute the claim that manners are in decline across the board. It is normal, in comparing the past and the present, to conclude that a great deal has been lost. It is also normal to exaggerate feelings of discomfort in the present. But manners are today more complex than ever before. As I have suggested, new social relationships entail new social codes. The intricacy of modern relationships and the wealth of channels through which we pursue them are reflected in the convoluted nature of modern manners. Rather than there being no manners, there are multitudes of conflicting manners, fraught with ambiguity. In the words of David Brooks, 'technological and social revolution . . . put greater and greater demands on human cognition. People are now compelled to absorb and process a much more complicated array of information streams. They are compelled to navigate much more complicated social environments.'[18]

In some areas of life, there is a glut of manners, or rather of the empty pleasantries that have taken the place of real courtesy – and of discretion, incisiveness and practicality. At work, we may well be judged according to technical criteria rather than on personal qualities; accordingly, we play roles that illustrate our competence, or have such roles imposed on us. Think, for instance, of those scripted phone conversations you have with 'customer service providers', in which the courtesies appear to be full of beans but smell of soap: 'Thank you for your continued interest in our range of services, Mr Hitchings. Please enjoy the rest of your day.'

Fake politeness is all around us, a meaningless hum. Lynne Truss provides a nice list of reasons ('mostly lapsed', she says) to show *real* politeness to others. Among them: they know more than you do, they got here first, they have educational qualifications in the subject under discussion, you are in their house, you work for them, they work for you, they paid for the tickets, you phoned them, they are less fortunate than you.[19] Reading this list, I realize that, in addition to having been on the receiving end of behaviour that violates this homely set of principles, I have perpetrated such behaviour – many times.

Truss's list accuses us of a failure to stand back from the

immediacy of our own experience and fathom other people's perspectives. We live in an age of narcissistic self-absorption; we are addicted to immediate rewards and short-term gains. Unrestrained individualism is rife. Evelyn Waugh once made the piquant claim that 'manners are especially the need of the plain. The pretty can get away with anything.'[20] The trouble is, we all think we're pretty now – or deserve to be. We gorge on advertisements and other images that encourage us to believe that the way we look is our most important feature; they sap our self-worth, and we react with a paroxysm of exaggerated confidence or a noisy sense of entitlement. Who needs to be empathetic when you can be omnipotent? But behind this apparent shamelessness are flickers of self-disgust and boredom, as well as a persistent feeling of being unfulfilled.

Ours is also a fearful age. The last few decades of the twentieth century saw the concern with familiar threats to physical existence replaced in part by nebulous anxieties: the belief that changes, in every area of life, are speeding up, and that threats are all around us, in the food we eat, the air we breathe, the sun and the soil.[21] The language of risk is everywhere, too: it is a plastic idiom, capable of being used to justify both intuitive, personal decisiveness and a deliberate, highly technical caution. At least as inescapable is the language of therapy, which does away with moral categories and gives priority to causal explanations, while also positing an adversarial model of human relations, full of conflict, secret motives, suppressed desires and defensiveness. Terms such as *anxiety*, *trauma*, *stress* and *addiction*, once the vocabulary of the specialist, are at the heart of a worldview in which feelings matter more than beliefs – and in which we are urged, even coerced, into feeling vulnerable.

One of the results is the increasingly common notion that criticism is a form of violence.[22] Accordingly, we perform rituals of respect and sensitivity, for fear of prosecution or losing our jobs, rather than out of a genuine concern for others' well-being. Forget enlightenment, the scaremongers insinuate: your goal should just be to survive.

Yet in truth material comfort insulates most of us from the deprivation that manners used to palliate. The most shocking rudeness is not that of the poor and downtrodden, but that of people whose lives are by comparison idyllic. Ever since the doctrine of etiquette took the marrow out of manners, replacing discretion and nuance with black and white legislation, the whole question of manners has had an image problem, tending to be represented as a set of traps for the unwary, a smirk-inducing test enabling smart folk to celebrate their privileges. Manners are associated with pretentiousness, a soulless caution, a denial of progress or even a hollow duplicity – and with conformism, drabness, the quenching of personality. But the ability to evaluate and regulate the effects we have on other people is part of a fine awareness of our selves. If we stop thinking about those effects, if we stop caring, we are not expressing the freedom and wonder of our selves, but limiting them. If we do not control our desires, they control us.

Acknowledgements

In the course of writing *Sorry!* I have incurred a number of debts of gratitude. I want to begin by thanking Eleanor Birne, who took on this project at John Murray, and Roland Philipps, who has proved a sensitive editor. I am grateful also to Nikki Barrow, James Spackman and Caroline Westmore at John Murray, and to my agents Peter Straus and Melanie Jackson.

Further thanks, for kindnesses in some cases only loosely related to this book, go to Andrew Brooke, Alex Burghart, Jesse Coleman, Molly Crockett, Nick de Somogyi, Katie Drummond, Susan Goldfarb, Gesche Ipsen, Kwasi Kwarteng, Will le Fleming, Daniel Light, Morag Lyall, Lucy Mangan, Douglas Matthews, Edouard Métrailler, Sybil Pincus, Miranda Popkey, Aliceson Robinson, James Scudamore, Roger Stacey, Craig Taylor and Mary Wellesley. I am grateful to the staff of the British Library and the London Library for their patience. Thanks are also due to my companions on the Japan Study Tour in the summer of 2001, as well as to the strangers who agreed to be interviewed about their attitudes to manners (their names have been changed).

My deepest thanks are reserved for Jessica Edwards, Robert Macfarlane and Leo Robson, and for my father, who provided the initial inspiration for this book.

Notes

I have not given individual page references for quotations from works that I cite liberally, such as Chesterfield's letters, or for quotations from works that can very easily be located, such as Jane Austen's novels.

Chapter 1: The stars' tennis balls: or, a short introduction from an unusual angle

1. Clive James, *Glued to the Box: Television Criticism from the Observer, 1979–82* (London: Jonathan Cape, 1983), 100, 140.
2. John McEnroe, *Serious* (London: Time Warner, 2003), 91.
3. See Eugene Oswald, 'Early German Courtesy Books', in F. J. Furnivall (ed.), *Queen Elizabethes Academy, etc.*, 2 vols. (London: Trübner, 1869), II, 79–147.
4. http://www.dailymail.co.uk/news/article-562464/Bad-manners -biggest-problem-facing-Britain-says-study--parents-blame .html, retrieved 29 June 2012.
5. Howard Association, *Juvenile Offenders* (London: Wertheimer, Lea, 1898), 22–3. Robert Wallace, *Characteristics of the Present Political State of Great Britain*, 2nd edn (London: Andrew Millar, 1758), 200.

6. http://www.telegraph.co.uk/comment/telegraph-view/8757595 /A-sorry-tally.html, retrieved 3 July 2012.

Chapter 2: 'I'ma get medieval on yo ass': manners in the age of chivalry

1. Ian Mortimer, *The Time Traveller's Guide to Medieval England* (London: Vintage, 2009), 196.

2. Aldo Scaglione, *Knights at Court: Courtliness, Chivalry, and Courtesy from Ottonian Germany to the Italian Renaissance* (Berkeley: University of California Press, 1991), 6.

3. Philippe Ariès, *Centuries of Childhood*, trans. Robert Baldick (London: Jonathan Cape, 1962), 398.

4. See the excellent coverage of this subject in J. A. Burrow, *Gestures and Looks in Medieval Narrative* (Cambridge: Cambridge University Press, 2002).

5. Norbert Elias, *The Civilizing Process*, trans. Edmund Jephcott, rev. edn (Oxford: Blackwell, 2000), 389, 191.

6. Robert Muchembled, *A History of Violence: From the End of the Middle Ages to the Present*, trans. Jean Birrell (Cambridge: Polity, 2012), 2.

7. For a full evocation of this, see Johan Huizinga, *The Waning of the Middle Ages*, trans. Fritz Hopman (London: Edward Arnold, 1924), 1–2.

8. Steven Pinker, *The Better Angels of Our Nature: The Decline of Violence in History and Its Causes* (London: Penguin Allen Lane, 2011), 61, 64.

9. Kenelm Digby, *The Broad Stone of Honour: or, The True Sense and Practice of Chivalry. The First Book, Godefridus* (London: Joseph Booker, 1829), 89.

10. Maurice Keen, *Chivalry* (New Haven, Connecticut: Yale University Press, 1984), 239.

11. Richard Brathwait, *The English Gentlewoman* (London: Alsop and Fawcet, 1631), 82–94, 219.

Chapter 3: Lubricants and filters:
'a kind of lesser morality'

1. David Hume, *An Enquiry Concerning the Principles of Morals*, ed. Tom L. Beauchamp (Oxford: Clarendon Press, 1998), 30, 67, 80.

2. See Paul J. Zak, *The Moral Molecule: The Source of Love and Prosperity* (London: Bantam, 2012).

3. Cited in Edward O. Wilson, *On Human Nature* (New York: Bantam, 1979), 22–3.

4. See George Lakoff and Mark Johnson, *Metaphors We Live By* (Chicago: University of Chicago Press, 1980), 5.

5. Michel Foucault, *The History of Sexuality*, trans. Robert Hurley, 3 vols. (New York: Pantheon, 1978–86), I, 86.

6. Thorstein Veblen, *The Theory of the Leisure Class* (New York: Macmillan, 1899), 47. Henri Bergson, *Mélanges*, ed. André Robinet (Paris: Presses Universitaires de France, 1972), 320.

7. Jilly Cooper, *Class: An Exposé of the English Class System* (London: Corgi, 1999), 176, 11.

8. George Bernard Shaw, *Pygmalion* (London: Penguin, 2000), 5. Kate Fox, *Watching the English: The Hidden Rules of English Behaviour* (London: Hodder and Stoughton, 2004), 73.

9. Freud coined the phrase in his essay 'The Virginity Taboo'; see Sigmund Freud, *The Psychology of Love*, trans. Shaun Whiteside (London: Penguin, 2006), 268. He was influenced here by the work of the British anthropologist Ernest Crawley.

Chapter 4: Godspeed, babe: or, meetings and greetings

1. Waldemar Heckel, *The Conquests of Alexander the Great* (Cambridge: Cambridge University Press, 2008), 109.

2. John Wade, *British History, Chronologically Arranged; Comprehending a Classified Analysis of Events and Occurrences in Church and State*, 5th edn (London: Henry G. Bohn, 1847), 827.

3. Erving Goffman, *Relations in Public: Microstudies of the Public Order* (London: Penguin Allen Lane, 1971), 79–80.

4. *The Correspondence of Erasmus 1484–1500*, trans. R. A. B. Mynors and D. F. S. Thomson (Toronto: University of Toronto Press, 1974), 193.

5. Glenda Cooper, 'Kiss of Death or Friendly Salute?', *Daily Telegraph*, 14 August 2011.

6. This is treated at length in Stephen Greenblatt, *Renaissance Self-Fashioning: From More to Shakespeare* (Chicago: University of Chicago Press, 1980).

Chapter 5: Of courtiers and codpieces: fashioning Renaissance identity

1. John Guy, *Tudor England* (Oxford: Oxford University Press, 1988), 46.

2. This subject is treated at length in Anna Bryson, *From Courtesy to Civility: Changing Codes of Conduct in Early Modern England* (Oxford: Clarendon Press, 1998).

3. Benet Davetian, *Civility: A Cultural History* (Toronto: University of Toronto Press, 2009), 61.

4. William Fiston, *The School of Good Manners* (London: J. Danter, 1595), 1.

5. Alister E. McGrath, *Christianity's Dangerous Idea: The Protestant*

Revolution – A History from the Sixteenth Century to the Twenty-First (New York: HarperOne, 2007), 254. Davetian, *Civility*, 89.

6. Jacob Burckhardt, *The Civilization of the Renaissance in Italy*, trans. S. G. C. Middlemore (London: Phaidon, 1960), 85, 232.

7. Keith Thomas, *The Ends of Life: Roads to Fulfilment in Early Modern England* (Oxford: Oxford University Press, 2009), 118–20.

8. Ian Mortimer, *The Time Traveller's Guide to Elizabethan England* (London: Bodley Head, 2012), 254, 261.

9. Ulinka Rublack, *Dressing Up: Cultural Identity in Renaissance Europe* (Oxford: Oxford University Press, 2010), 18.

10. Giovanni della Casa, *Galateo*, trans. Konrad Eisenbichler and Kenneth R. Bartlett (Toronto: Centre for Reformation and Renaissance Studies, 1986), 6–7.

Chapter 6: But who was the Renaissance man?

1. Its English title was *A Lytell Booke of Good Maners for Chyldren*.

2. Desiderius Erasmus, *A Handbook on Good Manners for Children*, trans. Eleanor Merchant (London: Preface, 2008), 25, 82.

3. John Ruskin, *Modern Painters*, 5 vols. (London: Smith, Elder, 1843–60), V, 268.

4. See Joaneath Spicer, 'The Renaissance Elbow', in Jan Bremmer and Herman Roodenburg (eds.), *A Cultural History of Gesture* (Cambridge: Polity, 1991), 84–128.

5. Baldassare Castiglione, *The Book of the Courtier . . . Done into English by Sir Thomas Hoby* (London: David Nutt, 1900), 374–7.

6. Details from Adam Nicolson, *The Gentry: Stories of the English* (London: HarperPress, 2011), xv, xviii.

7. Quoted in Anna Bryson, *From Courtesy to Civility*, 204.

8. Richard Brathwait, *The English Gentleman* (London: John Haviland, 1630), 457–58.

9. *Selected Writings of Daniel Defoe*, ed. James T. Boulton (Cambridge: Cambridge University Press, 1975), 248.

10. Quoted in Ron Chernow, *The House of Morgan: An American Banking Dynasty and the Rise of Modern Finance* (New York: Touchstone, 1991), 48.

11. The phrase is Ernest Barker's in *The Character of England* (1947). Quoted in Judy Giles and Tim Middleton (eds.), *Writing Englishness, 1900–1950* (London: Routledge, 1995), 59.

12. Quoted in Nancy Mitford et al., *Noblesse Oblige: An Enquiry into the Identifiable Characteristics of the English Aristocrat* (London: Hamish Hamilton, 1956), 74.

13. See Robin Gilmour, *The Idea of the Gentleman in the Victorian Novel* (London: George Allen & Unwin, 1981).

Chapter 7: Table manners: or, how to eat a cobra's heart

1. *Coryat's Crudities*, 2 vols. (Glasgow: James MacLehose, 1905), I, 236.

2. John F. Kasson, *Rudeness and Civility: Manners in Nineteenth-Century Urban America* (New York: Hill and Wang, 1990), 185.

3. *The Habits of Good Society: A Handbook of Etiquette for Ladies and Gentlemen* (London: James Hogg, 1859), 307, 319.

4. See Judith Flanders, *The Victorian House: Domestic Life from Childbirth to Deathbed* (London: HarperCollins, 2003), 112.

5. Anthony Bourdain, *A Cook's Tour* (London: Bloomsbury, 2002), 269. Sir Walter Scott, *Tales of a Grandfather; with Stories Taken from Scottish History* (Paris: Baudry's European Library, 1833), 220–21.

6. http://www.vanityfair.com/business/features/2011/10/china -201110, retrieved 5 July 2012.

7. John George Wood, *The Uncivilized Races of Men in All Countries of the World*, 2 vols. (Hartford, Connecticut: J. B. Burr, 1870), II, 1431.

8. See Margaret Visser, *The Rituals of Dinner: The Origins, Evolution, Eccentricities, and Meaning of Table Manners* (London: Viking, 1992), xii.
9. Colin McGinn, *The Meaning of Disgust* (Oxford: Oxford University Press, 2011), 203.

Chapter 8: *The Clothes Show*: 'When in doubt, opt for navy'

1. Quoted in Lauren Collins, 'Sole Mate', *New Yorker*, 28 March 2011.
2. J. C. Flügel, *The Psychology of Clothes* (London: Hogarth Press, 1930), 35, 22, 26.
3. Ibid., 139.
4. See Wade, *British History*, 759–60, and Kimberly Chrisman, 'Unhoop the Fair Sex: The Campaign Against the Hoop Petticoat in Eighteenth-Century England', *Eighteenth-Century Studies* 30 (1996), 5–23.
5. http://www.torturegarden.com/dress/, retrieved 30 July 2012.
6. Margaret Visser, *The Way We Are* (London: Viking, 1995), 208.
7. Laurie Graham, *Getting It Right: A Survival Guide to Modern Manners* (London: Chatto & Windus, 1989), 82.

Chapter 9: Mr Sex

1. Thomas Shadwell, *The Humorists* (London: Henry Herringman, 1671), 2.
2. *Rochester: The Critical Heritage*, ed. David Farley-Hills (London: Routledge & Kegan Paul, 1972), 57.
3. *The Works of John Wilmot, Earl of Rochester*, ed. Harold Love (Oxford: Oxford University Press, 1999), 89.

4. http://www.hrp.org.uk/discoverthepalaces/Historyandstories /Lifeinthepalaces/Mannersandetiquette, retrieved 6 July 2012.

5. Elizabeth Stone, *Chronicles of Fashion, from the Time of Elizabeth to the Early Part of the Nineteenth Century*, 2 vols. (London: Richard Bentley, 1845), II, 4.

6. The subject is illuminated by Peter Burke in *The Fabrication of Louis XIV* (New Haven, Connecticut: Yale University Press, 1992).

7. Francis Osborne, *Advice to a Son* (London: David Nutt, 1896), 48–9, 79.

8. The seventeenth-century phenomenon of libertine 'anti-civility' is discussed in Anna Bryson, *From Courtesy to Civility*, 243–75.

9. John Locke, *Some Thoughts Concerning Education*, 5th edn (London: A. and J. Churchill, 1705), 87. William Hazlitt, *Table-Talk: Original Essays on Men and Manners*, 2 vols. (London: C. Templeman, 1861), II, 315.

10. John Playford, *The English Dancing Master* (London: Thomas Harper, 1651), 2.

11. Jonas Hanway, *A Journal of Eight Days Journey . . . to which is added An Essay on Tea*, 2nd edn, 2 vols. (London: H. Woodfall, 1757), II, 2, 276, 273.

12. The phrase occurs in Isaac D'Israeli, *Curiosities of Literature*, 9th edn, 6 vols. (London: Edward Moxon, 1834), III, 307.

13. This subject is discussed by Jorge Arditi in *A Genealogy of Manners: Transformations of Social Relations in France and England from the Fourteenth to the Eighteenth Century* (Chicago: University of Chicago Press, 1998), 122–54.

14. Quoted in Joan Wildeblood and Peter Brinson, *The Polite World: A Guide to English Manners and Deportment from the Thirteenth to the Nineteenth Century* (London: Oxford University Press, 1965), 197.

15. Richard Allestree, *The Ladies Calling* (Oxford: printed at the Theatre, 1673), 259. Mary Astell, *A Serious Proposal to the Ladies*, ed.

Patricia Springborg (Peterborough, Ontario: Broadview Press, 2002), 109.

16. Jerry White, *London in the Eighteenth Century* (London: Bodley Head, 2012), 3.

17. Cited in David G. Hey, *An English Rural Community: Myddle Under the Tudors and Stuarts* (Leicester: Leicester University Press, 1974), 227.

18. G. J. Barker-Benfield, *The Culture of Sensibility: Sex and Society in Eighteenth-Century Britain* (Chicago: Chicago University Press, 1992), 80.

Chapter 10: Not Mr Sex: when 'coffee' doesn't mean coffee

1. George Mikes, *How To Be A Brit* (London: Penguin, 1986), 35.

2. Lawrence Stone, *The Family, Sex and Marriage in England 1500–1800*, abr. edn (London: Penguin, 1990), 324.

3. Philip Stubbes, *The Anatomie of Abuses* (London: Richard Jones, 1583), 120, 89–91.

4. Faramerz Dabhoiwala, *The Origins of Sex: A History of the First Sexual Revolution* (London: Penguin Allen Lane, 2012), 44.

5. *Aristotle's Masterpiece, or The Secrets of Generation Displayed in All the Parts Thereof* (London: J. How, 1684), 6, 49.

6. http://www.guardian.co.uk/lifeandstyle/2009/jan/24/online -dating-etiquette-advice, retrieved 14 September 2012.

7. See Steven Pinker, *The Stuff of Thought: Language as a Window into Human Nature* (London: Penguin, 2008), 23.

8. Osborne, *Advice to a Son*, 41, 38, 44, 54, 49, 55–6.

Chapter 11: The elephant and the bad baby: the everyday language of manners

1. This is discussed at greater length in Anna Wierzbicka, *English: Meaning and Culture* (Oxford: Oxford University Press, 2006), 204–96.
2. Bertrand Russell, *Mortals and Others* (London: Routledge, 2009), 337.
3. The question of 'polite lies' is discussed by Karen Stohr in *On Manners* (New York: Routledge, 2012), 92–113.
4. Thomas Hobbes, *Leviathan*, ed. Richard Tuck (Cambridge: Cambridge University Press, 1996), 69.
5. This is explored more fully in Anna Wierzbicka, *Experience, Evidence, and Sense: The Hidden Cultural Legacy of English* (New York: Oxford University Press, 2010).
6. Wierzbicka, *English: Meaning and Culture*, 160–67.
7. The book, written by Elfrida Vipont, has lovely illustrations by Raymond Briggs.
8. Seneca, *Moral and Political Essays*, ed. and trans. John M. Cooper and J. F. Procopé (Cambridge: Cambridge University Press, 1995), 203, 218.

Chapter 12: Spectators and stratagems: the polite, commercial eighteenth century

1. See Dabhoiwala, *The Origins of Sex*, 320–21.
2. Richard Steele and Joseph Addison, *Selections from the Tatler and the Spectator*, ed. Angus Ross (London: Penguin, 1988), 210, 277.
3. This subject is treated at length in Steven Shapin, *A Social History of Truth: Civility and Science in Seventeenth-Century England* (Chicago: University of Chicago Press, 1994).

4. James Boswell, *The Life of Samuel Johnson*, ed. David Womersley (London: Penguin, 2008), 373.

5. Quoted in the Introduction to *Selections from the Tatler and the Spectator*, ed. Ross, 54.

6. *Selections from the Tatler and the Spectator*, ed. Ross, 210.

7. Emily Cockayne, *Hubbub: Filth, Noise and Stench in England, 1600–1770* (New Haven, Connecticut: Yale University Press, 2007), 237.

8. Craig Koslofsky, *Evening's Empire: A History of the Night in Early Modern Europe* (Cambridge: Cambridge University Press, 2011), 184.

9. Anthony Ashley Cooper, Third Earl of Shaftesbury, *Characteristics of Men, Manners, Opinions, Times*, ed. Lawrence E. Klein (Cambridge: Cambridge University Press, 1999), 31.

10. *The Works of Jonathan Swift*, 19 vols. (Edinburgh: Constable, 1814), IX, 453.

11. Ibid., XI, 406, 419, 389.

12. *Wise Sayings and Favourite Passages from the Works of Henry Fielding* (Cedar Rapids, Iowa: Torch Press, 1909), 120.

13. *The Correspondence of Jonathan Swift*, ed. Harold Williams, 5 vols. (Oxford: Clarendon Press, 1963–5), III, 341, 383. *The Works of Jonathan Swift*, XII, 392–3.

14. Jane Collier, *An Essay on the Art of Ingeniously Tormenting* (London: Andrew Millar, 1753), 27, 142, 232.

15. Peter Beckford, *Familiar Letters from Italy, to a Friend in England*, 2 vols. (Salisbury: J. Easton, 1805), I, 9.

16. Hannah Cowley, *The Belle's Stratagem* (Dublin: 1781), 8, 26–7.

17. Mary Wollstonecraft, *A Vindication of the Rights of Woman*, 3rd edn (London: Joseph Johnson, 1796), 112.

Chapter 13: Lord Chesterfield and the invention of etiquette

1. *Gentleman's Magazine* 7 (1737), 34–5.
2. Eliza Cheadle, *Manners of Modern Society: Being A Book of Etiquette* (London: Cassell, Petter & Galpin, 1878), 35.
3. *The Works of George Savile, Marquis of Halifax*, ed. Mark N. Brown, 3 vols. (Oxford: Clarendon Press, 1989), II, 390, 393, 363, 373, 390.
4. This is the date of the first letter to Philip in Bonamy Dobrée's six-volume edition, though in his introduction Dobrée gives the date as 1738; Lord Chesterfield, *Letters*, ed. Bonamy Dobrée, 6 vols. (London: Eyre & Spottiswoode, 1932), I, 162; II, 306.
5. *World*, 12 August 1756.
6. *Mark Twain at Your Fingertips*, ed. Caroline Thomas Harnsberger (New York: Beechhurst Press, 1948), 33.
7. Harriet Martineau, *Society in America*, 2 vols. (Paris: A. and W. Galignani, 1837), II, 109.
8. Fanny Burney, *Journals and Letters*, ed. Peter Sabor and Lars E. Troide (London: Penguin, 2001), 33.
9. Boswell, *The Life of Samuel Johnson*, ed. Womersley, 144.
10. *Boswell's London Journal, 1762–1763*, ed. Frederick A. Pottle (Edinburgh: Edinburgh University Press, 1991), 272.
11. George Edward Ayscough, *Letters from an Officer in the Guards to his Friend in England* (London: Thomas Cadell, 1778), 23.
12. John Brown, *An Estimate of the Manners and Principles of the Times*, 5th edn (London: Davis and Reymers, 1757), 135–7, 141.
13. Arthur Young, *Travels, During the Years 1787, 1788, and 1789* (Bury St Edmunds: J. Rackham, 1792), 277.
14. Hobbes, *Leviathan*, ed. Tuck, 43.
15. Béat-Louis de Muralt, *Letters Describing the Character and*

Customs of the English and French Nations (London: Thomas Edlin, 1726), 11.

16. J. A. Sharpe, 'Civility, Civilizing Processes, and the End of Public Punishment in England', in Peter Burke, Brian Harrison and Paul Slack (eds.), *Civil Histories: Essays Presented to Sir Keith Thomas* (Oxford: Oxford University Press, 2000), 227.

17. Paul Langford, *Englishness Identified: Manners and Character 1650–1850* (Oxford: Oxford University Press, 2000), 76.

18. Robert Lesuire, *The Savages of Europe* (London: Dryden Leach, 1764), 21. Kielmansegge is quoted in Langford, *Englishness Identified*, 56.

19. Carl Philip Moritz, *Journeys of a German in England*, trans. Reginald Nettel (London: Eland, 2009), 176, 61.

20. Johann Wilhelm von Archenholz, *A Picture of England*, 2 vols. (London: Edward Jeffery, 1789), I, 60.

21. William Godwin, *The Enquirer: Reflections on Education, Manners, and Literature* (London: G. G. and J. Robinson, 1797), 326.

22. *The Letters of William Godwin: Volume I, 1778–1797*, ed. Pamela Clemit (Oxford: Oxford University Press, 2011), 71–3.

Chapter 14: Letters and social change:
Jane Austen and Fanny Burney

1. See Charles Bazerman, 'Letters and the Social Grounding of Differentiated Genres', in David Barton and Nigel Hall (eds.), *Letter Writing as a Social Practice* (Amsterdam: John Benjamins, 2000).

2. *The Young Lady's Companion; or, Beauty's Looking-Glass* (London: printed and sold by the booksellers of London and Westminster, 1740), 41.

3. Jane Austen, *Selected Letters*, ed. Vivien Jones (Oxford: Oxford University Press, 2004), 85, 49.

4. See Tony Tanner, *Jane Austen* (Basingstoke: Macmillan, 1986), 12.

5. Burney, *Journals and Letters*, ed. Sabor and Troide, 252.

6. Ibid., 230.

Chapter 15: The Englishness of English manners

1. Edmund Burke, *Reflections on the Revolution in France*, 2nd edn (London: James Dodsley, 1790), 112–13.

2. Edmund Burke, *Two Letters Addressed to a Member of the Present Parliament* (Dublin: William Porter, 1796), 72.

3. Burke, *Reflections on the Revolution in France*, 2nd edn, 128, 144.

4. W. C. Sellar and R. J. Yeatman, *1066 and All That: A Memorable History of England*, 6th edn (London: Methuen, 1930), 17.

5. Roger Scruton, *England: An Elegy* (London: Pimlico, 2001), 10, 122.

6. Doris Lessing, *In Pursuit of the English: A Documentary* (London: MacGibbon & Kee, 1960), 9.

7. Arthur Bryant, *The National Character* (London: Longmans, Green, 1934), 6.

8. Bill Bryson, *Notes from A Small Island* (London: Black Swan, 1996), 32.

9. Quoted in Giles and Middleton (eds.), *Writing Englishness*, 101.

10. Julian Barnes, *England, England* (London: Jonathan Cape, 1998), 83–5.

11. George Orwell, *Essays*, ed. John Carey (London: Everyman, 2002), 292, 1026–8.

12. Fox, *Watching the English*, 256–7.

13. Hobbes, *Leviathan*, ed. Tuck, 89–90.

Chapter 16: Island Man and his discontents:
'They do things differently there'

1. One of those advertisements can be seen at http://
www.youtube.com/watch?v=JK_NinOmFWw, retrieved 9
August 2012.

2. For details of this, see Margaret Visser, *The Gift of Thanks: The
Roots and Rituals of Gratitude* (Boston: Houghton Mifflin
Harcourt, 2009), 36–46.

3. Peter Hessler, *Country Driving: A Chinese Road Trip* (Edinburgh:
Canongate, 2011), 274.

4. Ralph Waldo Emerson, *Essays & Lectures*, ed. Joel Porte (New
York: Library of America, 1983), 826.

5. Christopher Hitchens, *The Monarchy: A Critique of Britain's
Favourite Fetish* (London: Chatto & Windus, 1990), 3.

6. Pearl Binder, *The English Inside Out* (London: Weidenfeld and
Nicolson, 1961), 32, 128, 131, 151, 244, 68, 243, 111.

7. Mikes, *How To Be A Brit*, 30, 42, 22, 54.

8. Peter Mandler, *The English National Character: The History of an
Idea from Edmund Burke to Tony Blair* (New Haven, Connecticut:
Yale University Press, 2006), 179.

9. G. J. Renier, *The English: Are They Human?* (London: Williams
& Norgate, 1949), 171, 194, 18.

10. Orwell, *Essays*, ed. Carey, 294.

11. *Debrett's Etiquette and Modern Manners*, ed. Elsie Burch Donald
(London: Debrett's, 1981), 279.

12. George Slythe Street, *People and Questions* (London: Martin
Secker, 1910), 103.

13. Alan F. Westin, *Privacy and Freedom* (New York: Atheneum,
1967), 24.

14. Theodore Zeldin, *The French* (London: Collins, 1983), 35.

15. Hermann Muthesius, *The English House*, ed. Dennis Sharp, trans.

Janet Seligman and Stewart Spencer, 3 vols. (London: Frances Lincoln, 2007), II, 108.

16. Quoted in Christopher Ricks, *T. S. Eliot and Prejudice* (London: Faber, 1988), 200.

Chapter 17: Fanny Trollope and the domestic manners of Americans

1. Anthony Trollope, *An Autobiography* (Berkeley, California: University of California Press, 1978), 20. Twain is quoted in Pamela Neville-Sington, *Fanny Trollope: The Life and Adventures of a Clever Woman* (London: Viking, 1997), 176.

2. Charles Dickens, *American Notes for General Circulation* (New York: Harper, 1842), 44. Philip Kelland, *Transatlantic Sketches* (Edinburgh: A. & C. Black, 1858), 5, 25.

3. *The Life and Writings of Benjamin Franklin*, 2 vols. (Philadelphia: McCarty & Davis, 1834), I, 34.

4. Gerald Carson, *The Polite Americans* (London: Macmillan, 1967), 71, 79.

5. Alexis de Tocqueville, *Democracy in America*, trans. Arthur Goldhammer (New York: Library of America, 2004), 713. *The Journal of Henry D. Thoreau*, 2 vols. (New York: Dover, 1962), II, 332.

6. Andrew St George, *The Descent of Manners: Etiquette, Rules and the Victorians* (London: Chatto & Windus, 1993), 175.

7. Sarah Josepha Hale, *Manners; or, Happy Homes and Good Society All the Year Round* (Boston: J. E. Tilton, 1868), 244, 143, 6.

8. L. J. Ransone, *'Good Form' in England, by an American Resident in the United Kingdom* (New York: Appleton, 1888), 160–61, 6, 100. Florence Burton Kingsland, *Etiquette for All Occasions* (New York: Doubleday, Page, 1901), 500.

Chapter 18: 'You're the most important person!': the trouble with children

1. Stephen L. Carter, *Civility: Manners, Morals, and the Etiquette of Democracy* (New York: Harper Perennial, 1998), 230.
2. These are some of the lessons Robert Fulghum recalls learning at Sunday school, in *All I Really Need to Know I Learned in Kindergarten* (London: Grafton, 1989), 6–7.
3. John Locke, *Some Thoughts Concerning Education*, 5th edn, 52, 92, 86, 81, 390, 91.
4. *The Works of Jonathan Swift*, XI, 313. Locke, *Some Thoughts Concerning Education*, 92–3.
5. Jean-Jacques Rousseau, *The Social Contract and Other Later Political Writings*, ed.Victor Gourevitch (Cambridge: Cambridge University Press, 1997), 191.
6. Peter N. Stearns, *Childhood in World History* (New York: Routledge, 2006), 108.
7. Tina Fey, *Bossypants* (London: Sphere, 2012), 54.
8. Elizabeth Kolbert, 'Spoiled Rotten', *New Yorker*, 2 July 2012.
9. Pamela Druckerman, *French Children Don't Throw Food: Parenting Secrets from Paris* (London: Doubleday, 2012), 4, 28, 91, 301.

Chapter 19: What were Victorian values?

1. Quoted in M. Dorothy George, *London Life in the Eighteenth Century* (London: Penguin, 1987), 18.
2. J. Robinson, *A Manual of Manners; or, Hints for the Proper Deportment of School Boys* (London: Hamilton, Adams, 1829), ix.
3. Friedrich Engels, *The Condition of the Working Class in England*, trans. Florence Wischnewetzky, ed. Victor Kiernan (London: Penguin, 2009), 68–71, 266. *The Works of Jonathan Swift*, XIV, 96.

4. Lawrence Wright, *Clean and Decent: The History of the Bath and Loo*, rev. edn (London: Routledge & Kegan Paul, 1980), 139.

5. Margaret Thatcher, *The Downing Street Years* (London: Harper Perennial, 1995), 627.

6. John Stuart Mill, *On Liberty and Other Writings*, ed. Stefan Collini (Cambridge: Cambridge University Press, 1989), 183.

7. See Marjorie Morgan, *Manners, Morals and Class in England, 1774–1858* (London: St Martin's Press, 1994).

8. See Arditi, *A Genealogy of Manners*, 5.

9. John Browne, *Tobacco Morally and Physically Considered* (Driffield: B. Fawcett, 1842), 9. *A Present for an Apprentice* (London: Thomas Tegg, 1838), 117, 320–22.

10. Thomas Carlyle, *Sartor Resartus* (London: Chapman and Hall, 1858), 134.

11. http://www.guardian.co.uk/media/2007/nov/22/television business, retrieved 13 June 2012.

12. Beatrice Knollys, *The Gentle Art of Good Talking* (London: James Bowden, 1899), 33. George Seaton Bowes, *Conversation: Why Don't We Do More Good by It?* (London: James Nisbet, 1886), xi, xiii.

13. Langford, *Englishness Identified*, 181. James Sully, 'Civilization and Noise', *Fortnightly Review* 24 (1878), 715.

14. See John M. Picker, 'The Soundproof Study: Victorian Professionals, Work Space, and Urban Noise', *Victorian Studies* 42 (1999–2000), 427–53.

15. David Goldblatt, *The Ball Is Round: A Global History of Soccer* (New York: Riverhead, 2008), 17, 27.

16. Martin Tupper, *Proverbial Philosophy: A Book of Thoughts and Arguments, Originally Treated* (London: Joseph Rickerby, 1839), 156.

17. Sarah Stickney Ellis, *The Wives of England* (London: Fisher, 1843), 242, 250, 267, 268–9.

18. *Mrs Beeton's Book of Household Management*, ed. Nicola Humble (Oxford: Oxford University Press, 2000), 7.

19. *The Young Lady's Book: A Manual of Elegant Recreations, Exercises, and Pursuits* (London: Vizetelly, Branston, 1829), 24, 57, 283, 424–5. Sarah Stickney Ellis, *The Wives of England*, 281.

20. Quoted in Judith Flanders, *The Victorian House: Domestic Life from Childbirth to Deathbed* (London: HarperCollins, 2003), 232.

21. Michael Curtin, *Propriety and Position: A Study of Victorian Manners* (New York: Garland, 1987), 277.

22. *A Present for an Apprentice*, 275–6.

23. Oliver Bell Bunce, *Don't: A Manual of Mistakes and Improprieties More or Less Prevalent in Conduct and Speech* (London: Field & Tuer, 1883), 61, 52–3, 56, 60.

24. Theodore Zeldin, *An Intimate History of Humanity* (London: Minerva, 1995), 40.

25. Hester Lynch Piozzi, *British Synonymy* (London: G. G. and J. Robinson, 1794), 14. Bharat Tandon writes in *Jane Austen and the Morality of Conversation* (London: Anthem, 2003) that Piozzi's work 'raises the possibility that vulgarisms might issue infectiously from the mouths of the poor, like germs or bad breath, and *British Synonymy* repeatedly attempts to keep the objects of its disapproval at least at arm's length' (31).

26. The subject is explored at length in Richard W. Bailey, *Nineteenth-Century English* (Ann Arbor: University of Michigan Press, 1996).

27. Gertrude Himmelfarb, *The De-Moralization of Society: From Victorian Virtues to Modern Values* (New York: Knopf, 1995), 259–63.

Chapter 20: Curb your enthusiasm: new ways for new times

1. Elizabeth Kolbert, 'Place Settings', *New Yorker*, 20 October 2008. Helen Huntington Smith, 'Lady Chesterfield', *New Yorker*, 16 August 1930.

2. Edmund Wilson, 'Books of Etiquette and Emily Post', *New Yorker*, 19 July 1947.

3. Emily Post, *Etiquette: The Blue Book of Social Usage*, 10th edn (New York: Funk & Wagnalls, 1960), 61.

4. Ibid., 602.

5. Ibid., 45, 456, 525, 576.

6. Amy Vanderbilt, 'Bad Manners in America', *Annals of the American Academy of Political and Social Science* 378 (1968), 90, 92, 96, 98.

7. *Letitia Baldrige's New Manners for New Times* (New York, Scribner, 2003), 53.

8. Judith Martin, *Miss Manners' Guide to Excruciatingly Correct Behavior* (London: Hamish Hamilton, 1983), 158, 211, 384.

9. This is reported by Margaret Y. Han in the *Harvard Crimson*, 11 May 1984.

10. See Bret Easton Ellis, *American Psycho*, rev. edn (London: Picador, 1998).

11. 'Miss Manners on Office Etiquette', *Fortune*, 6 November 1989.

12. Elizabeth Wyse et al., *Debrett's A–Z of Modern Manners* (Richmond: Debrett's, 2008), 90, 176, 173, 128, 231.

13. Anne Edwards and Drusilla Beyfus, *Lady Behave: A Guide to Modern Manners for the 1970s* (London: Cassell, 1969), 160.

Chapter 21: Creative hubs and 'extreme phenomena':
negotiating the modern city

1. *Inedited Tracts. Illustrating the Manners, Opinions and Occupations of Englishmen During the Sixteenth and Seventeenth Centuries* (London: Whittingham and Wilkins for the Roxburghe Library, 1868), 31. The quoted words are in fact Valentine's, not Vincent's, but they support Vincent's arguments.

2. Jonathan Raban, *Soft City* (London: Picador, 2008), 26–7, 68.

3. Orwell, *Essays*, ed. Carey, 295.

4. Georg Simmel, *On Individuality and Social Forms*, ed. Donald N. Levine (Chicago: University of Chicago Press, 1971), 324, 329, 338.

5. See John Reader, *Cities* (London: Vintage, 2005), 111.

6. See Emily Cockayne, *Cheek by Jowl: A History of Neighbours* (London: Bodley Head, 2012).

7. Evelyn Waugh, 'Manners and Morals', in *The Essays, Articles and Reviews of Evelyn Waugh*, ed. Donat Gallagher (London: Methuen, 1983), 591.

8. Torbjörn Lundmark, *Tales of Hi and Bye: Greeting and Parting Rituals Around the World* (Cambridge: Cambridge University Press, 2009), 146.

9. Fox, *Watching the English*, 170–71.

10. Quoted in Frank Victor Dawes, *Not In Front of the Servants* (London: Hutchinson, 1984), 35.

11. Joe Moran, *Queuing for Beginners: The Story of Daily Life from Breakfast to Bedtime* (London: Profile, 2007), 39.

Chapter 22: Location, location, location: the rules of place

1. Philip Smith, Timothy L. Phillips and Ryan D. King, *Incivility: The Rude Stranger in Everyday Life* (Cambridge: Cambridge University Press, 2010), 64.

2. Bill Bryson, *At Home: A Short History of Private Life* (London: Doubleday, 2010), 48.

3. Mark Girouard, *Life in the English Country House* (New Haven, Connecticut: Yale University Press, 1978), 194.

4. The experiment is cited in Jonathan Haidt, *The Righteous Mind: Why Good People Are Divided by Politics and Religion* (London: Penguin Allen Lane, 2012), 61.

Chapter 23: A fluid world:
or, 'Are you suggesting that I should call you Eric?'

1. These figures come from Kevin Cahill, 'The Great Property Swindle', *New Statesman*, 11 March 2011.
2. Richard Pomfret, *The Age of Equality: The Twentieth Century in Economic Perspective* (Cambridge, Mass.: Belknap Press, 2011), 1.
3. Alice-Leone Moats, *No Nice Girl Swears* (London: Cassell, 1933), 23.
4. Quoted in David Attenborough, *Life on Air: Memoirs of a Broadcaster* (London: BBC Books, 2002), 143.
5. Lady Troubridge, *Etiquette and Entertaining* (London: Amalgamated Press, 1939), 10. Lady Troubridge, *The Book of Etiquette* (Kingswood: The World's Work, 1926), 302–3.
6. David Kynaston, *Austerity Britain: 1945–51* (London: Bloomsbury, 2007), 19.
7. Geoffrey Gorer, *Exploring English Character* (London: Cresset Press, 1955), 52.
8. Ibid.
9. Betty Friedan, *The Feminine Mystique* (New York: Norton, 1963), 296–7. Zeldin, *An Intimate History of Humanity*, 75.
10. Clive Aslet, *Anyone for England? A Search for British Identity* (London: Little, Brown, 1997), 155.
11. Pinker, *The Better Angels of Our Nature*, 692, 125, 128.
12. *Manners and Rules of Good Society*, 17th edn (London: Frederick Warne, 1891), 32, 185, 225.
13. http://www.nytimes.com/2006/04/27/technology/27myspace.html, retrieved 29 June 2012. http://www.dailymail.co.uk/debate/article-2075133/Christopher-Hitchens-death-In-Memoriam-courageous-sibling-Peter-Hitchens.html, retrieved 29 June 2012.

Chapter 24: Technology and the revenge effect

1. Lynne Truss, *Talk to the Hand* (London: Profile, 2005), 23.
2. Sherry Turkle, *Alone Together: Why We Expect More from Technology and Less from Each Other* (New York: Basic Books, 2011), 1.
3. http://www.edge.org/3rd_culture/foreman05/foreman05_index .html, retrieved 31 May 2012.
4. Jonathan Franzen, *Farther Away* (New York: Farrar, Straus and Giroux, 2012), 145–50.
5. This image is used, a little differently, by a character in a Max Frisch novel. See Max Frisch, *Homo Faber*, trans. Michael Bullock (London: Penguin, 2006), 182.

Chapter 25: 'Are we there yet?': manners now

1. Benjamin DeMott, 'Seduced by Civility: Political Manners and the Crisis of Democratic Values', *Nation*, 9 December 1996.
2. http://www.guardian.co.uk/uk/interactive/2011/dec/14 /reading-the-riots-investigating-england-s-summer-of-disorder -full-report, retrieved 29 June 2012.
3. Phoebe Griffith, Will Norman, Carmel O'Sullivan and Rushanara Ali, *Charm Offensive: Cultivating Civility in 21st Century Britain* (London: The Young Foundation, 2011), 18.
4. Edward Shils, *The Virtue of Civility: Selected Essays on Liberalism, Tradition, and Civil Society*, ed. Steven Grosby (Indianapolis: Liberty Fund, 1997), 4.
5. Griffith et al., *Charm Offensive*, 10, 43.
6. Robert D. Putnam, *Bowling Alone: The Collapse and Revival of American Community* (New York: Simon & Schuster, 2000), 132.
7. Richard Sennett, *Respect: The Formation of Character in An Age of Inequality* (London: Penguin Allen Lane, 2003), 207.

8. Charles Murray, *Coming Apart: The State of White America, 1960–2010* (New York: Crown Forum, 2012), 200–201, 286–7.

9. Florence Bell, *The Minor Moralist* (London: Edward Arnold, 1903), 39.

10. http://www.standard.co.uk/news/two-year-asbo-for-10yearold - tearaway-7200957.html, retrieved 30 August 2012. http://www.messengernewspapers.co.uk/news/8671336.11_year_old_Hale_Barns_boy_gets_five_year_ASBO/, retrieved 30 August 2012. http://www.dailymail.co.uk/news/article-469670/Asbo-12-year-old-thug-nicknamed-Chucky.html, retrieved 30 August 2012.

11. See Martin Ingram, 'Sexual Manners: The Other Face of Civility in Early Modern England', in Burke, Harrison and Slack (eds.), *Civil Histories*, 99.

12. For the review in question, by Theo Tait, see http://www.guardian.co.uk/books/2012/jun/08/lionel-asbo-martin-amis-review, retrieved 29 August 2012.

13. Wyse et al., *Debrett's A–Z of Modern Manners*, 264, 111, 277.

14. John Morgan, *The Times Book of Modern Manners* (London: HarperCollins, 2000), 60, 116–17, 132.

15. Anne de Courcy, *A Guide to Modern Manners* (London: Thames and Hudson, 1985), 145.

16. *Scots Magazine* 44 (1782), 368.

17. The questions are intended to be rhetorical. Still, responding spontaneously, I would give the following answers:

   I don't know, but I expect I'll find out if I have a daughter. Straightforwardly.

   Rarely; on the whole you should choose something that you can eat or should choose to eat elsewhere, but in a restaurant where you are a regular a special request of this kind is permissible.

   Yes, but only in extreme circumstances, and don't expect to win any prizes for doing so.

Yes, although you will probably think I need to loosen up a little.

Well . . . it's so uncool that it's almost cool, but, on hygiene grounds, no.

Yes, if it's not raining or snowing and there's a suitable space for smoking, such as a balcony or indeed a garden.

Just about, if it is done briefly and unintrusively, but it's a bit creepy.

18. David Brooks, *The Social Animal: A Story of How Success Happens* (London: Short Books, 2012), 394.

19. Truss, *Talk to the Hand*, 152–3.

20. Waugh, 'Manners and Morals', 587.

21. See Joanna Bourke, *Fear: A Cultural History* (London: Virago, 2005).

22. See Frank Furedi, *Therapy Culture: Cultivating Vulnerability in an Uncertain Age* (London: Routledge, 2004).

Bibliography

Peter Ackroyd, *Albion: The Origins of the English Imagination* (London: Chatto & Windus, 2002)

Petrus Alfonsi, *Disciplina Clericalis*, ed. and trans. Eberhard Hermes, trans. into English P. R. Quarrie (London: Routledge & Kegan Paul, 1977)

Henry Alford, *Would It Kill You to Stop Doing That? A Modern Guide to Manners* (New York: Twelve, 2012)

Richard Allestree, *The Ladies Calling* (Oxford: printed at the Theatre, 1673)

_____, *The Causes of the Decay of Christian Piety* (London: E. and R. Pawlet, 1704)

_____, *The Whole Duty of Man* (London: John Eyres, William Mount and Thomas Page, 1735)

Nicholas Amhurst, *Terrae-Filius*, ed. William E. Rivers (Newark, Delaware: University of Delaware Press, 2004)

Martin Amis, *Lionel Asbo: State of England* (London: Jonathan Cape, 2012)

Digby Anderson (ed.), *Gentility Recalled: Mere Manners and the Making of Social Order* (London: Social Affairs Unit, 1996)

Anon., *The Institucion of a Gentleman* (London: Thomas Marshe, 1555)

_____, *Civil and Uncivil Life* (London: Richard Jones, 1579)

_____, *Aristotle's Masterpiece, or The Secrets of Generation Displayed in All the Parts Thereof* (London: J. How, 1684)

_____, *The Young Lady's Companion; or, Beauty's Looking-Glass* (London: printed and sold by the booksellers of London and Westminster, 1740)

_____, *The Ladies Complete Letter-Writer*, 2nd edn (London: T. Lownds, 1765)

_____, *The Young Lady's Book: A Manual of Elegant Recreations, Exercises, and Pursuits* (London: Vizetelly, Branston, 1829)

_____, *The Habits of Good Society: A Handbook of Etiquette for Ladies and Gentlemen* (London: James Hogg, 1859)

_____, *Inedited Tracts. Illustrating the Manners, Opinions and Occupations of Englishmen During the Sixteenth and Seventeenth Centuries* (London: Whittingham and Wilkins for the Roxburghe Library, 1868)

_____, *Manners and Rules of Good Society*, 17th edn (London: Frederick Warne, 1891)

Jorge Arditi, *A Genealogy of Manners: Transformations of Social Relations in France and England from the Fourteenth to the Eighteenth Century* (Chicago: University of Chicago Press, 1998)

Esther B. Aresty, *The Best Behavior* (New York: Simon and Schuster, 1970)

Philippe Ariès, *Centuries of Childhood*, trans. Robert Baldick (London: Jonathan Cape, 1962)

Philippe Ariès and Georges Duby (gen. eds.), *A History of Private Life*, 5 vols. (Cambridge, Mass.: Belknap Press, 1987–91)

Nancy Armstrong and Leonard Tennenhouse (eds.), *The Ideology of Conduct: Essays in Literature and the History of Sexuality* (New York: Methuen, 1987)

Roger Ascham, *Toxophilus: The Schole of Shootinge* (London: Edward Whytchurch, 1545)

Katherine Ashenburg, *Clean: The Unsanitized History of Washing* (London: Profile, 2008)

Kathleen Ashley and Robert L. A. Clark (eds.), *Medieval Conduct* (Minneapolis: University of Minnesota Press, 2001)

Clive Aslet, *Anyone for England? A Search for British Identity* (London: Little, Brown, 1997)

Mary Astell, *A Serious Proposal to the Ladies*, ed. Patricia Springborg (Peterborough, Ontario: Broadview Press, 2002)

David Attenborough, *Life on Air: Memoirs of a Broadcaster* (London: BBC Books, 2002)

Arthur Aughey, *The Politics of Englishness* (Manchester: Manchester University Press, 2007)

Jane Austen, *Selected Letters*, ed. Vivien Jones (Oxford: Oxford University Press, 2004)

George Edward Ayscough, *Letters from an Officer in the Guards to his Friend in England* (London: Thomas Cadell, 1778)

Julian Baggini, *Welcome to Everytown: A Journey into the English Mind* (London: Granta, 2007)

Richard W. Bailey, *Nineteenth-Century English* (Ann Arbor: University of Michigan Press, 1996)

Letitia Baldrige's New Manners for New Times (New York: Scribner, 2003)

E. Digby Baltzell, *Sporting Gentlemen: Men's Tennis from the Age of Honour to the Cult of the Superstar* (New York: Free Press, 1995)

Ernest Barker, *National Character and the Factors in its Formation*, 4th edn (Westport, Connecticut: Hyperion Press, 1979)

G. J. Barker-Benfield, *The Culture of Sensibility: Sex and Society in Eighteenth-Century Britain* (Chicago: Chicago University Press, 1992)

Julian Barnes, *England, England* (London: Jonathan Cape, 1998)

David Barton and Nigel Hall (eds.), *Letter Writing as a Social Practice* (Amsterdam: John Benjamins, 2000)

Ian Baucom, *Out of Place: Englishness, Empire, and the Locations of Identity* (Princeton, NJ: Princeton University Press, 1999)

Peter Beckford, *Familiar Letters from Italy, to a Friend in England*, 2 vols. (Salisbury: J. Easton, 1805)

Mrs Beeton's Book of Household Management, ed. Nicola Humble (Oxford: Oxford University Press, 2000)

Florence Bell, *The Minor Moralist* (London: Edward Arnold, 1903)

Joseph Bensman and Robert Lilienfeld, *Between Public and Private: The Lost Boundaries of the Self* (New York: Free Press, 1979)

Henri Bergson, *Mélanges*, ed. André Robinet (Paris: Presses Universitaires de France, 1972)

Drusilla Beyfus, *Modern Manners: The Essential Guide to Living in the '90s* (London: Hamlyn, 1992)

Pearl Binder, *The English Inside Out* (London: Weidenfeld and Nicolson, 1961)

James Boswell, *The Life of Samuel Johnson*, ed. David Womersley (London: Penguin, 2008)

Boswell's London Journal, 1762–1763, ed. Frederick A. Pottle (Edinburgh: Edinburgh University Press, 1991)

Anthony Bourdain, *A Cook's Tour* (London: Bloomsbury, 2002)

Pierre Bourdieu, *Outline of a Theory of Practice*, trans. Richard Nice (Cambridge: Cambridge University Press, 1977)

Joanna Bourke, *Fear: A Cultural History* (London: Virago, 2005)

George Seaton Bowes, *Conversation: Why Don't We Do More Good By It?* (London: James Nisbet, 1886)

Richard Brathwait, *The English Gentleman* (London: John Haviland, 1630)

_____, *The English Gentlewoman* (London: Alsop and Fawcet, 1631)

Fernand Braudel, *The Structures of Everyday Life*, trans. Miriam Kochan, rev. Siân Reynolds (New York: Harper & Row, 1985)

Jan Bremmer and Herman Roodenburg (eds.), *A Cultural History of Gesture* (Cambridge: Polity, 1991)

Mary Theresa Brentano, *Relationship of the Latin* Facetus *Literature to the Medieval English Courtesy Poems* (Lawrence, Kansas: University of Kansas, Department of Journalism Press, 1935)

John Brewer, *The Pleasures of the Imagination: English Culture in the Eighteenth Century* (London: HarperCollins, 1997)

David Brooks, *The Social Animal: A Story of How Success Happens* (London: Short Books, 2012)

John Brown, *An Estimate of the Manners and Principles of the Times,* 5th edn (London: Davis and Reymers, 1757)

Penelope Brown and Stephen C. Levinson, *Politeness: Some Universals in Language Usage* (Cambridge: Cambridge University Press, 1987)

John Browne, *Tobacco Morally and Physically Considered* (Driffield: B. Fawcett, 1842)

Arthur Bryant, *The National Character* (London: Longmans, Green, 1934)

Anna Bryson, *From Courtesy to Civility: Changing Codes of Conduct in Early Modern England* (Oxford: Clarendon Press, 1998)

Bill Bryson, *Notes from A Small Island* (London: Black Swan, 1996)

_____, *At Home: A Short History of Private Life* (London: Doubleday, 2010)

Oliver Bell Bunce, *Don't: A Manual of Mistakes and Improprieties More or Less Prevalent in Conduct and Speech* (London: Field & Tuer, 1883)

Jacob Burckhardt, *The Civilization of the Renaissance in Italy,* trans. S. G. C. Middlemore (London: Phaidon, 1960)

Edmund Burke, *Reflections on the Revolution in France,* 2nd edn (London: James Dodsley, 1790)

_____, *Two Letters Addressed to a Member of the Present Parliament* (Dublin: William Porter, 1796)

Peter Burke, *The Fabrication of Louis XIV* (New Haven, Connecticut: Yale University Press, 1992)

_____, *The Fortunes of the Courtier: The European Reception of Castiglione's Cortegiano* (Cambridge: Polity, 1995)

Peter Burke, Brian Harrison and Paul Slack (eds.), *Civil Histories: Essays Presented to Sir Keith Thomas* (Oxford: Oxford University Press, 2000)

Fanny Burney, *Journals and Letters*, ed. Peter Sabor and Lars E. Troide (London: Penguin, 2001)

J. A. Burrow, *Gestures and Looks in Medieval Narrative* (Cambridge: Cambridge University Press, 2002)

Ian Buruma, *Voltaire's Coconuts* (London: Weidenfeld & Nicolson, 1999)

Kevin Cahill, 'The Great Property Swindle', *New Statesman*, 11 March 2011

Mark Caldwell, *A Short History of Rudeness: Manners, Morals, and Misbehavior in Modern America* (New York: Picador, 1999)

D. K. Campbell-Meiklejohn et al., 'Modulation of Social Influence by Methylphenidate', *Neuropsychopharmacology* 37 (2012), 1517–25

David Cannadine, *Class in Britain* (New Haven, Connecticut: Yale University Press, 1998)

Thomas Carlyle, *Sartor Resartus* (London: Chapman and Hall, 1858)

Gerald Carson, *The Polite Americans* (London: Macmillan, 1967)

Stephen L. Carter, *Civility: Manners, Morals, and the Etiquette of Democracy* (New York: Harper Perennial, 1998)

Baldassare Castiglione, *The Book of the Courtier . . . Done into English by Sir Thomas Hoby* (London: David Nutt, 1900)

_____, *The Courtier*, trans. George Bull (London: Penguin, 2003)

Edwin Chadwick, *Report on the Sanitary Condition of the Labouring Population of Great Britain*, ed. M. W. Flinn (Edinburgh: Edinburgh University Press, 1965)

Eliza Cheadle, *Manners of Modern Society: Being A Book of Etiquette* (London: Cassell, Petter & Galpin, 1878)

Ron Chernow, *The House of Morgan: An American Banking Dynasty and the Rise of Modern Finance* (New York: Touchstone, 1991)

Lord Chesterfield, *Letters*, ed. Bonamy Dobrée, 6 vols. (London: Eyre & Spottiswoode, 1932)

_____, *Letters*, ed. David Roberts (Oxford: Oxford University Press, 2008)

Kimberly Chrisman, 'Unhoop the Fair Sex: The Campaign Against the Hoop Petticoat in Eighteenth-Century England', *Eighteenth-Century Studies* 30 (1996), 5–23

Cicero, *On Duties*, ed. M. T. Griffin and E. M. Atkins (Cambridge: Cambridge University Press, 1991)

Constance Classen (ed.), *The Book of Touch* (Oxford: Berg, 2005)

Emily Cockayne, *Hubbub: Filth, Noise and Stench in England, 1600–1770* (New Haven, Connecticut: Yale University Press, 2007)

————, *Cheek by Jowl: A History of Neighbours* (London: Bodley Head, 2012)

Linda Colley, *Britons: Forging the Nation, 1707–1837* (New Haven, Connecticut: Yale University Press, 1992)

Jane Collier, *An Essay on the Art of Ingeniously Tormenting* (London: Andrew Millar, 1753)

Lauren Collins, 'Sole Mate', *New Yorker*, 28 March 2011

Confucius, *The Analects*, trans. D. C. Lau (Harmondsworth: Penguin, 1979)

Stephanie Coontz, *The Way We Never Were: American Families and the Nostalgia Trap* (New York: Basic Books, 1992)

Anthony Ashley Cooper, Third Earl of Shaftesbury, *Characteristics of Men, Manners, Opinions, Times*, ed. Lawrence E. Klein (Cambridge: Cambridge University Press, 1999)

Glenda Cooper, 'Kiss of Death or Friendly Salute?', *Daily Telegraph*, 14 August 2011

Jilly Cooper, *Class: An Exposé of the English Class System* (London: Corgi, 1999)

Coryat's Crudities, 2 vols. (Glasgow: James MacLehose, 1905)

Hannah Cowley, *The Belle's Stratagem* (Dublin: 1781)

Michael Curtin, *Propriety and Position: A Study of Victorian Manners* (New York: Garland, 1987)

Faramerz Dabhoiwala, *The Origins of Sex: A History of the First Sexual Revolution* (London: Penguin Allen Lane, 2012)

Leo Damrosch, *Jean-Jacques Rousseau: Restless Genius* (New York: Houghton Mifflin Harcourt, 2005)

Daniel of Beccles, *Urbanus Magnus: The Book of the Civilized Man*, comp. Anne Frith, Dorothy Smith and Susan Treggiari (Beccles: Bidnall Press, 2007)

Benet Davetian, *Civility: A Cultural History* (Toronto: University of Toronto Press, 2009)

Leonore Davidoff, *The Best Circles: Society Etiquette and the Season* (London: Croom Helm, 1973)

Leonore Davidoff and Catherine Hall, *Family Fortunes: Men and Women of the English Middle Class 1780–1850*, rev. edn (London: Routledge, 2002)

Jenny Davidson, *Hypocrisy and the Power of Politeness: Manners and Morals from Locke to Austen* (Cambridge: Cambridge University Press, 2004)

_____, *Breeding: A Partial History of the Eighteenth Century* (New York: Columbia University Press, 2009)

Frank Victor Dawes, *Not In Front of the Servants* (London: Hutchinson, 1984)

Debrett's Etiquette and Modern Manners, ed. Elsie Burch Donald (London: Debrett's, 1981)

Geoffroi de Charny, *A Knight's Own Book of Chivalry*, trans. Elspeth Kennedy (Philadelphia: University of Pennsylvania Press, 2005)

Anne de Courcy, *A Guide to Modern Manners* (London: Thames and Hudson, 1985)

Selected Writings of Daniel Defoe, ed. James T. Boulton (Cambridge: Cambridge University Press, 1975)

Giovanni della Casa, *Galateo*, trans. Konrad Eisenbichler and Kenneth R. Bartlett (Toronto: Centre for Reformation and Renaissance Studies, 1986)

Benjamin DeMott, 'Seduced by Civility: Political Manners and the Crisis of Democratic Values', *Nation*, 9 December 1996

Béat-Louis de Muralt, *Letters Describing the Character and Customs of the English and French Nations* (London: Thomas Edlin, 1726)

Madame de Sévigné, *Selected Letters*, trans. Leonard Tancock (Harmondsworth: Penguin, 1982)

Alexis de Tocqueville, *Democracy in America*, trans. Arthur Goldhammer (New York: Library of America, 2004)

Charles Dickens, *American Notes for General Circulation* (New York: Harper, 1842)

Kenelm Digby, *The Broad Stone of Honour: or, The True Sense and Practice of Chivalry. The First Book, Godefridus* (London: Joseph Booker, 1829)

Isaac D'Israeli, *Curiosities of Literature*, 9th edn, 6 vols. (London: Edward Moxon, 1834)

Richard Donkin, *Blood, Sweat and Tears: The Evolution of Work* (New York: Texere, 2001)

Pamela Druckerman, *French Children Don't Throw Food: Parenting Secrets from Paris* (London: Doubleday, 2012)

Charles Duhigg, *The Power of Habit: Why We Do What We Do and How to Change* (London: William Heinemann, 2012)

John Dunton, *The Night-walker: or, Evening Rambles in Search of Lewd Women* (London: J. Orme, 1696)

Anne Edwards and Drusilla Beyfus, *Lady Behave: A Guide to Modern Manners for the 1970s* (London: Cassell, 1969)

Norbert Elias, *The Civilizing Process*, trans. Edmund Jephcott, rev. edn (Oxford: Blackwell, 2000)

Bret Easton Ellis, *American Psycho*, rev. edn (London: Picador, 1998)

Sarah Stickney Ellis, *The Wives of England* (London: Fisher, 1843)

Thomas Elyot, *The Boke Named the Governour*, ed. Donald W. Rude (New York: Garland, 1992)

Ralph Waldo Emerson, *Essays & Lectures*, ed. Joel Porte (New York: Library of America, 1983)

Friedrich Engels, *The Condition of the Working Class in England*, trans.

Florence Wischnewetzky, ed. Victor Kiernan (London: Penguin, 2009)

The Correspondence of Erasmus 1484–1500, trans. R. A. B. Mynors and D. F. S. Thomson (Toronto: University of Toronto Press, 1974)

Desiderius Erasmus, *A Handbook on Good Manners for Children*, trans. Eleanor Merchant (London: Preface, 2008)

David Farley-Hills (ed.), *Rochester: The Critical Heritage* (London: Routledge & Kegan Paul, 1972)

Ellen Fein and Sherrie Schneider, *The Rules: Time-tested Secrets for Capturing the Heart of Mr Right* (New York: Grand Central, 1995)

Tina Fey, *Bossypants* (London: Sphere, 2012)

Wise Sayings and Favourite Passages from the Works of Henry Fielding (Cedar Rapids, Iowa: Torch Press, 1909)

Joanne Finkelstein, *Dining Out: A Sociology of Modern Manners* (Cambridge: Polity, 1989)

Valeria Finucci, *The Lady Vanishes: Subjectivity and Representation in Castiglione and Ariosto* (Stanford, California: Stanford University Press, 1992)

William Fiston, *The School of Good Manners* (London: J. Danter, 1595)

Judith Flanders, *The Victorian House: Domestic Life from Childbirth to Deathbed* (London: HarperCollins, 2003)

J. C. Flügel, *The Psychology of Clothes* (London: Hogarth Press, 1930)

Carole R. Fontaine, 'A Modern Look at Ancient Wisdom: The Instruction of Ptahhotep Revisited', *Biblical Archaeologist* 44 (1981), 155–60

James Fordyce, *Sermons to Young Women*, 5th edn, 2 vols. (London: Andrew Millar and Thomas Cadell, 1768)

P. M. Forni, *Choosing Civility: The Twenty-Five Rules of Considerate Conduct* (New York: St Martin's Griffin, 2002)

Michel Foucault, *The History of Sexuality*, trans. Robert Hurley, 3 vols. (New York: Pantheon, 1978–86)

Kate Fox, *Watching the English: The Hidden Rules of English Behaviour* (London: Hodder and Stoughton, 2004)

The Life and Writings of Benjamin Franklin, 2 vols. (Philadelphia: McCarty & Davis, 1834)

Jonathan Franzen, *Farther Away* (New York: Farrar, Straus and Giroux, 2012)

Sigmund Freud, *Civilization and Its Discontents*, trans. David McLintock (London: Penguin, 2002)

_____, *Beyond the Pleasure Principle*, trans. John Reddick (London: Penguin, 2003)

_____, *The Psychology of Love*, trans. Shaun Whiteside (London: Penguin, 2006)

Betty Friedan, *The Feminine Mystique* (New York: Norton, 1963)

Max Frisch, *Homo Faber*, trans. Michael Bullock (London: Penguin, 2006)

Robert Fulghum, *All I Really Need to Know I Learned in Kindergarten* (London: Grafton, 1989)

P. N. Furbank, *Unholy Pleasure: or The Idea of Social Class* (Oxford: Oxford University Press, 1985)

Frank Furedi, *Therapy Culture: Cultivating Vulnerability in an Uncertain Age* (London: Routledge, 2004)

F. J. Furnivall (ed.), *The Babees Book, Aristotle's ABC, etc.* (London: Trübner, 1868)

_____, *Queen Elizabethes Academy, etc.*, 2 vols. (London: Trübner, 1869)

Clifford Geertz, *Local Knowledge: Further Essays in Interpretive Anthropology* (London: Fontana, 1993)

M. Dorothy George, *London Life in the Eighteenth Century* (London: Penguin, 1987)

Judy Giles and Tim Middleton (eds.), *Writing Englishness, 1900–1950* (London: Routledge, 1995)

John Gillingham, 'War and Chivalry in the *History of William the*

Marshal' in P. R. Coss and S. D. Lloyd (eds.), *Thirteenth Century England* (Woodbridge: Boydell Press, 1988)

_____, 'From Civilitas to Civility: Codes of Manners in Medieval and Early Modern England', *Transactions of the Royal Historical Society,* 6th series, 12 (2002), 267–89

Robin Gilmour, *The Idea of the Gentleman in the Victorian Novel* (London: George Allen & Unwin, 1981)

Mark Girouard, *Life in the English Country House* (New Haven, Connecticut: Yale University Press, 1978)

William Godwin, *The Enquirer: Reflections on Education, Manners, and Literature* (London: G. G. and J. Robinson, 1797)

The Letters of William Godwin: Volume I, 1778–1797, ed. Pamela Clemit (Oxford: Oxford University Press, 2011)

Erving Goffman, *Relations in Public: Microstudies of the Public Order* (London: Penguin Allen Lane, 1971)

_____, *The Presentation of Self in Everyday Life* (London: Penguin, 1990)

David Goldblatt, *The Ball Is Round: A Global History of Soccer* (New York: Riverhead, 2008)

Geoffrey Gorer, *Exploring English Character* (London: Cresset Press, 1955)

Mina Gorji (ed.), *Rude Britannia* (Oxford: Routledge, 2007)

Ignacio L. Götz, *Manners and Violence* (Westport, Connecticut: Praeger, 2000)

Richard Gough, *The History of Myddle,* ed. David Hey (Harmondsworth: Penguin, 1981)

Laurie Graham, *Getting It Right: A Survival Guide to Modern Manners* (London: Chatto & Windus, 1989)

Stephen Greenblatt, *Renaissance Self-Fashioning: From More to Shakespeare* (Chicago: University of Chicago Press, 1980)

Thomas M. Greene, 'Roger Ascham: The Perfect End of Shooting', *English Literary History* 36 (1969), 609–25

Phoebe Griffith, Will Norman, Carmel O'Sullivan and Rushanara Ali, *Charm Offensive: Cultivating Civility in 21st Century Britain* (London: The Young Foundation, 2011)

Stefano Guazzo, *The Art of Conversation* (London: J. Brett, 1738)

John Guy, *Tudor England* (Oxford: Oxford University Press, 1988)

Jonathan Haidt, *The Righteous Mind: Why Good People Are Divided by Politics and Religion* (London: Penguin Allen Lane, 2012)

Richard Hakluyt, *The Tudor Venturers*, ed. John Hampden (London: Folio Society, 1970)

Sarah Josepha Hale, *Manners; or, Happy Homes and Good Society All the Year Round* (Boston: J. E. Tilton, 1868)

Stephen Halliday, *The Great Filth: The War Against Disease in Victorian England* (Stroud: Sutton, 2007)

Philip Gilbert Hamerton, *French and English: A Comparison* (London: Macmillan, 1889)

Jonas Hanway, *A Journal of Eight Days Journey . . . to which is added An Essay on Tea*, 2nd edn, 2 vols. (London: H. Woodfall, 1757)

George Harris, 'Domestic Everyday Life, and Manners and Customs in This Country, from the Earliest Period to the End of the Last Century', *Transactions of the Royal Historical Society* 5 (1877), 83–116; 6 (1877), 86–130; 7 (1878), 176–211; 8 (1880), 36–63; 9 (1881), 224–53; 10 (1882), 203–31

William Hazlitt, *Table-Talk: Original Essays on Men and Manners*, 2 vols. (London: C. Templeman, 1861)

Waldemar Heckel, *The Conquests of Alexander the Great* (Cambridge: Cambridge University Press, 2008)

Joyce Hemlow, 'Fanny Burney and the Courtesy Books', *Publications of the Modern Language Association of America* 65 (1950), 732–61

Peter Hessler, *Country Driving: A Chinese Road Trip* (Edinburgh: Canongate, 2011)

David G. Hey, *An English Rural Community: Myddle Under the Tudors and Stuarts* (Leicester: Leicester University Press, 1974)

Colin Heywood, *A History of Childhood* (Cambridge: Polity, 2001)

Gertrude Himmelfarb, *The De-Moralization of Society: From Victorian Virtues to Modern Values* (New York: Knopf, 1995)

Christopher Hitchens, *The Monarchy: A Critique of Britain's Favourite Fetish* (London: Chatto & Windus, 1990)

_____, *Blood, Class and Nostalgia: Anglo-American Ironies* (London: Vintage, 1991)

Thomas Hobbes, *Leviathan*, ed. Richard Tuck (Cambridge: Cambridge University Press, 1996)

Howard Association, *Juvenile Offenders* (London: Wertheimer, Lea, 1898)

Ford Madox Hueffer, *The Spirit of the People: An Analysis of the English Mind* (London: Alston Rivers, 1907)

Johan Huizinga, *The Waning of the Middle Ages*, trans. Fritz Hopman (London: Edward Arnold, 1924)

David Hume, *An Enquiry Concerning the Principles of Morals*, ed. Tom L. Beauchamp (Oxford: Clarendon Press, 1998)

Clive James, *Glued to the Box: Television Criticism from the Observer, 1979–82* (London: Jonathan Cape, 1983)

Peter Johnson, *The Philosophy of Manners* (Bristol: Thoemmes, 1999)

Edwin Jones, *The English Nation: The Great Myth* (Stroud: Sutton, 1998)

Owen Jones, *Chavs: The Demonization of the Working Class* (London: Verso, 2012)

Vivien Jones (ed.), *Women and Literature in Britain 1700–1800* (Cambridge: Cambridge University Press, 2000)

Daniel Kahneman, *Thinking, Fast and Slow* (New York: Farrar, Straus and Giroux, 2011)

John F. Kasson, *Rudeness and Civility: Manners in Nineteenth-Century Urban America* (New York: Hill and Wang, 1990)

Maurice Keen, *Chivalry* (New Haven, Connecticut: Yale University Press, 1984)

Philip Kelland, *Transatlantic Sketches* (Edinburgh: A. & C. Black, 1858)

Ann Cline Kelly, 'Swift's "Polite Conversation": An Eschatological Vision', *Studies in Philology* 73 (1976), 204–24

Florence Burton Kingsland, *Etiquette for All Occasions* (New York: Doubleday, Page, 1901)

Paul Kingsnorth, *Real England: The Battle Against the Bland* (London: Portobello Books, 2009)

Lawrence E. Klein, *Shaftesbury and the Culture of Politeness: Moral Discourse and Cultural Politics in Early Eighteenth-Century England* (Cambridge: Cambridge University Press, 1994)

Beatrice Knollys, *The Gentle Art of Good Talking* (London: James Bowden, 1899)

Elizabeth Kolbert, 'Place Settings', *New Yorker*, 20 October 2008

_____, 'Spoiled Rotten', *New Yorker*, 2 July 2012

Craig Koslofsky, *Evening's Empire: A History of the Night in Early Modern Europe* (Cambridge: Cambridge University Press, 2011)

Krishan Kumar, *The Making of English National Identity* (Cambridge: Cambridge University Press, 2003)

David Kynaston, *Austerity Britain: 1945–51* (London: Bloomsbury, 2007)

_____, *Family Britain: 1951–57* (London: Bloomsbury, 2009)

Paul Laity, 'Dazed and Confused', *London Review of Books*, 28 November 2002

George Lakoff and Mark Johnson, *Metaphors We Live By* (Chicago: University of Chicago Press, 1980)

David S. Landes, *The Wealth and Poverty of Nations: Why Some Are So Rich and Some So Poor* (London: Little, Brown, 1998)

Geoffroy de la Tour Landry, *The Book of the Knight of the Tower*, trans. Alexander Vance (London: Chapman and Hall, 1862)

Paul Langford, *Englishness Identified: Manners and Character 1650–1850* (Oxford: Oxford University Press, 2000)

Jaron Lanier, *You Are Not A Gadget: A Manifesto* (London: Penguin Allen Lane, 2010)

Doris Lessing, *In Pursuit of the English: A Documentary* (London: MacGibbon & Kee, 1960)

Robert Lesuire, *The Savages of Europe* (London: Dryden Leach, 1764)

Claude Lévi-Strauss, *The Origin of Table Manners*, trans. John and Doreen Weightman (London: Jonathan Cape, 1978)

The Lisle Letters, ed. Muriel St Clare Byrne, 6 vols. (Chicago: University of Chicago Press, 1981)

John Locke, *Some Thoughts Concerning Education*, 5th edn (London: A. and J. Churchill, 1705)

Torbjörn Lundmark, *Tales of Hi and Bye: Greeting and Parting Rituals Around the World* (Cambridge: Cambridge University Press, 2009)

Sarah Lyall, *A Field Guide to the English*, rev. edn (London: Quercus, 2009)

Niccolò Machiavelli, *The Prince*, ed. and trans. Robert M. Adams, 2nd edn (New York: Norton, 1992)

Alasdair MacIntyre, *After Virtue: A Study in Moral Theory*, 3rd edn (Notre Dame, Indiana: University of Notre Dame Press, 2007)

John McEnroe, *Serious* (London: Time Warner, 2003)

Iain McGilchrist, *The Master and His Emissary: The Divided Brain and the Making of the Western World* (New Haven, Connecticut: Yale University Press, 2009)

Colin McGinn, *The Meaning of Disgust* (Oxford: Oxford University Press, 2011)

Alister E. McGrath, *Christianity's Dangerous Idea: The Protestant Revolution – A History from the Sixteenth Century to the Twenty-First* (New York: HarperOne, 2007)

Bernard Mandeville, *The Fable of the Bees; or, Private Vices, Public Benefits* (London: J. Roberts, 1714)

Peter Mandler, *The English National Character: The History of an Idea from Edmund Burke to Tony Blair* (New Haven, Connecticut: Yale University Press, 2006)

Judith Martin, *Miss Manners' Guide to Excruciatingly Correct Behavior* (London: Hamish Hamilton, 1983)

_____, 'Miss Manners on Office Etiquette', *Fortune*, 6 November 1989

Harriet Martineau, *Society in America*, 2 vols. (Paris: A. and W. Galignani, 1837)

John E. Mason, *Gentlefolk in the Making* (Philadelphia: University of Pennsylvania Press, 1935)

Philip Mason, *The English Gentleman: The Rise and Fall of an Ideal* (London: André Deutsch, 1982)

George Mikes, *How to Be a Brit* (London: Penguin, 1986)

John Stuart Mill, *On Liberty and Other Writings*, ed. Stefan Collini (Cambridge: Cambridge University Press, 1989)

Nancy Mitford et al., *Noblesse Oblige: An Enquiry into the Identifiable Characteristics of the English Aristocrat* (London: Hamish Hamilton, 1956)

Alice-Leone Moats, *No Nice Girl Swears* (London: Cassell, 1933)

Joe Moran, *Queuing for Beginners: The Story of Daily Life from Breakfast to Bedtime* (London: Profile, 2007)

John Morgan, *The Times Book of Modern Manners* (London: HarperCollins, 2000)

Marjorie Morgan, *Manners, Morals and Class in England, 1774–1858* (London: St Martin's Press, 1994)

Carl Philip Moritz, *Journeys of a German in England*, trans. Reginald Nettel (London: Eland, 2009)

Ian Mortimer, *The Time Traveller's Guide to Medieval England* (London: Vintage, 2009)

_____, *The Time Traveller's Guide to Elizabethan England* (London: Bodley Head, 2012)

Ferdinand Mount, 'The Recovery of Civility: Notes for the Long Trek Back', *Encounter* 41 (1973), 31–43

_____, *Mind the Gap: The New Class Divide in Britain* (London: Short Books, 2004)

Harry Mount, *How England Made the English* (London: Viking, 2012)

Robert Muchembled, *A History of Violence: From the End of the Middle Ages to the Present*, trans. Jean Birrell (Cambridge: Polity, 2012)

Charles Murray, *Coming Apart: The State of White America, 1960–2010* (New York: Crown Forum, 2012)

Hermann Muthesius, *The English House*, ed. Dennis Sharp, trans. Janet Seligman and Stewart Spencer, 3 vols. (London: Frances Lincoln, 2007)

Tom Nairn, *The Break-Up of Britain: Crisis and Neo-Nationalism* (London: New Left Books, 1977)

N. E. Nelson, 'Cicero's *De Officiis* in Christian Thought: 300–1300', in *Essays and Studies in English and Comparative Literature* (Ann Arbor: University of Michigan Press, 1933), 59–160

Pamela Neville-Sington, *Fanny Trollope: The Life and Adventures of a Clever Woman* (London: Viking, 1997)

Adam Nicolson, *The Gentry: Stories of the English* (London: HarperPress, 2011)

Harold Nicolson, *Good Behaviour* (London: Constable, 1955)

Andrew O'Hagan, 'A Car of One's Own', *London Review of Books*, 11 June 2009

George Orwell, *Essays*, ed. John Carey (London: Everyman, 2002)

Francis Osborne, *Advice to a Son* (London: David Nutt, 1896)

Elsie Clews Parsons, *Fear and Conventionality* (Chicago: University of Chicago Press, 1997)

Talcott Parsons, *The Social System* (Glencoe, Illinois: Free Press, 1951)

Bethanne Patrick, *An Uncommon History of Common Courtesy* (Washington, DC: National Geographic, 2011)

Jeremy Paxman, *The English: A Portrait of A People* (London: Penguin, 1999)

Henry Peacham, *The Compleat Gentleman*, 2nd edn (London: Francis Constable, 1634)

_____, *The Art of Living in London* (London: John Gyles, 1642)

Arthur Stanley Pease, 'The Omen of Sneezing', *Classical Philology* 6 (1911), 429–43

Samuel Pepys, *Diary*, ed. Robert Latham and William Matthews, 11 vols. (London: Bell and Hyman, 1970–83)

Nikolaus Pevsner, *The Englishness of English Art* (Harmondsworth: Penguin, 1964)

John M. Picker, 'The Soundproof Study: Victorian Professionals, Work Space, and Urban Noise', *Victorian Studies* 42 (1999–2000), 427–53

Steven Pinker, *The Stuff of Thought: Language as a Window into Human Nature* (London: Penguin, 2008)

_____, *The Better Angels of Our Nature: The Decline of Violence in History and Its Causes* (London: Penguin Allen Lane, 2011)

Hester Lynch Piozzi, *British Synonymy* (London: G. G. and J. Robinson, 1794)

The Autobiography of Francis Place (1771–1854), ed. Mary Thale (Cambridge: Cambridge University Press, 1972)

John Playford, *The English Dancing Master* (London: Thomas Harper, 1651)

Richard Pomfret, *The Age of Equality: The Twentieth Century in Economic Perspective* (Cambridge, Mass.: Belknap Press, 2011)

Ithiel de Sola Pool (ed.), *The Social Impact of the Telephone* (Cambridge, Mass.: MIT Press, 1977)

Emily Post, *Etiquette: In Society, In Business, In Politics and At Home* (New York: Funk & Wagnalls, 1922)

_____, *Etiquette: The Blue Book of Social Usage*, 10th edn (New York: Funk & Wagnalls, 1960)

Michael Prestwich, *Knight: The Medieval Warrior's (Unofficial) Manual* (London: Thames & Hudson, 2010)

J. B. Priestley, *The English* (Harmondsworth: Penguin, 1975)

Robert D. Putnam, *Bowling Alone:The Collapse and Revival of American Community* (New York: Simon & Schuster, 2000)

Maurice J. Quinlan, *Victorian Prelude: A History of English Manners 1700–1830* (New York: Columbia University Press, 1941)

Jonathan Raban, *Soft City* (London: Picador, 2008)

L. J. Ransone, *'Good Form' in England, by an American Resident in the United Kingdom* (New York: Appleton, 1888)

John Reader, *Cities* (London: Vintage, 2005)

Bruce Redford, *The Converse of the Pen* (Chicago: University of Chicago Press, 1986)

G. J. Renier, *The English: Are They Human?* (London: Williams & Norgate, 1949)

Samuel Richardson, *Letters Written to and for Particular Friends, on the Most Important Occasions* (London: Rivington, Osborn and Leake, 1741)

Christopher Ricks, *T. S. Eliot and Prejudice* (London: Faber, 1988)

J. Robinson, *A Manual of Manners; or, Hints for the Proper Deportment of School Boys* (London: Hamilton, Adams, 1829)

The Works of John Wilmot, Earl of Rochester, ed. Harold Love (Oxford: Oxford University Press, 1999)

Ben Rogers, *Beef and Liberty: Roast Beef, John Bull and the English Nation* (London: Chatto & Windus, 2003)

Steve Roud, *The English Year* (London: Penguin, 2008)

Jean-Jacques Rousseau, *The Social Contract and Other Later Political Writings*, ed. Victor Gourevitch (Cambridge: Cambridge University Press, 1997)

Ulinka Rublack, *Dressing Up: Cultural Identity in Renaissance Europe* (Oxford: Oxford University Press, 2010)

John Ruskin, *Modern Painters*, 5 vols. (London: Smith, Elder, 1843–60)

Bertrand Russell, *Mortals and Others* (London: Routledge, 2009)

Joycelyne G. Russell, *The Field of Cloth of Gold: Men and Manners in 1520* (London: Routledge & Kegan Paul, 1969)

Andrew St George, *The Descent of Manners: Etiquette, Rules and the Victorians* (London: Chatto & Windus, 1993)

Michael J. Sandel, *What Money Can't Buy: The Moral Limits of Markets* (London: Penguin Allen Lane, 2012)

The Works of George Savile, Marquis of Halifax, ed. Mark N. Brown, 3 vols. (Oxford: Clarendon Press, 1989)

Aldo Scaglione, *Knights at Court: Courtliness, Chivalry, and Courtesy from Ottonian Germany to the Italian Renaissance* (Berkeley, California: University of California Press, 1991)

Ron Scapp and Brian Seitz (eds.), *Etiquette: Reflections on Contemporary Comportment* (Albany, NY: State University of New York Press, 2007)

Arthur M. Schlesinger, *Learning How to Behave: A Historical Study of American Etiquette Books* (New York: Macmillan, 1947)

Dietmar Schloss (ed.), *Civilizing America: Manners and Civility in American Literature and Culture* (Heidelberg: Universitätsverlag Winter, 2009)

George Schöpflin, *Nations, Identity, Power: The New Politics of Europe* (London: Hurst, 2000)

Susie Scott, *Making Sense of Everyday Life* (Cambridge: Polity, 2009)

Sir Walter Scott, *Tales of a Grandfather; with Stories Taken from Scottish History* (Paris: Baudry's European Library, 1833)

Roger Scruton, *England: An Elegy* (London: Pimlico, 2001)

W. C. Sellar and R. J. Yeatman, *1066 and All That: A Memorable History of England*, 6th edn (London: Methuen, 1930)

Seneca, *Moral and Political Essays*, ed. and trans. John M. Cooper and J. F. Procopé (Cambridge: Cambridge University Press, 1995)

Richard Sennett, *Respect: The Formation of Character in An Age of Inequality* (London: Penguin Allen Lane, 2003)

Thomas Shadwell, *The Humorists* (London: Henry Herringman, 1671)

Steven Shapin, *A Social History of Truth: Civility and Science in Seventeenth-Century England* (Chicago: University of Chicago Press, 1994)

Diane Shaw, 'The Construction of the Private in Medieval London', *Journal of Medieval and Early Modern Studies* 26 (1996), 447–66

George Bernard Shaw, *Pygmalion* (London: Penguin, 2000)

Nancy Sherman, 'Of Manners and Morals', *British Journal of Educational Studies* 53 (2005), 272–89

Edward Shils, *The Virtue of Civility: Selected Essays on Liberalism, Tradition, and Civil Society*, ed. Steven Grosby (Indianapolis: Liberty Fund, 1997)

Clay Shirky, *Cognitive Surplus: Creativity and Generosity in a Connected Age* (London: Penguin, 2011)

Georg Simmel, *On Individuality and Social Forms*, ed. Donald N. Levine (Chicago: University of Chicago Press, 1971)

Adam Smith, *The Theory of Moral Sentiments*, 3rd edn (London: Andrew Millar, 1767)

Helen Huntington Smith, 'Lady Chesterfield', *New Yorker*, 16 August 1930

Philip Smith, Timothy L. Phillips and Ryan D. King, *Incivility: The Rude Stranger in Everyday Life* (Cambridge: Cambridge University Press, 2010)

Richard J. Smith, John K. Fairbank and Katherine F. Bruner, *Robert Hart and China's Early Modernization: His Journals 1863–1866* (Cambridge, Mass.: Harvard University Press, 1991)

Oswald Spengler, *The Decline of the West*, abr. edn, ed. Arthur Helps from trans. Charles Francis Atkinson (Oxford: Oxford University Press, 1991)

Peter N. Stearns, *Childhood in World History* (New York: Routledge, 2006)

Richard Steele and Joseph Addison, *Selections from the Tatler and the Spectator*, ed. Angus Ross (London: Penguin, 1988)

Karen Stohr, *On Manners* (New York: Routledge, 2012)

Elizabeth Stone, *Chronicles of Fashion, from the Time of Elizabeth to the Early Part of the Nineteenth Century*, 2 vols. (London: Richard Bentley, 1845)

Lawrence Stone, *The Family, Sex and Marriage in England 1500–1800*, abr. edn (London: Penguin, 1990)

George Slythe Street, *People and Questions* (London: Martin Secker, 1910)

Philip Stubbes, *The Anatomie of Abuses* (London: Richard Jones, 1583)

James Sully, 'Civilization and Noise', *Fortnightly Review* 24 (1878), 704–20

The Works of Jonathan Swift, 19 vols. (Edinburgh: Constable, 1814)

The Correspondence of Jonathan Swift, ed. Harold Williams, 5 vols. (Oxford: Clarendon Press, 1963–5)

Bharat Tandon, *Jane Austen and the Morality of Conversation* (London: Anthem, 2003)

Tony Tanner, *Jane Austen* (Basingstoke: Macmillan, 1986)

Charles Taylor, *Sources of the Self: The Making of Modern Identity* (Cambridge, Mass.: Harvard University Press, 1989)

Thomas Tegg et al., *A Present for an Apprentice* (London: Thomas Tegg, 1838)

Margaret Thatcher, *The Downing Street Years* (London: Harper Perennial, 1995)

Keith Thomas, *Religion and the Decline of Magic* (London: Weidenfeld & Nicolson, 1971)

——————, *The Ends of Life: Roads to Fulfilment in Early Modern England* (Oxford: Oxford University Press, 2009)

Stephen Tignor, *High Strung: Bjorn Borg, John McEnroe, and the Untold Story of Tennis's Fiercest Rivalry* (New York: Harper, 2011)

Claire Tomalin, *Samuel Pepys: The Unequalled Self* (London: Viking, 2002)

Anthony Trollope, *An Autobiography* (Berkeley, California: University of California Press, 1978)

Frances Trollope, *Domestic Manners of the Americans* (Mineola, NY: Dover, 2003)

Lady Troubridge, *The Book of Etiquette* (Kingswood: The World's Work, 1926)

_____, *Etiquette and Entertaining* (London: Amalgamated Press, 1939)

Lynne Truss, *Talk to the Hand* (London: Profile, 2005)

Martin Tupper, *Proverbial Philosophy: A Book of Thoughts and Arguments, Originally Treated* (London: Joseph Rickerby, 1839)

Sherry Turkle, *Alone Together: Why We Expect More from Technology and Less from Each Other* (New York: Basic Books, 2011)

Mark Twain at Your Fingertips, ed. Caroline Thomas Harnsberger (New York: Beechhurst Press, 1948)

Jenny Uglow, *A Gambling Man: Charles II and the Restoration* (London: Faber, 2009)

Amy Vanderbilt, 'Bad Manners in America', *Annals of the American Academy of Political and Social Science* 378 (1968), 90–98

Wilbert van Vree, *Meetings, Manners and Civilization: The Development of Modern Meeting Behaviour*, trans. Kathleen Bell (London: Leicester University Press, 1999)

Thorstein Veblen, *The Theory of the Leisure Class* (New York: Macmillan, 1899)

Margaret Visser, *The Rituals of Dinner: The Origins, Evolution, Eccentricities, and Meaning of Table Manners* (London: Viking, 1992)

_____, *The Way We Are* (London: Viking, 1995)

_____, *The Gift of Thanks: The Roots and Rituals of Gratitude* (Boston: Houghton Mifflin Harcourt, 2009)

Johann Wilhelm von Archenholz, *A Picture of England*, 2 vols. (London: Edward Jeffery, 1789)

John Wade, *British History, Chronologically Arranged; Comprehending a*

Classified Analysis of Events and Occurrences in Church and State, 5th edn (London: Henry G. Bohn, 1847)

Robert Wallace, *Characteristics of the Present Political State of Great Britain,* 2nd edn (London: Andrew Millar, 1758)

Maureen Waller, *The English Marriage: Tales of Love, Money and Adultery* (London: John Murray, 2009)

Edward Ward, *The History of the London Clubs* (London: J. Dutten, 1709)

Nicola J. Watson, *Revolution and the Form of the British Novel, 1790–1825: Intercepted Letters, Interrupted Seductions* (Oxford: Clarendon Press, 1994)

Richard J. Watts, *Politeness* (Cambridge: Cambridge University Press, 2003)

Evelyn Waugh, 'Manners and Morals', in *The Essays, Articles and Reviews of Evelyn Waugh,* ed. Donat Gallagher (London: Methuen, 1983)

Alan F. Westin, *Privacy and Freedom* (New York: Atheneum, 1967)

Frank Whigham, *Ambition and Privilege: The Social Tropes of Elizabethan Courtesy Theory* (Berkeley, California: University of California Press, 1984)

Jerry White, *London in the Eighteenth Century* (London: Bodley Head, 2012)

Susan E. Whyman, *The Pen and the People: English Letter Writers 1660–1800* (Oxford: Oxford University Press, 2009)

Anna Wierzbicka, *English: Meaning and Culture* (Oxford: Oxford University Press, 2006)

_____, *Experience, Evidence, and Sense: The Hidden Cultural Legacy of English* (New York: Oxford University Press, 2010)

Joan Wildeblood and Peter Brinson, *The Polite World: A Guide to English Manners and Deportment from the Thirteenth to the Nineteenth Century* (London: Oxford University Press, 1965)

A. N. Wilson, *The Victorians* (London: Arrow, 2003)

Edmund Wilson, 'Books of Etiquette and Emily Post', *New Yorker*, 19 July 1947

Edward O. Wilson, *On Human Nature* (New York: Bantam, 1979)

K. J. Wilson, 'Ascham's *Toxophilus* and the Rules of Art', *Renaissance Quarterly* 29 (1976), 30–51

Mary Wollstonecraft, *A Vindication of the Rights of Woman*, 3rd edn (London: Joseph Johnson, 1796)

John George Wood, *The Uncivilized Races of Men in All Countries of the World*, 2 vols. (Hartford, Connecticut: J. B. Burr, 1870)

Michael Wood, *In Search of England: Journeys into the English Past* (London: Penguin, 2000)

Patrick Wormald, *Legal Culture in the Early Medieval West: Law as Text, Image and Experience* (London: Hambledon Press, 1999)

Cas Wouters, *Sex and Manners: Female Emancipation in the West, 1890–2000* (London: Sage, 2004)

_____, *Informalization: Manners and Emotions Since 1890* (London: Sage, 2007)

Lawrence Wright, *Clean and Decent: The History of the Bath and Loo*, rev. edn (London: Routledge & Kegan Paul, 1980)

Elizabeth Wyse et al., *Debrett's A–Z of Modern Manners* (Richmond: Debrett's, 2008)

Arthur Young, *Travels, During the Years 1787, 1788, and 1789* (Bury St Edmunds: J. Rackham, 1792)

Robert J. C. Young, *The Idea of English Ethnicity* (Oxford: Blackwell, 2008)

Paul J. Zak, *The Moral Molecule: The Source of Love and Prosperity* (London: Bantam, 2012)

Theodore Zeldin, *The French* (London: Collins, 1983)

_____, *An Intimate History of Humanity* (London: Minerva, 1995)

Index

CPSIA information can be obtained
at www.ICGtesting.com
Printed in the USA
LVHW011549280122
709456LV00002B/2